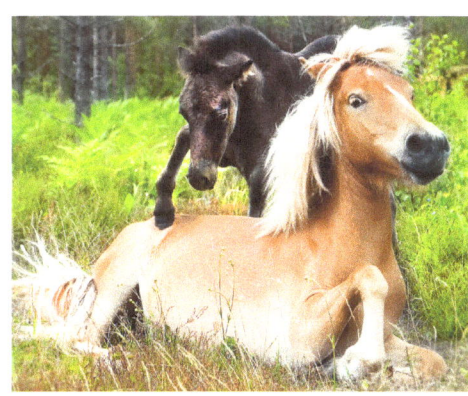
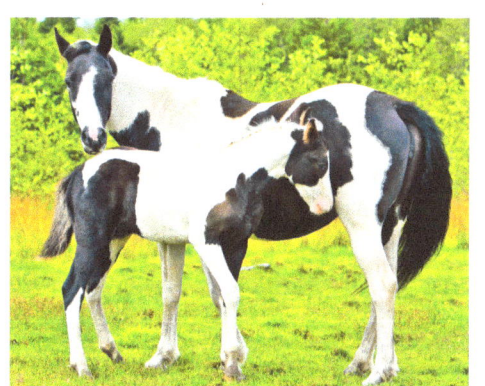
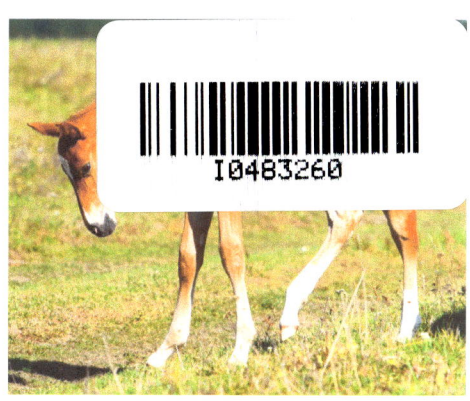

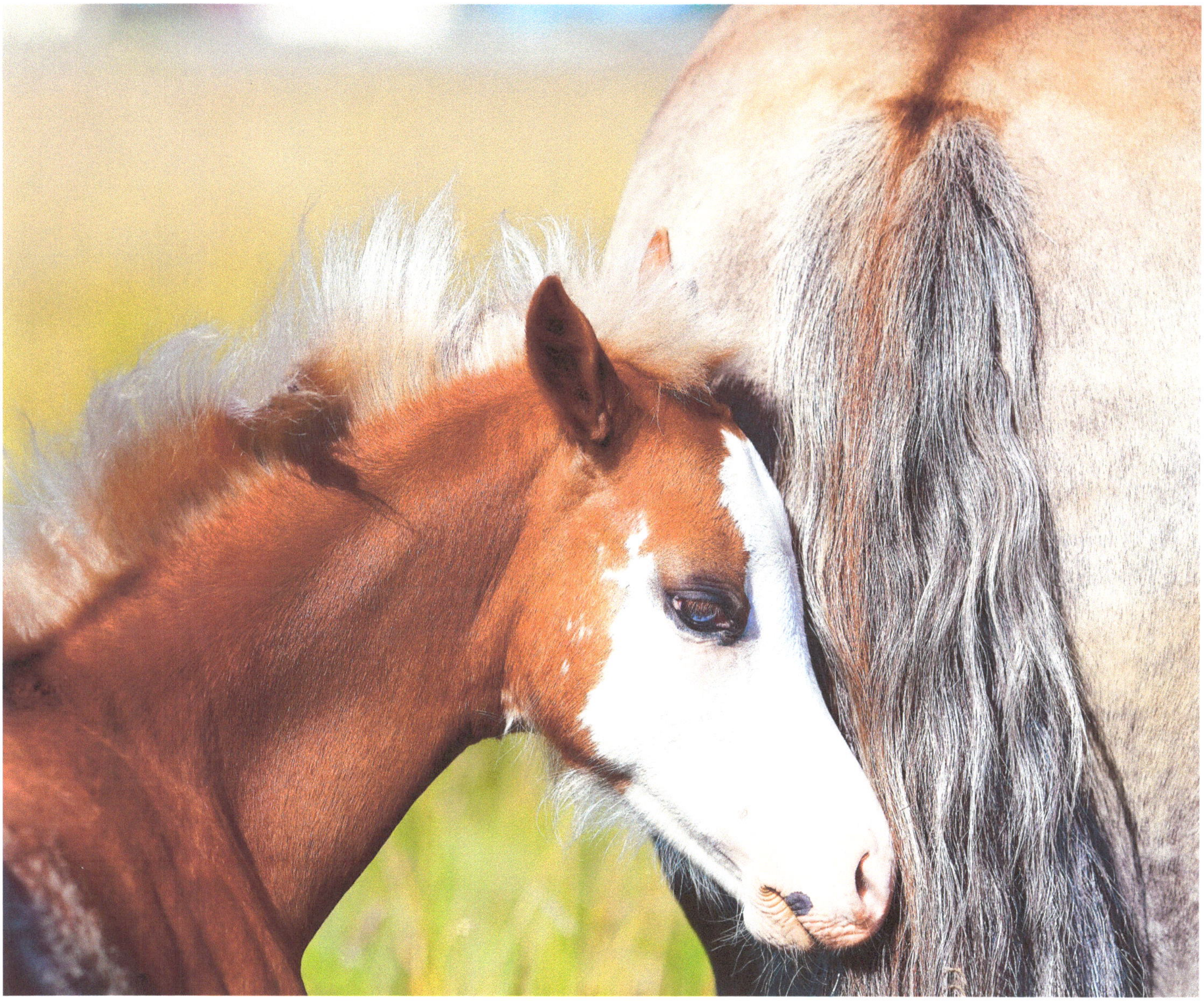

HORSE

Foals

Images for Artist's Reference & Inspiration

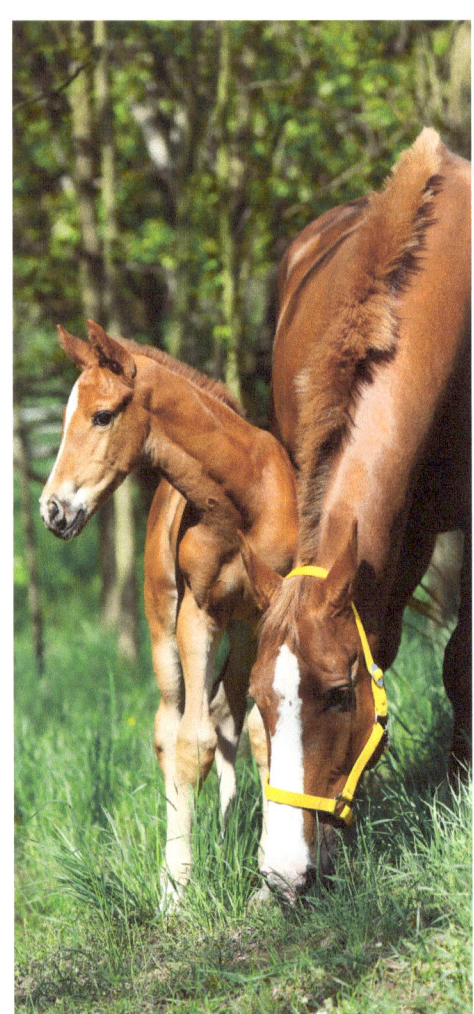

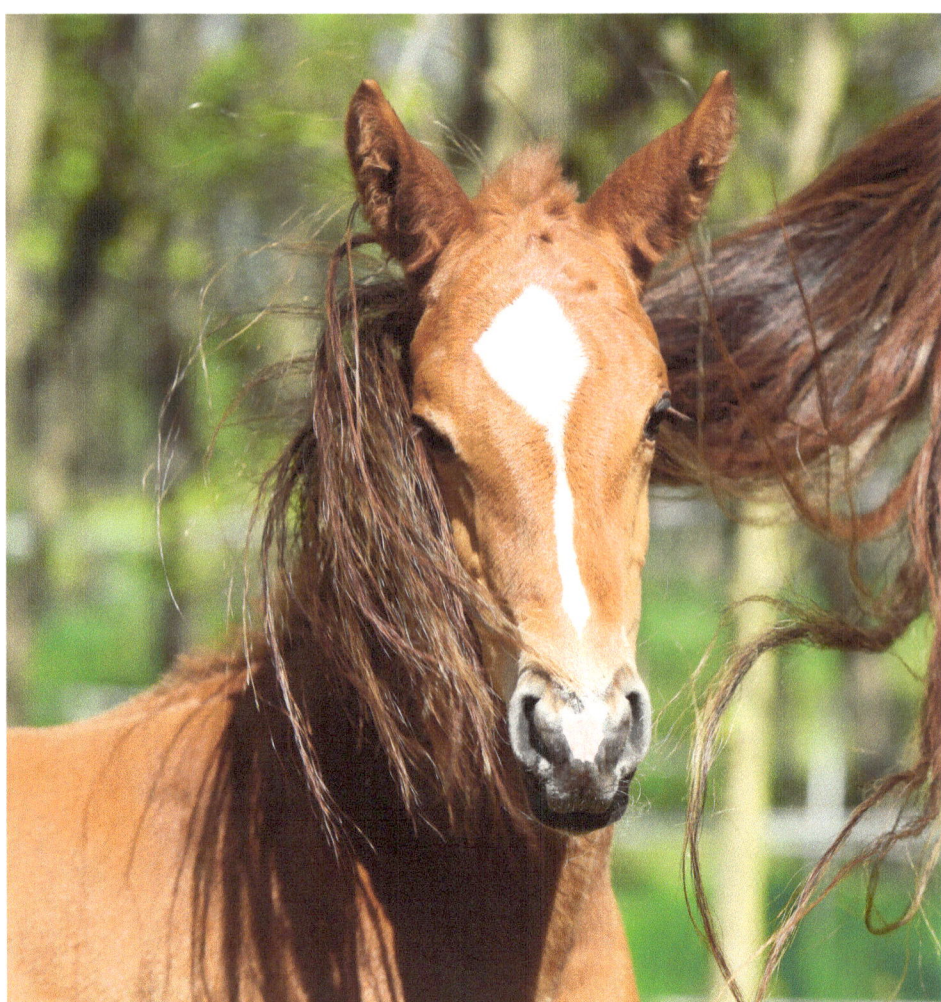

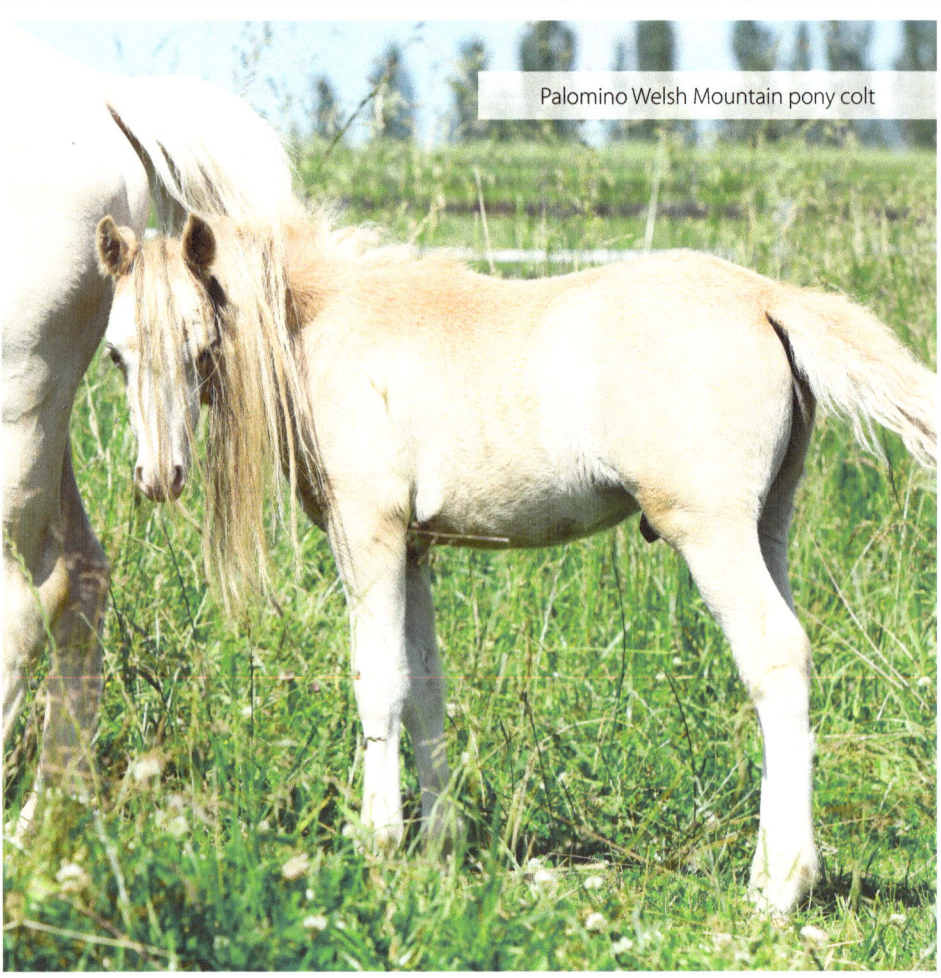
Palomino Welsh Mountain pony colt

Table of Contents

I would like to thank all of the talented photographers from around the world who have made their work available on Dreamstime, select stock photography sites. Their talent has made this book possible.

If you have purchased this book and would like to view, download, or purchase these photographs for your drawing, sculpting, or model horse show reference needs, please visit Dreamstime.com.

For more books in this series, please visit sarahtregay.com.

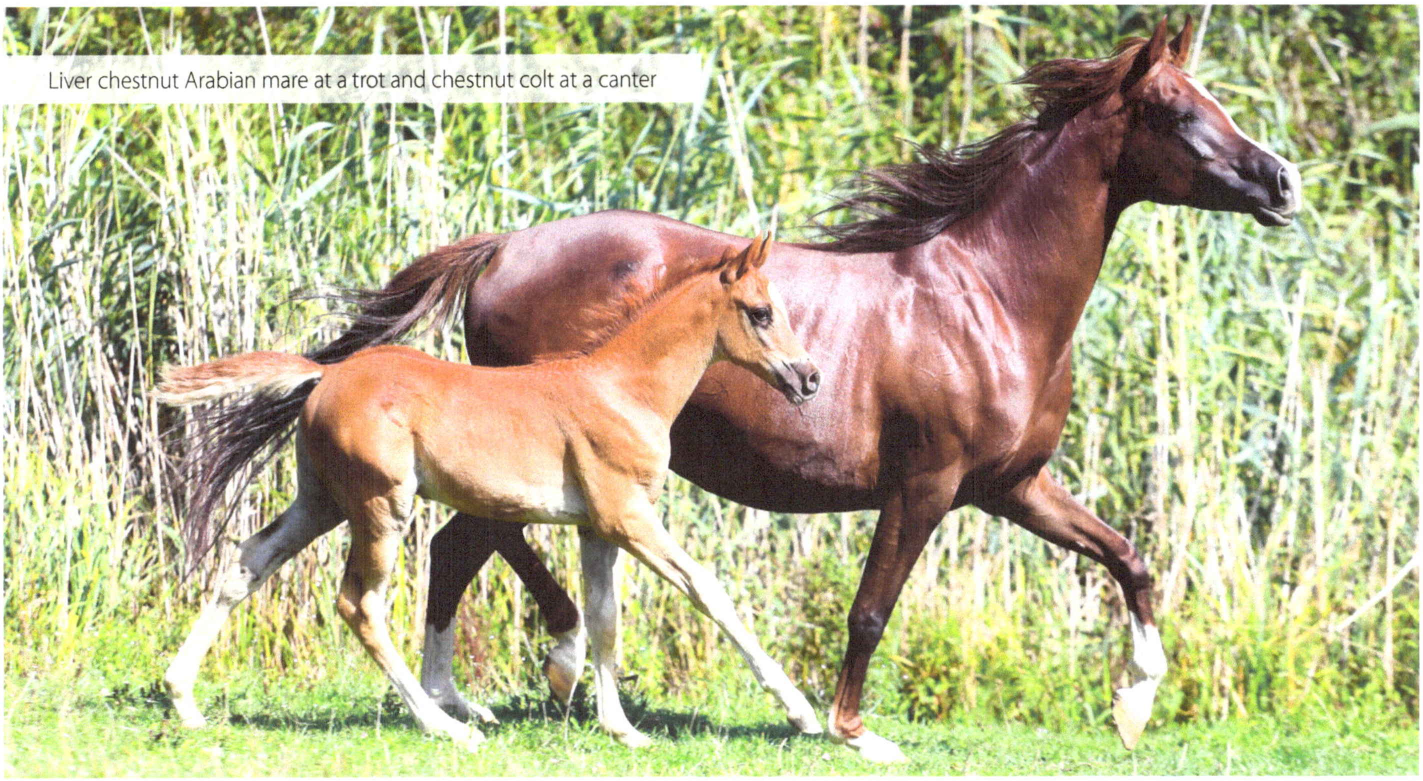

Liver chestnut Arabian mare at a trot and chestnut colt at a canter

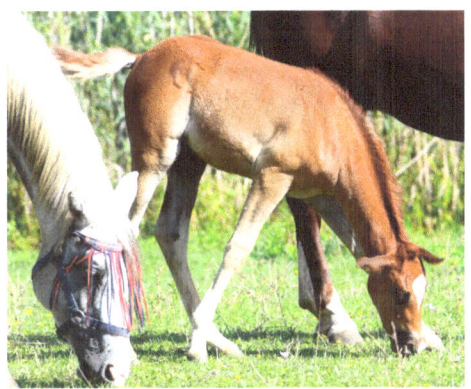
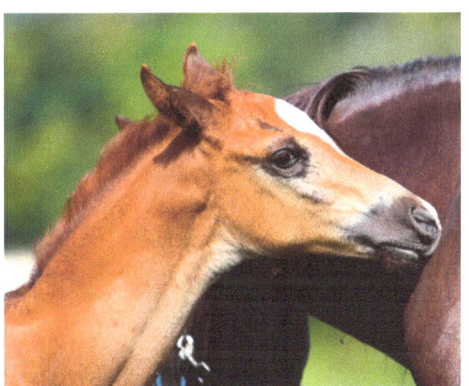
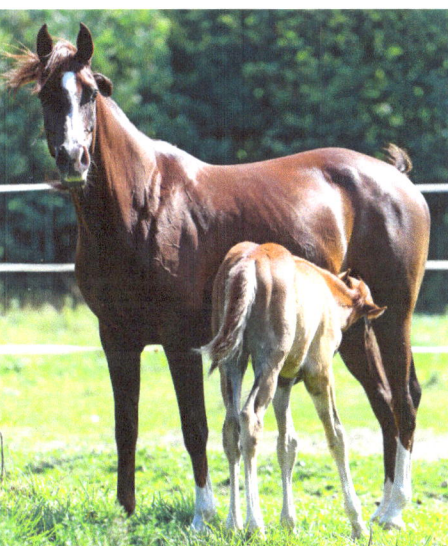
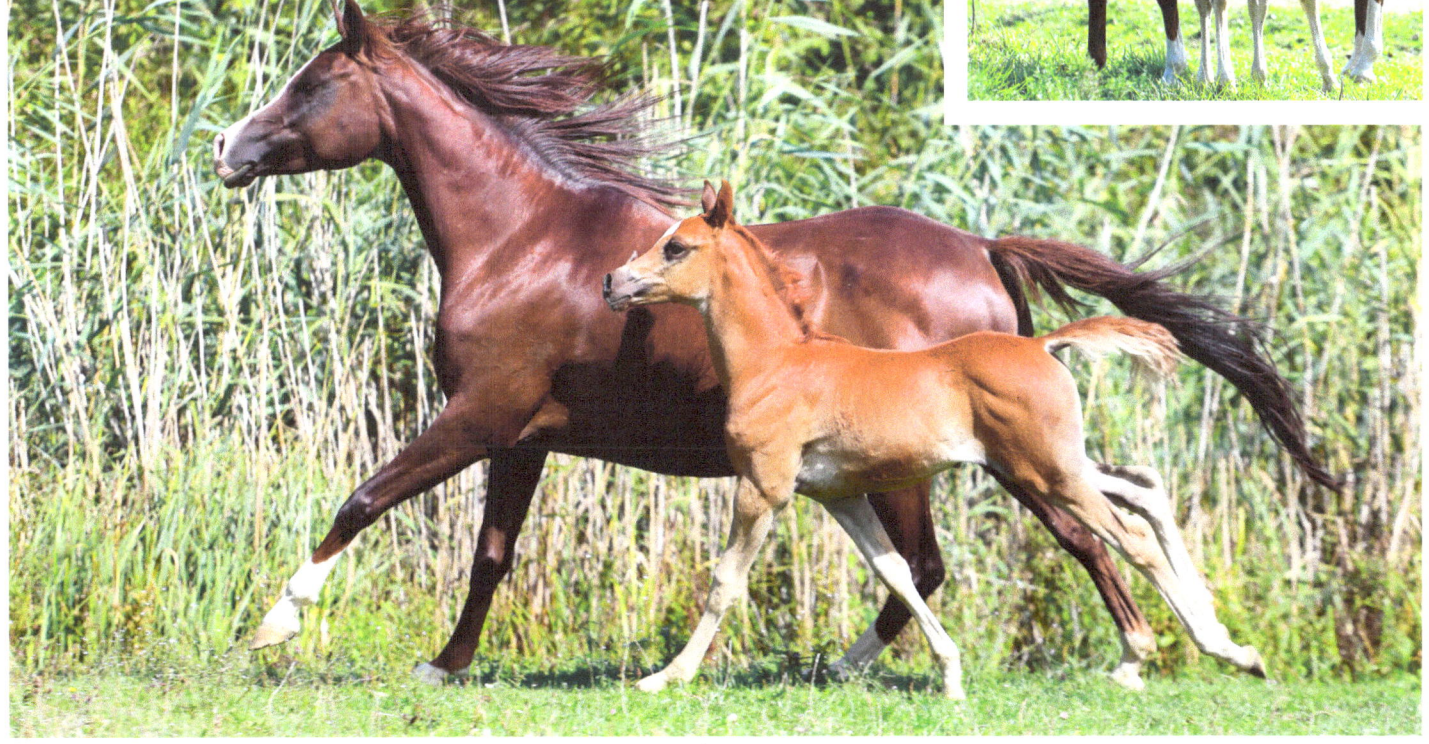

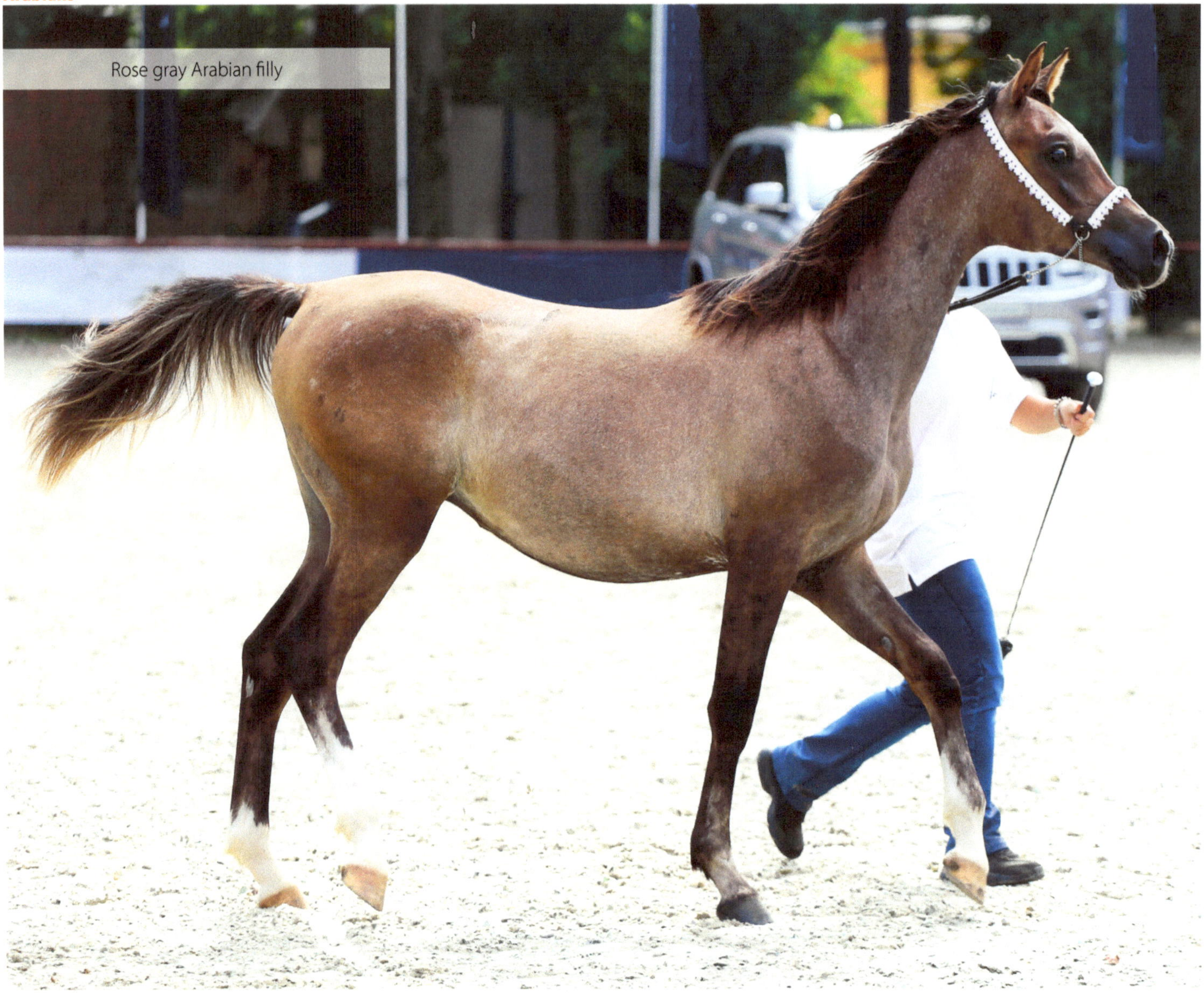

Rose gray Arabian filly

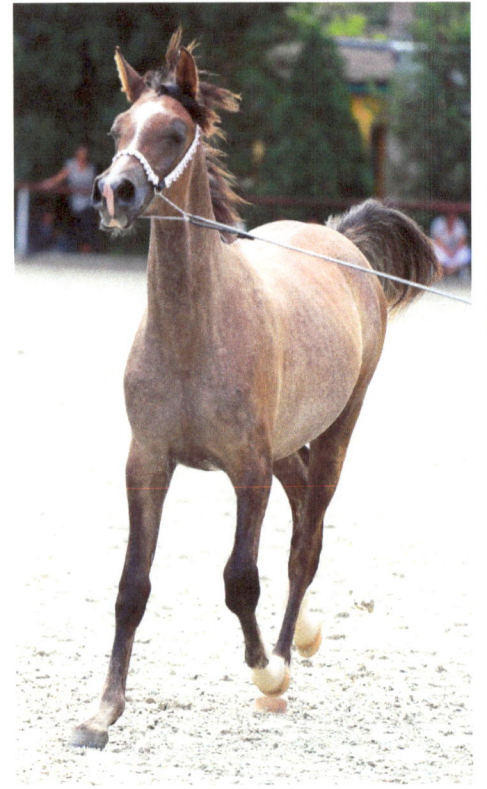

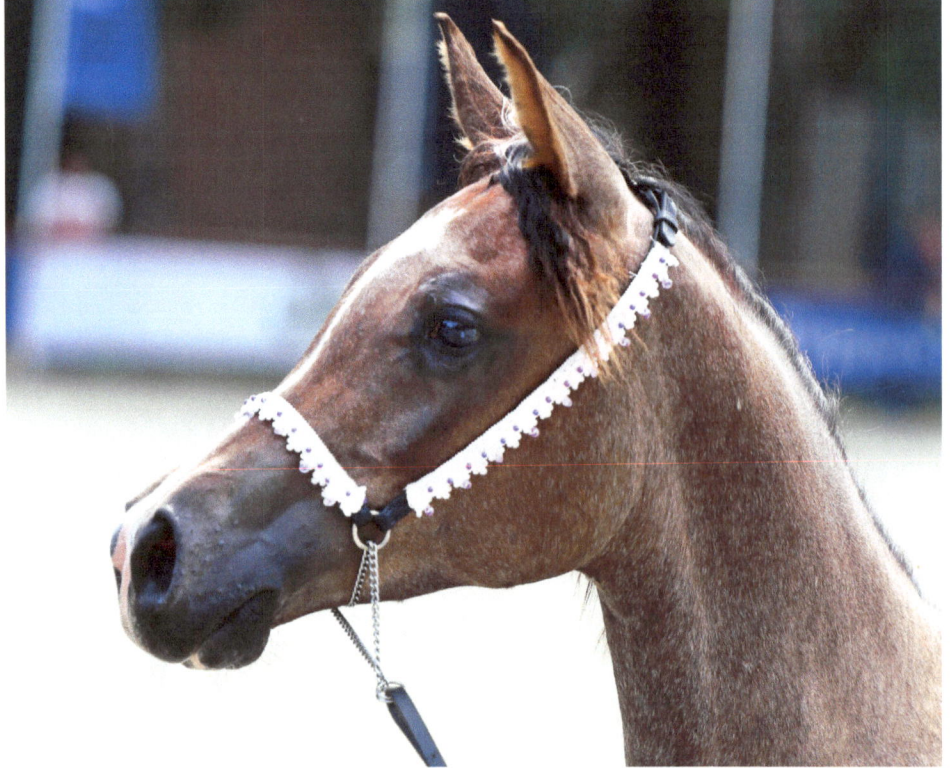

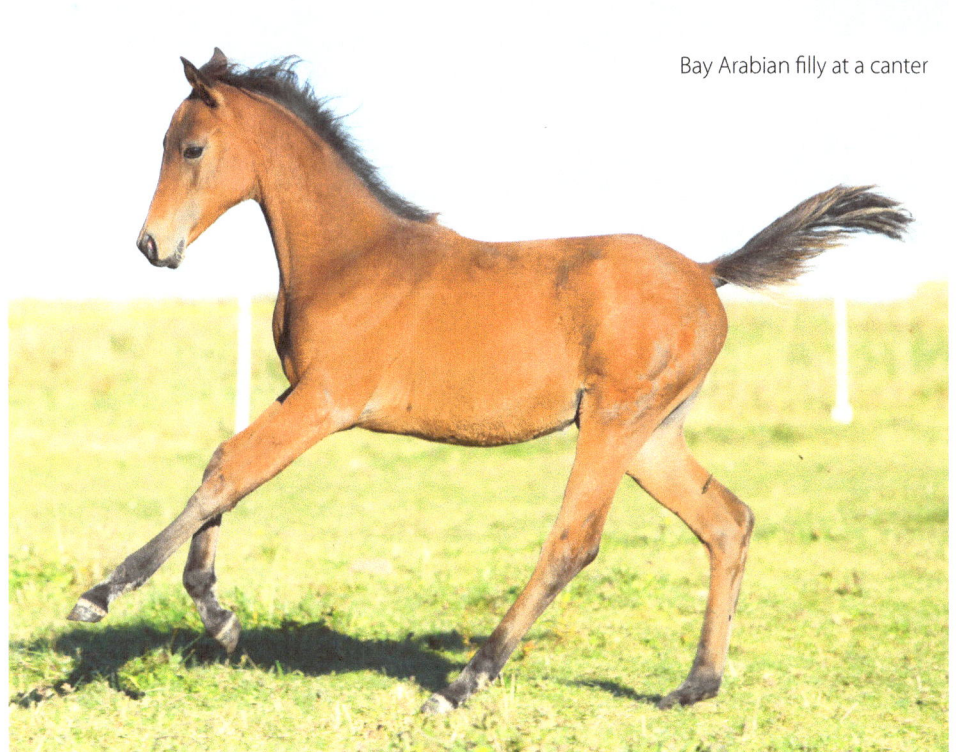

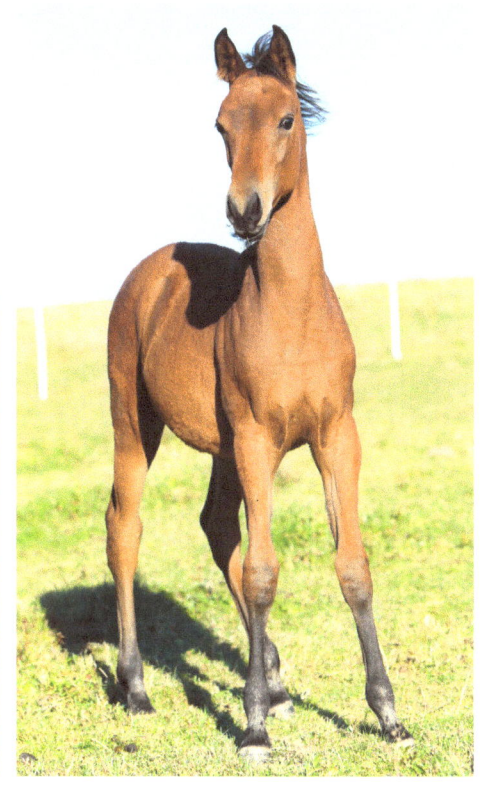

Bay Arabian filly at a canter

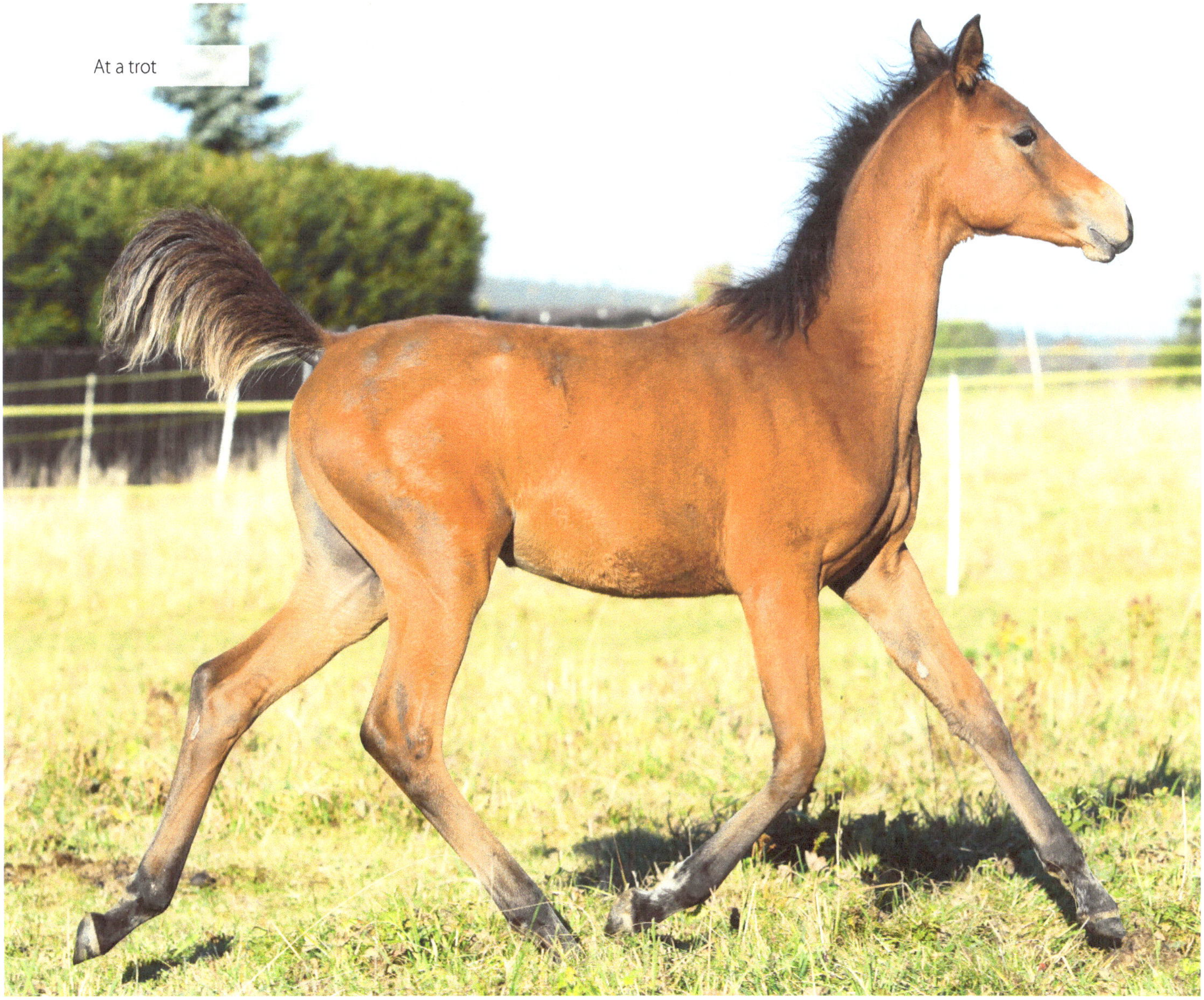

At a trot

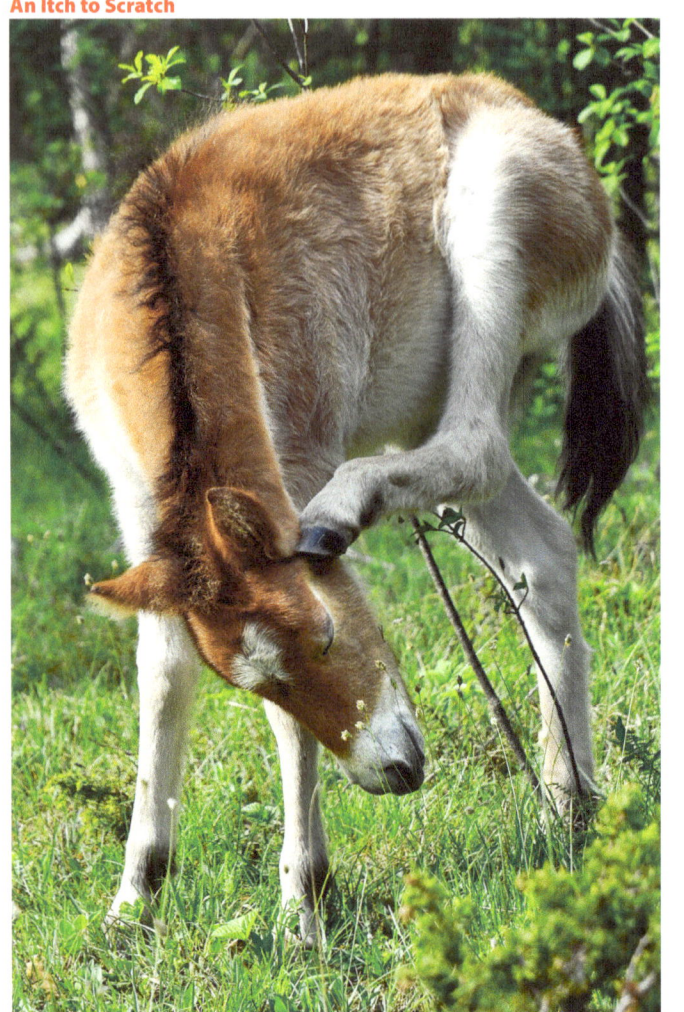

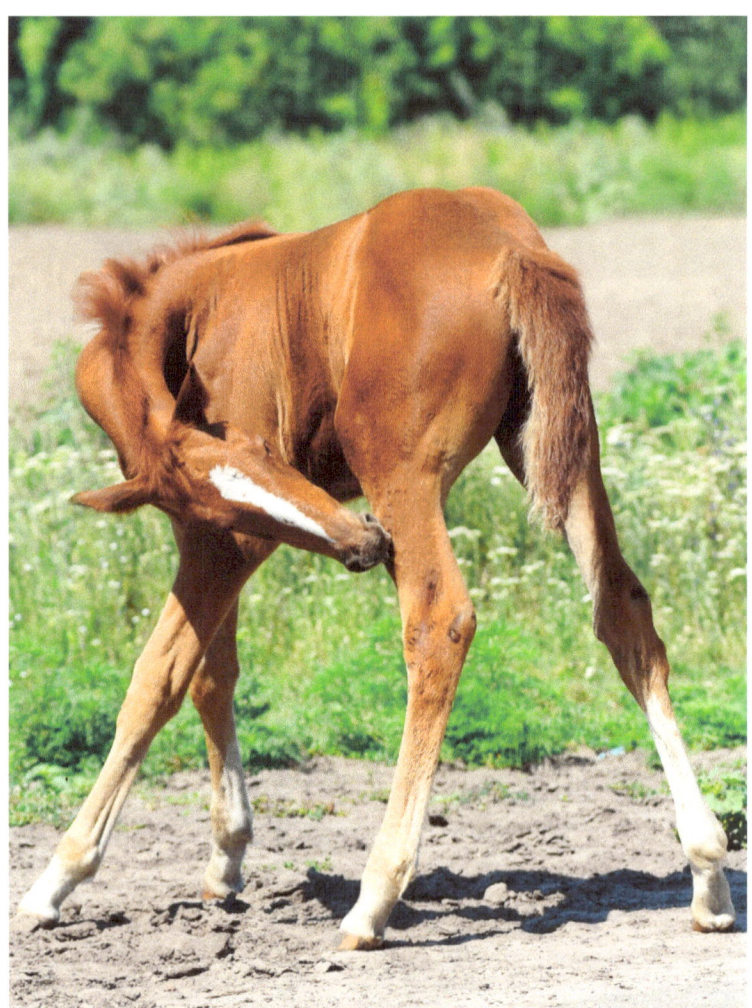

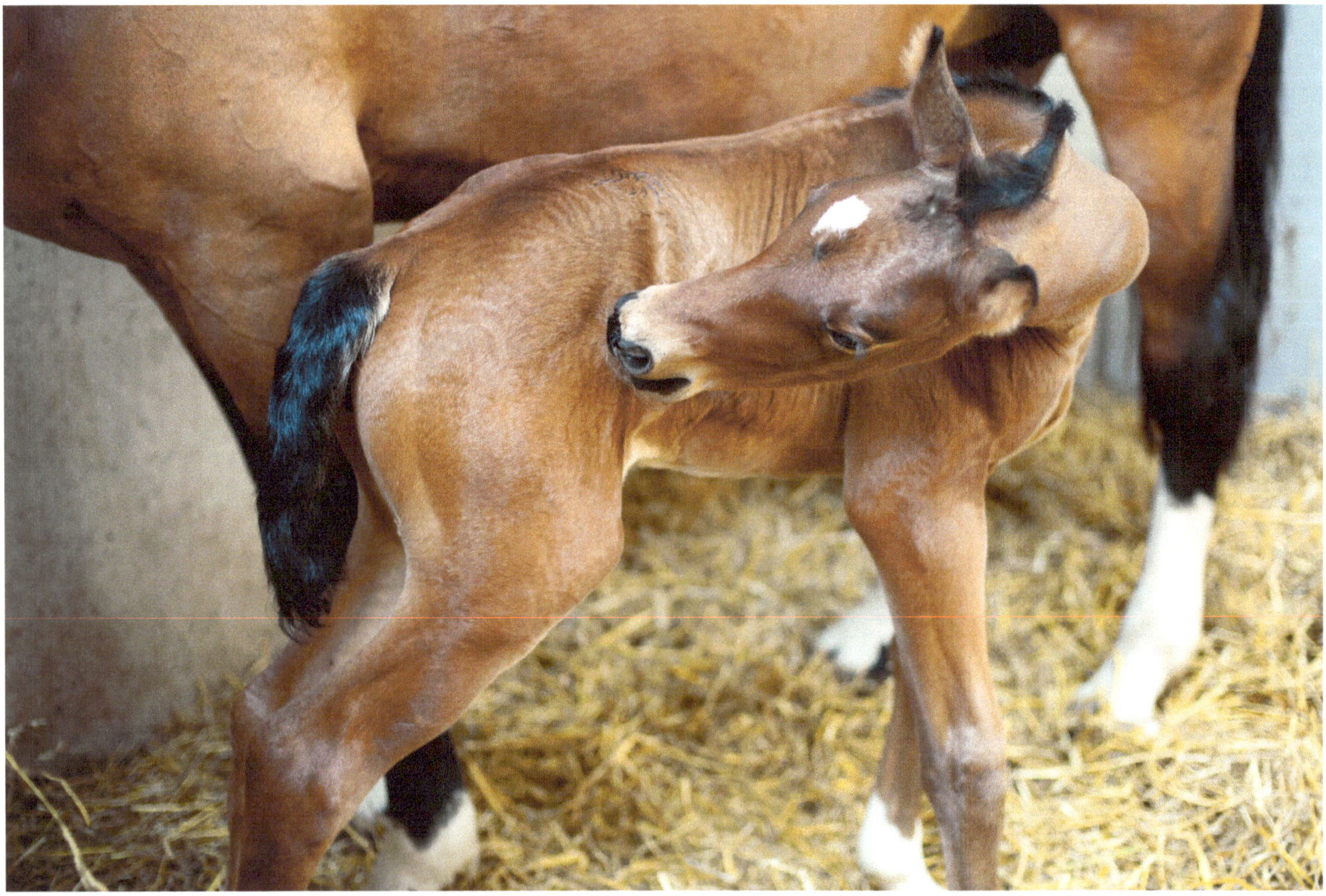

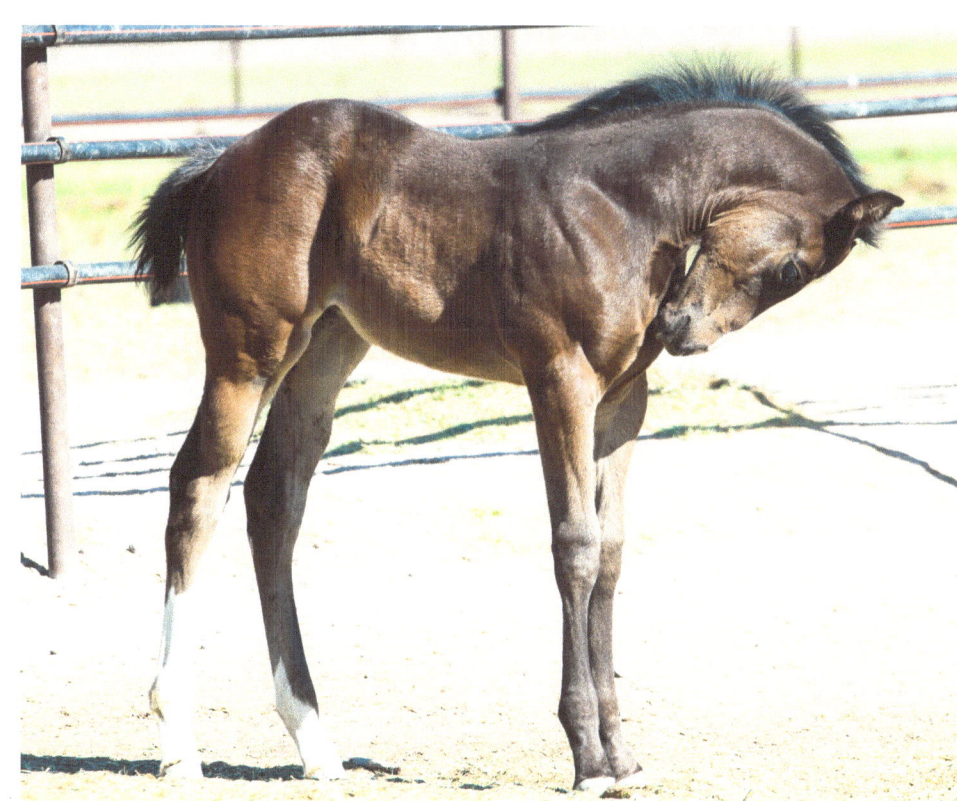

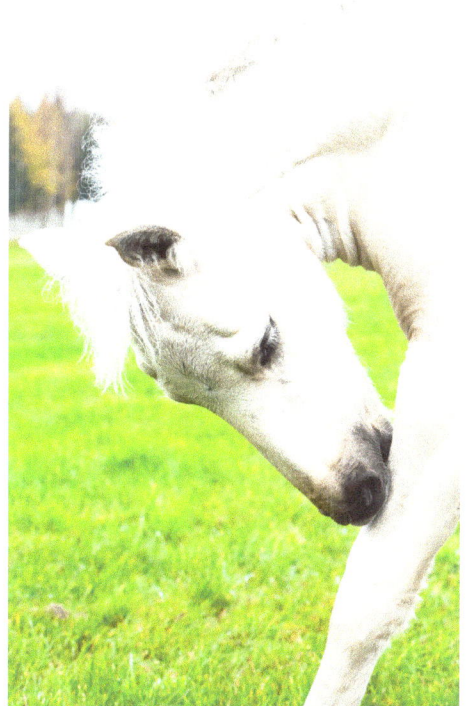

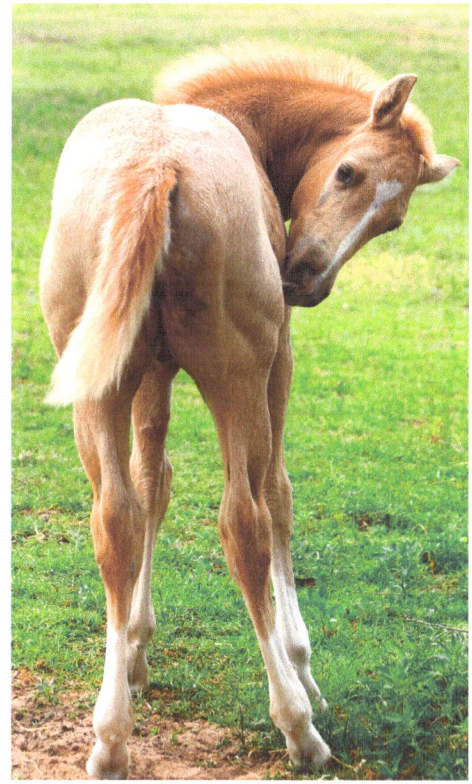

Bay Arabian with an itch

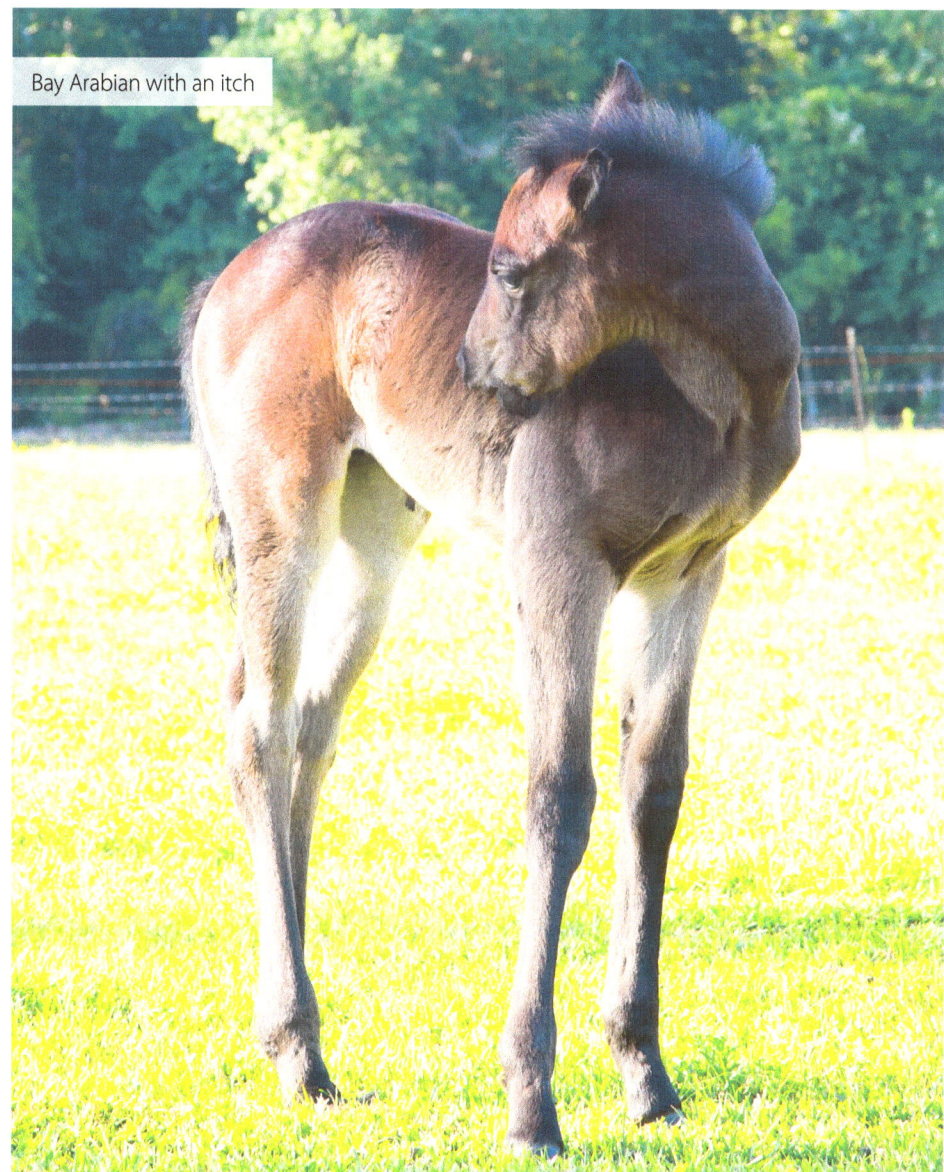

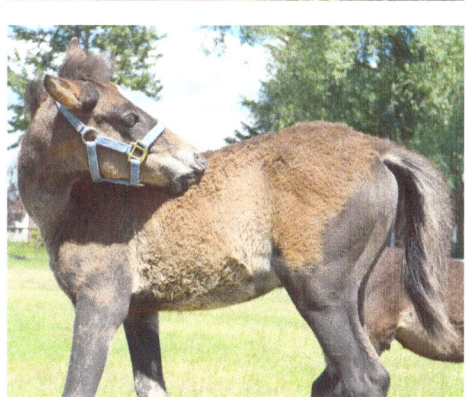

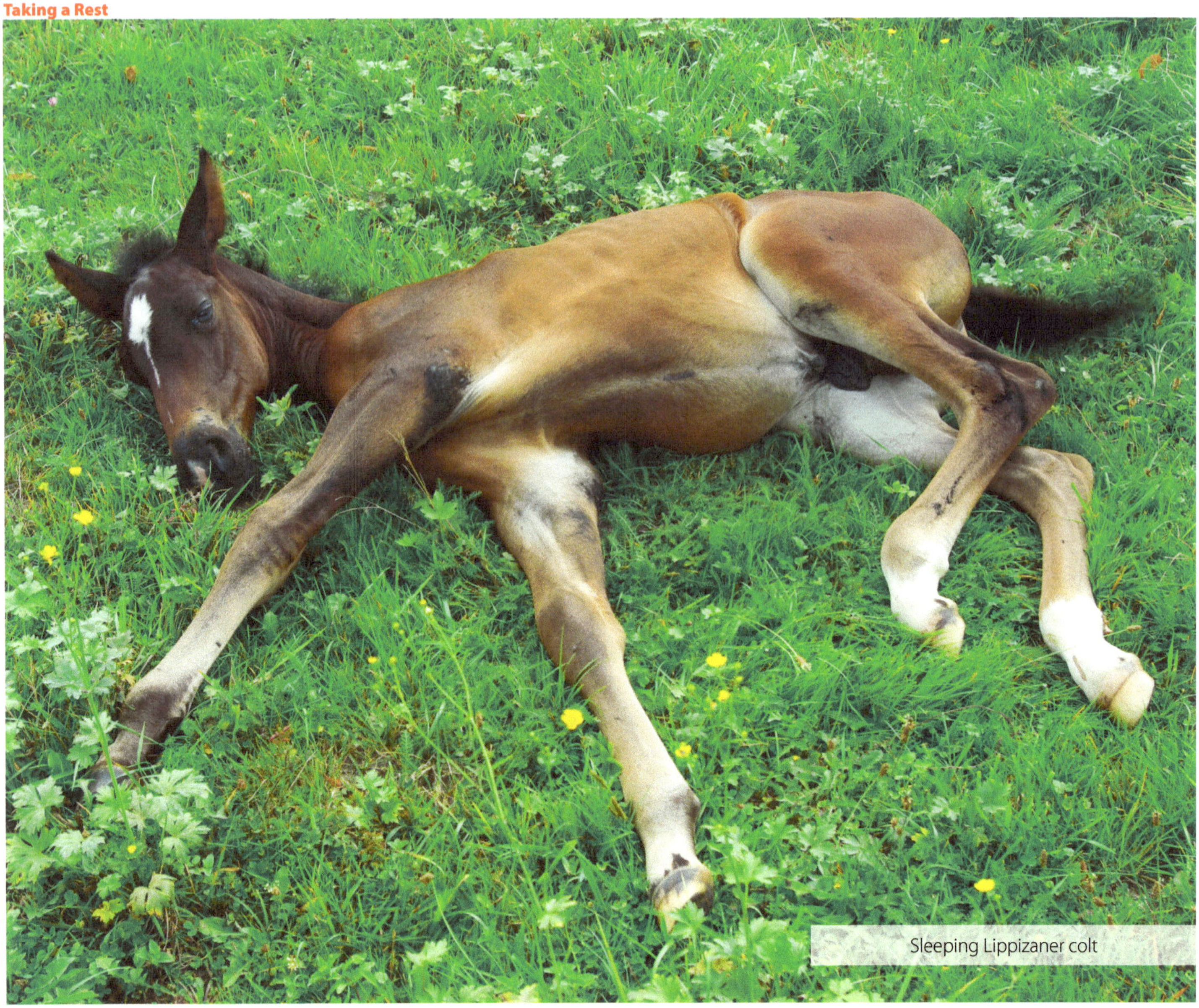

Sleeping Lippizaner colt

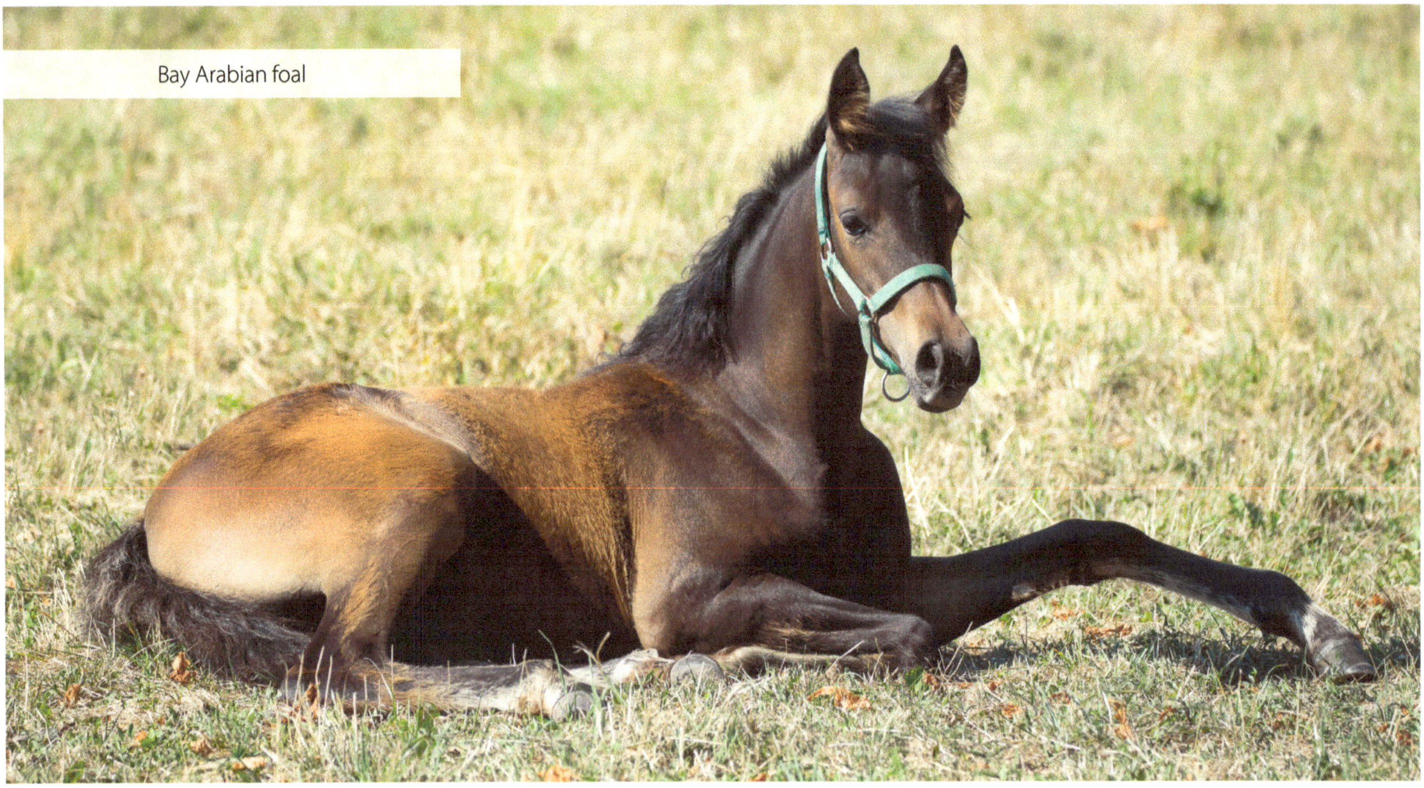

Bay Arabian foal

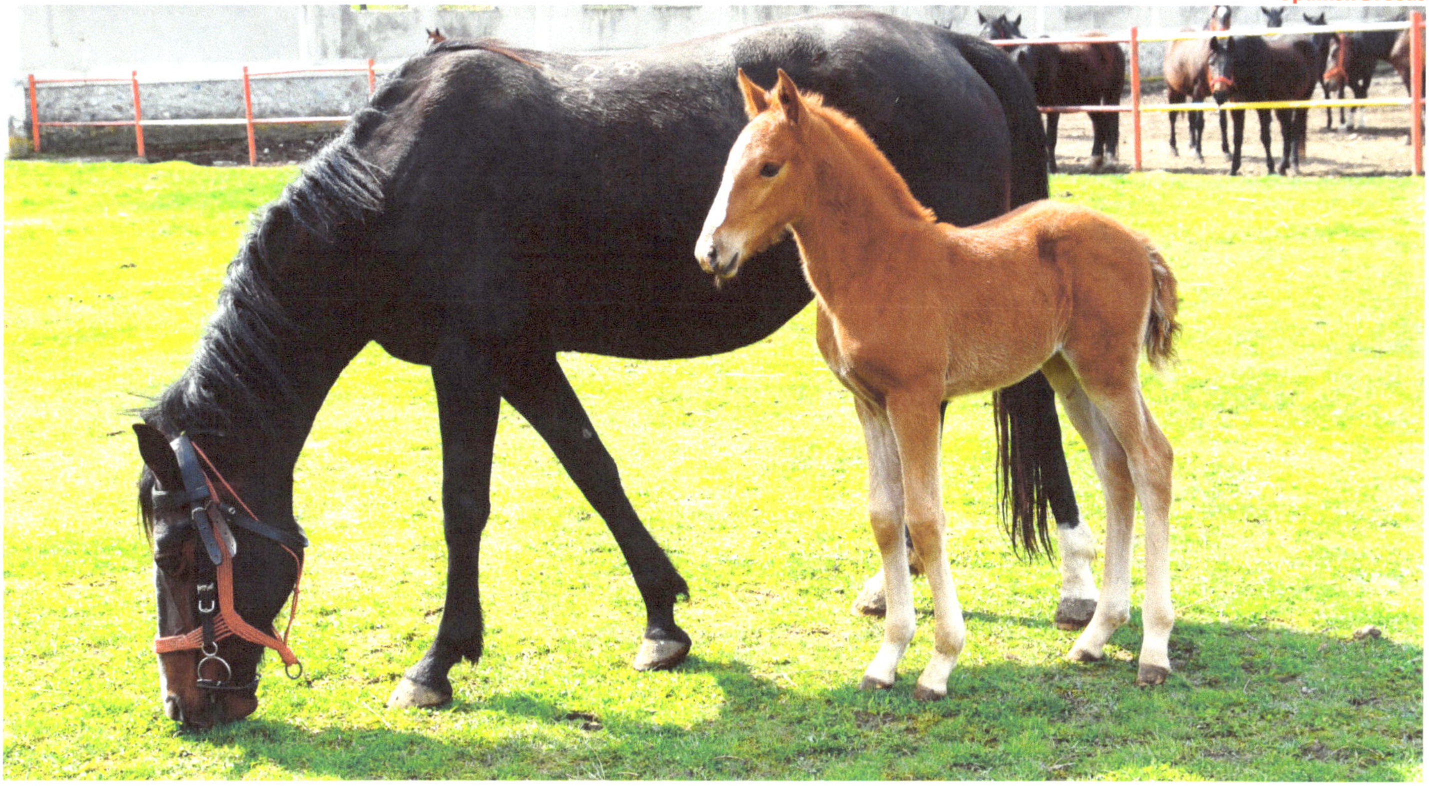

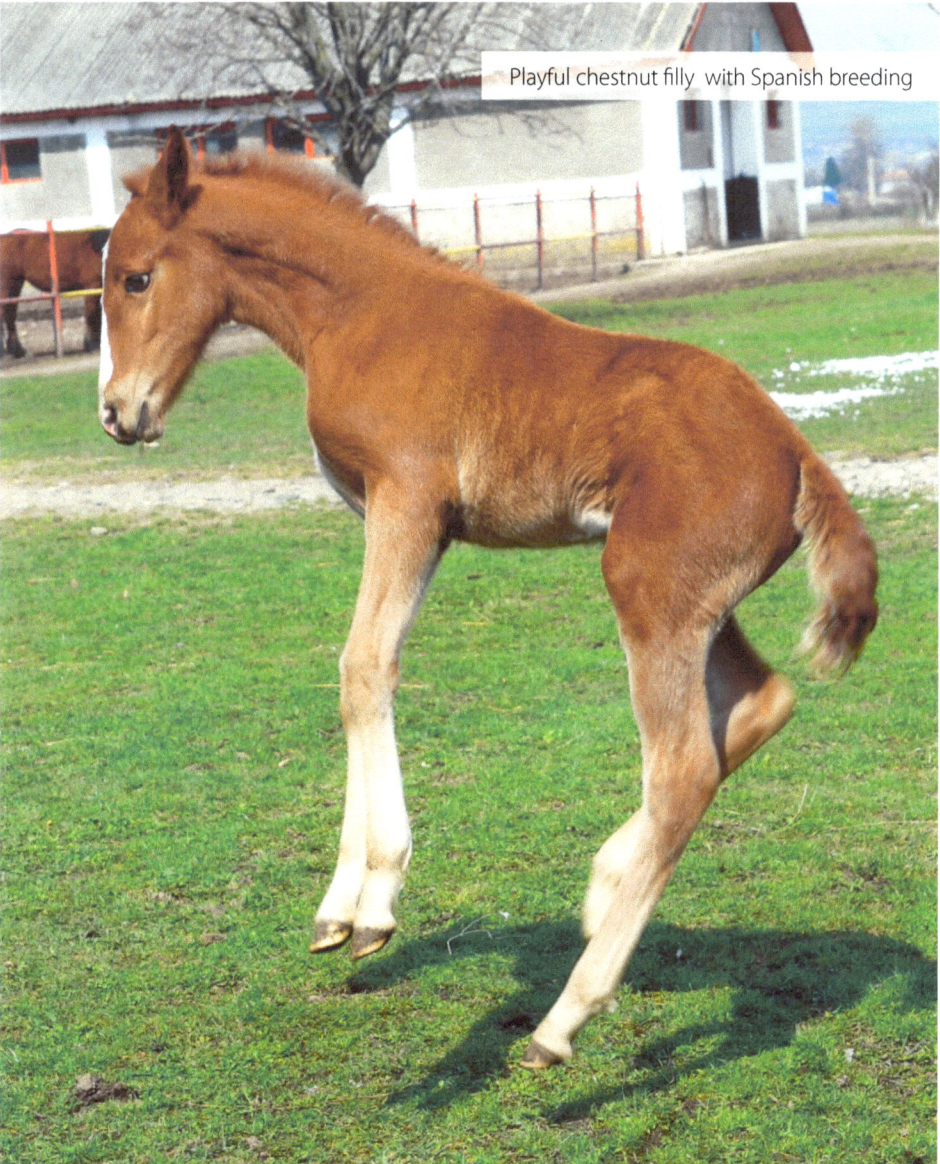

Playful chestnut filly with Spanish breeding

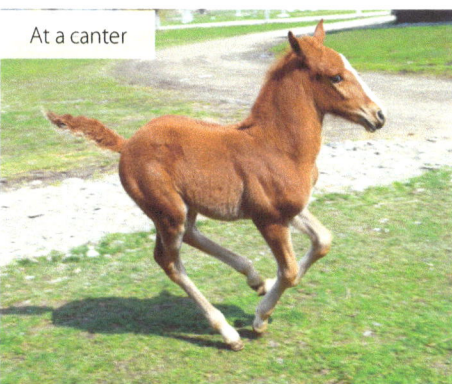

At a canter

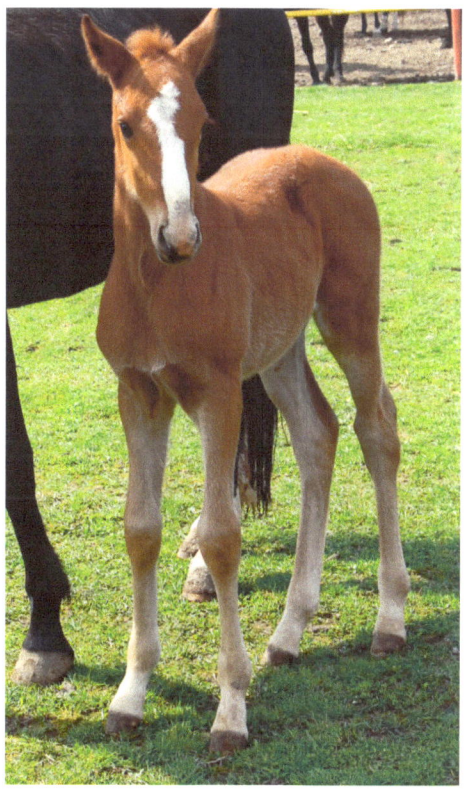

7

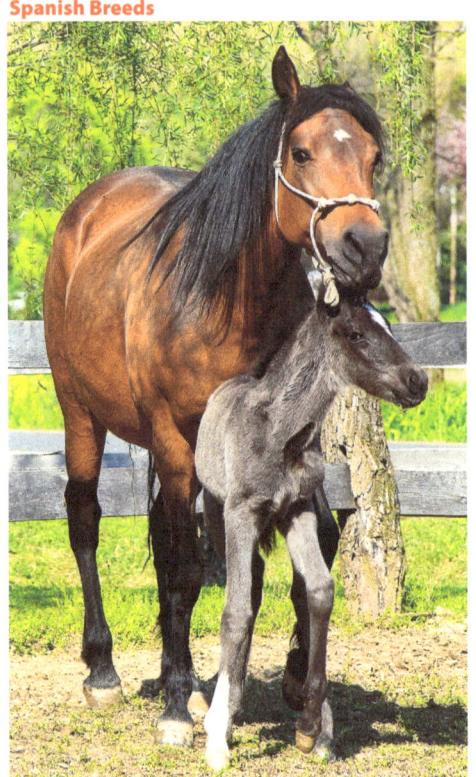
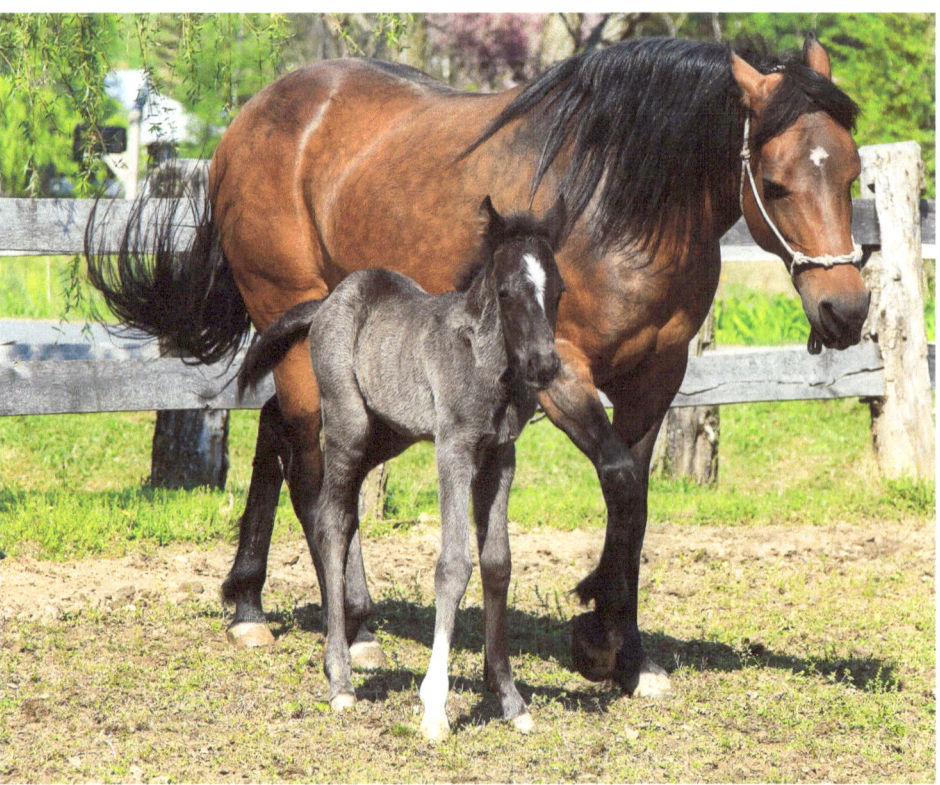

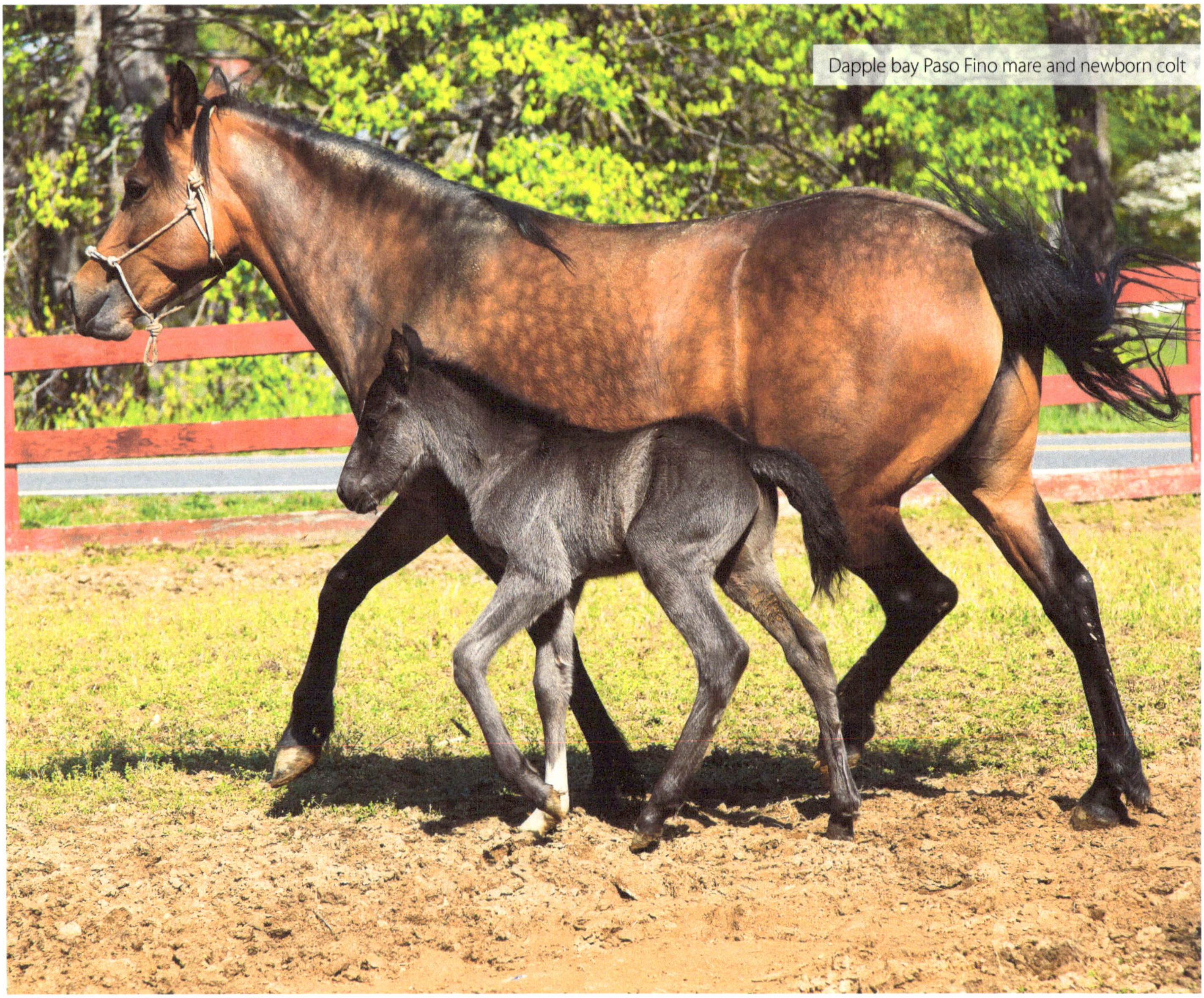

Dapple bay Paso Fino mare and newborn colt

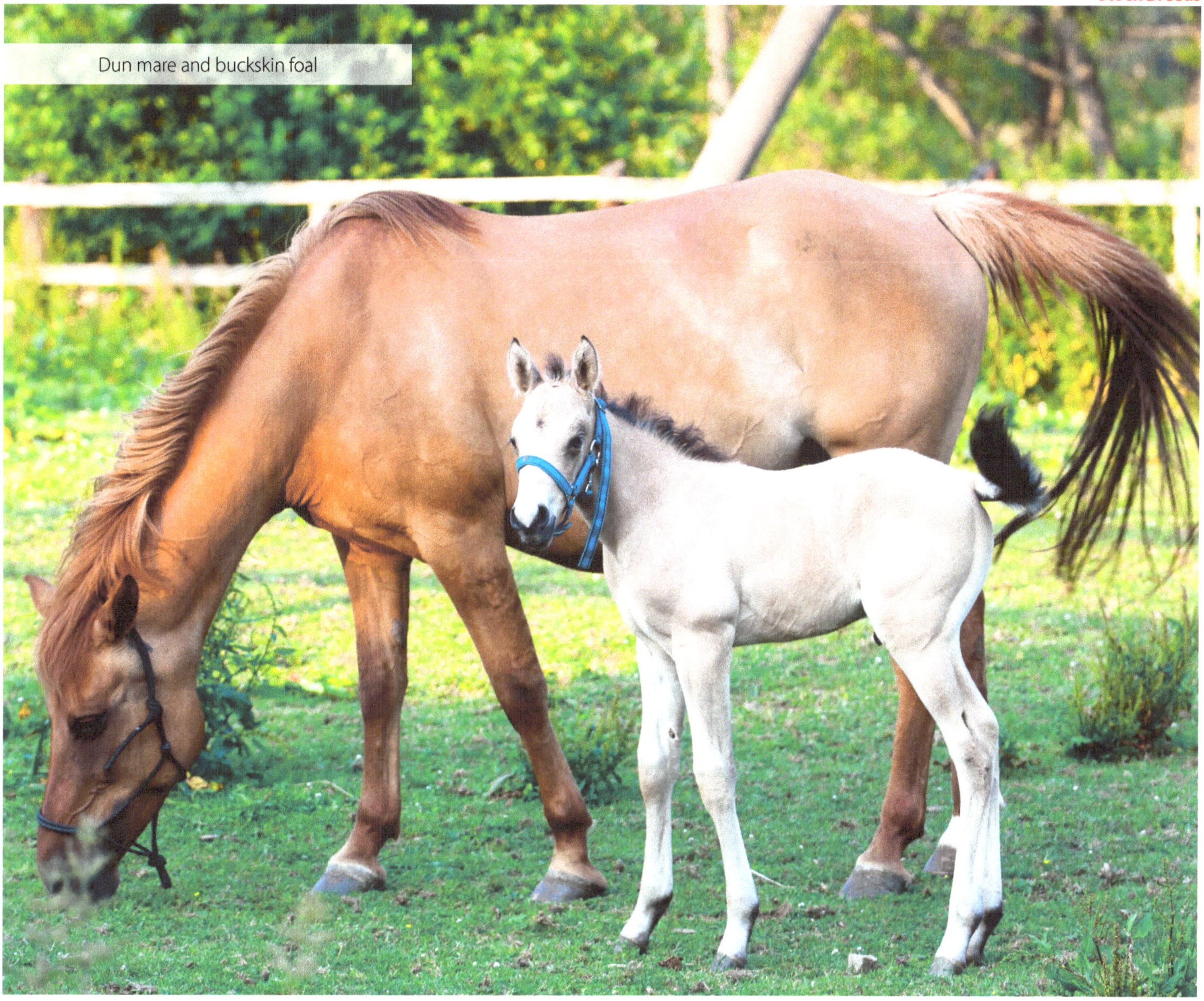

Dun mare and buckskin foal

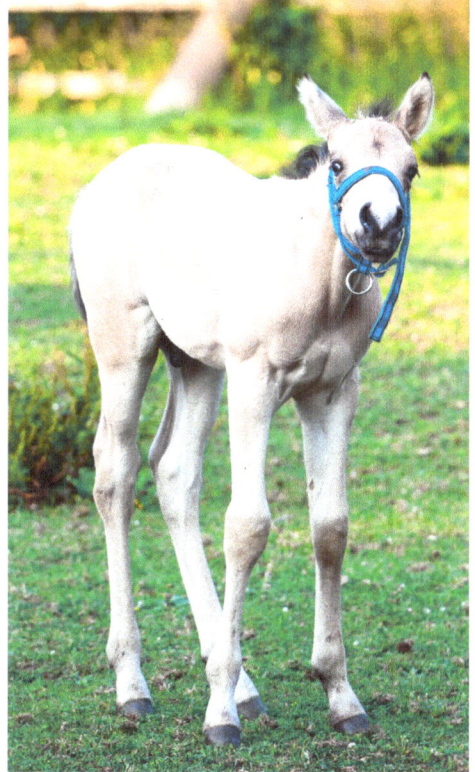

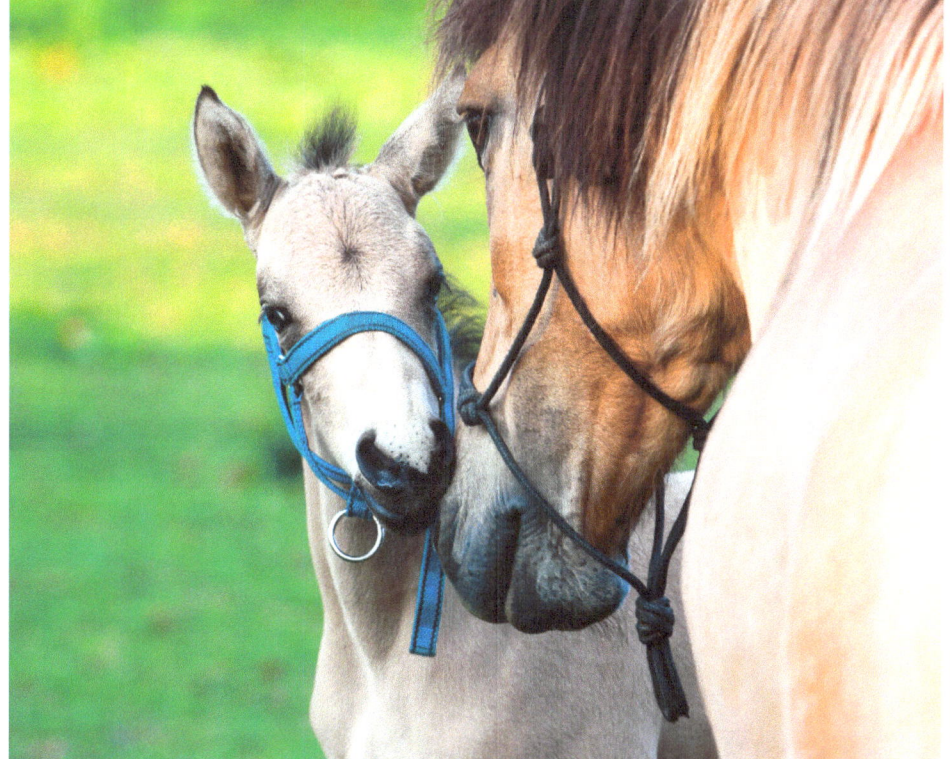

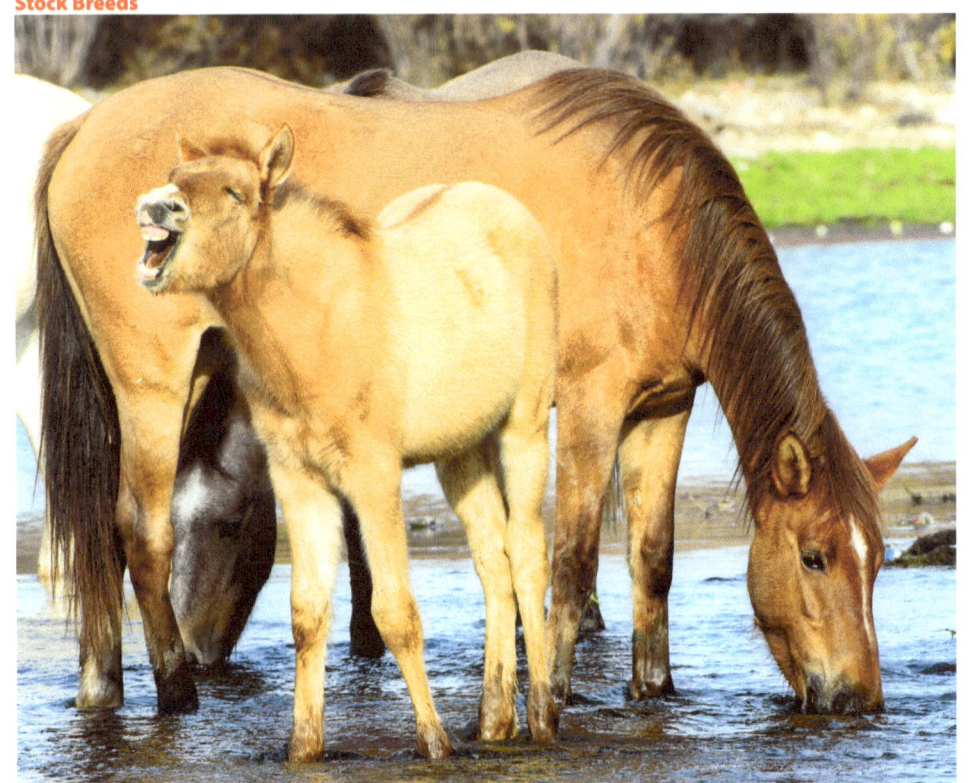

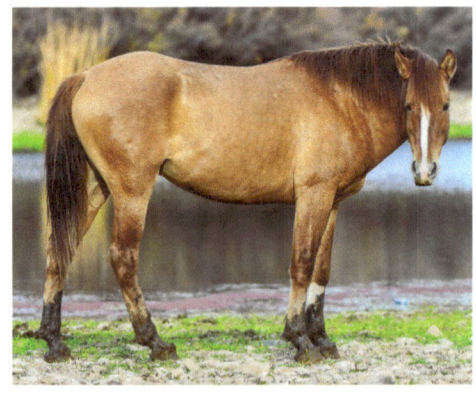

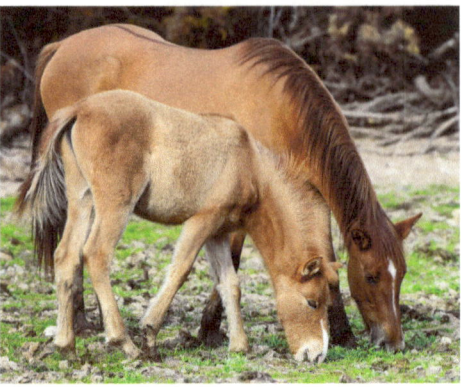

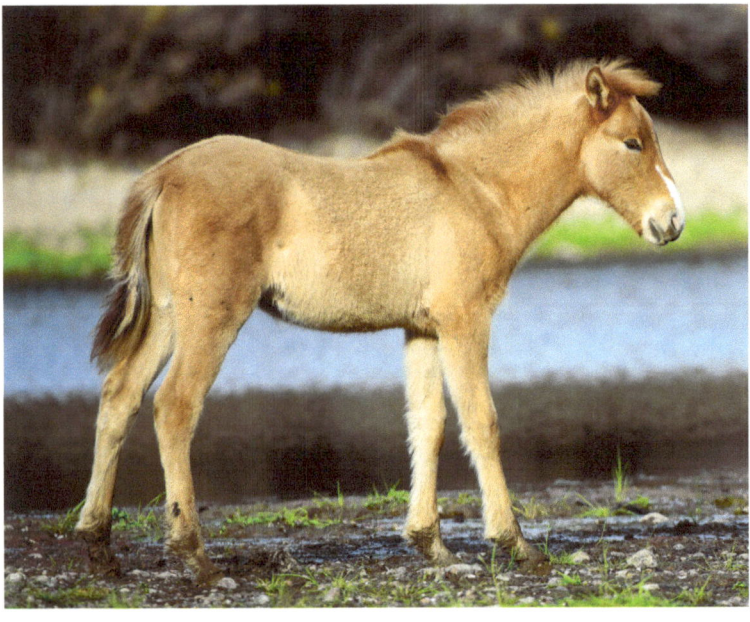

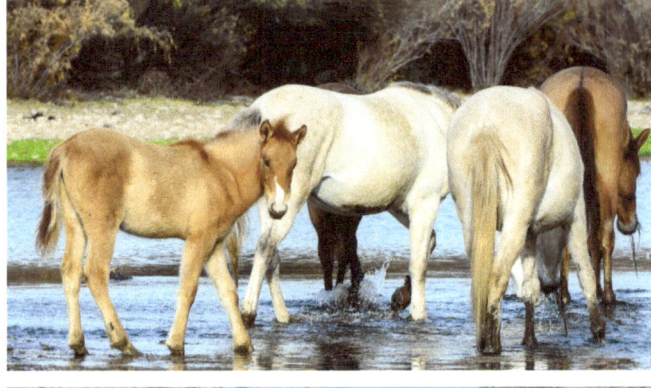

Claybank dun filly and her herd of Salt River wild Mustangs in the Tonto National Forest, Arizona

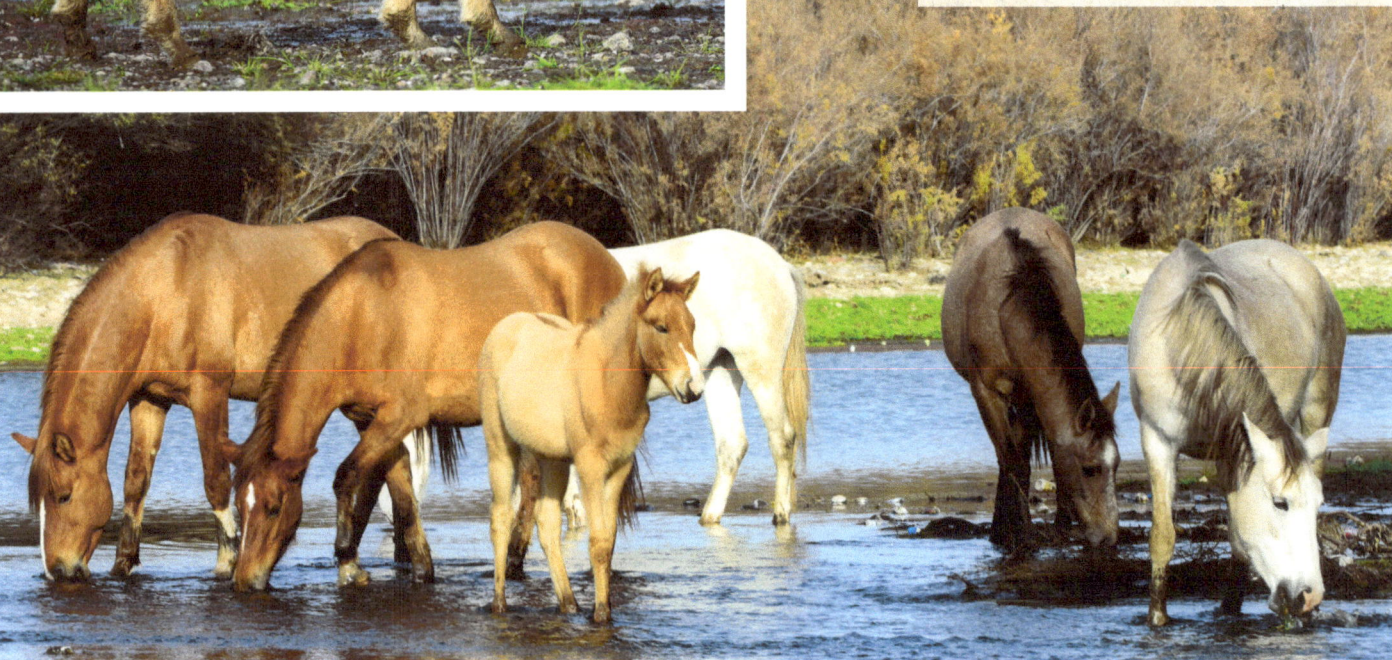

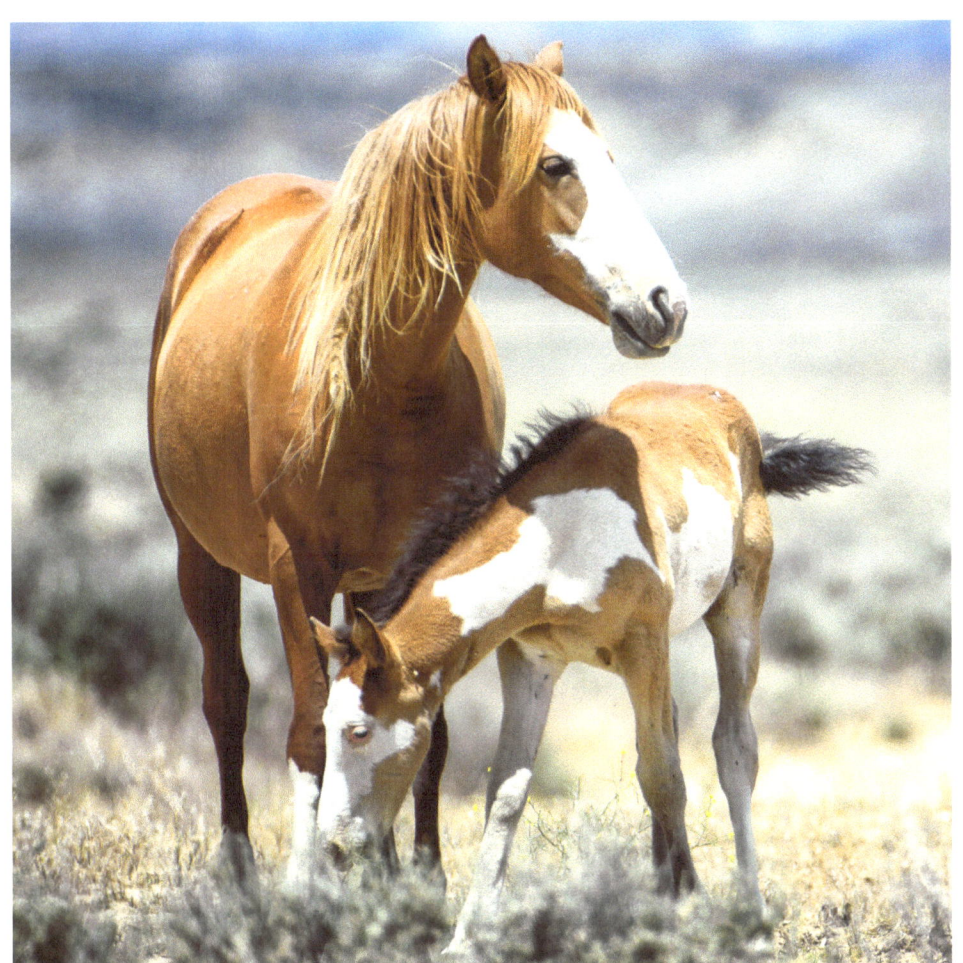

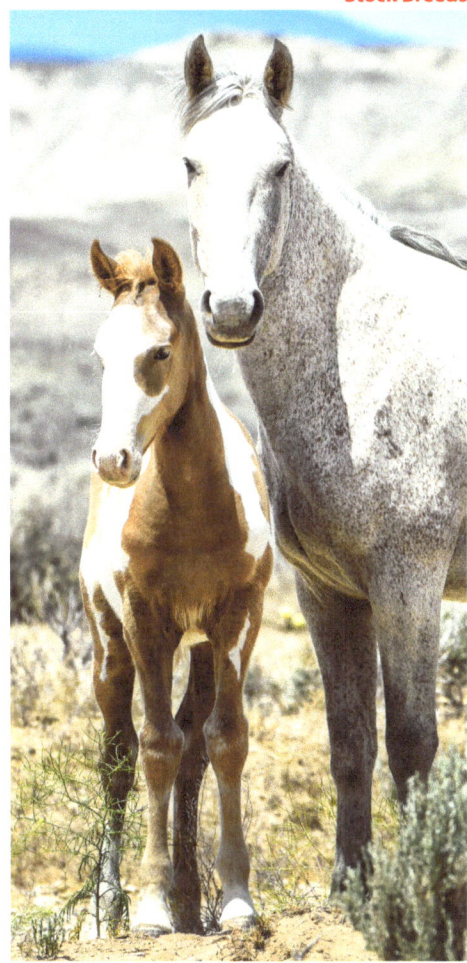

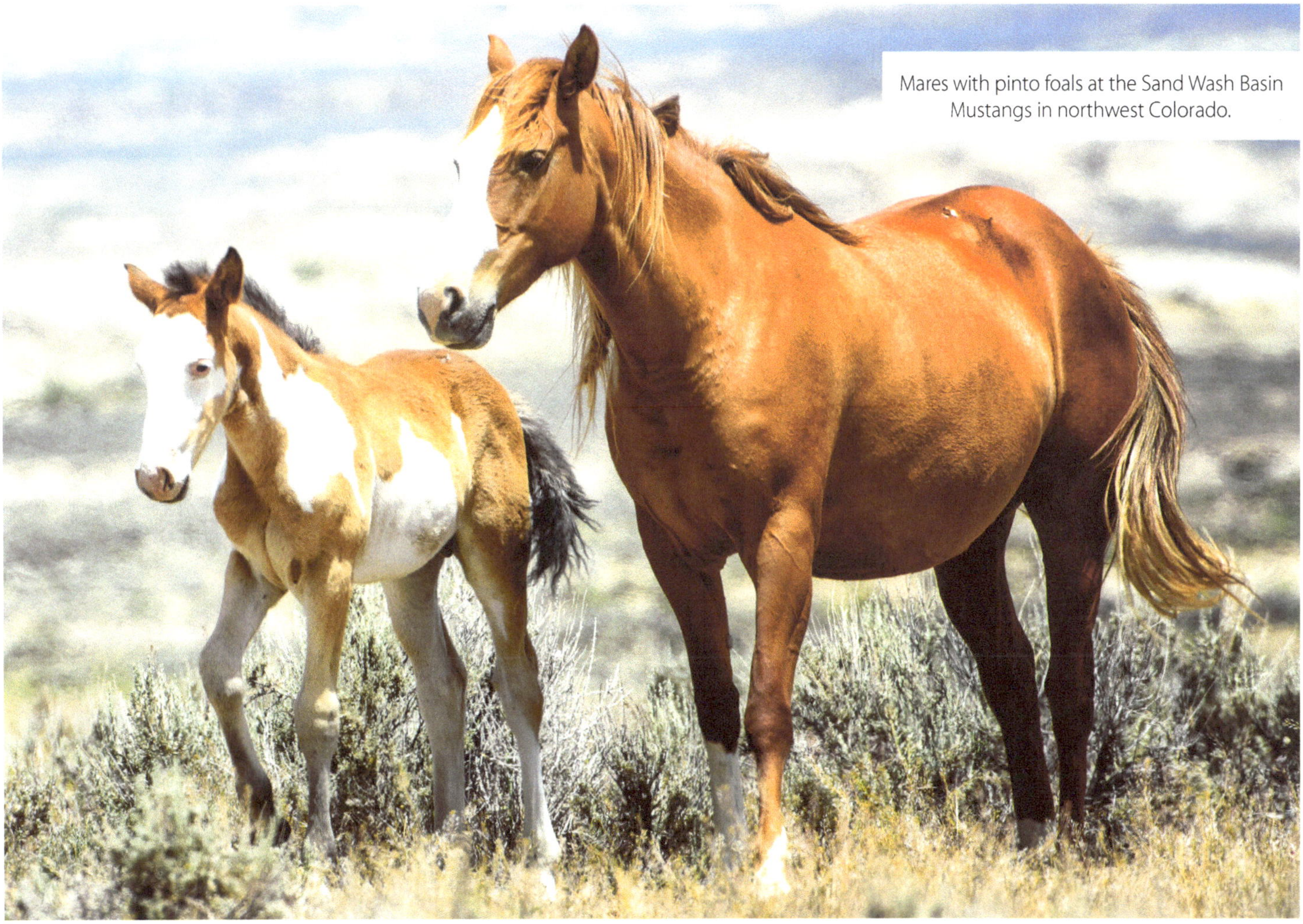

Mares with pinto foals at the Sand Wash Basin Mustangs in northwest Colorado.

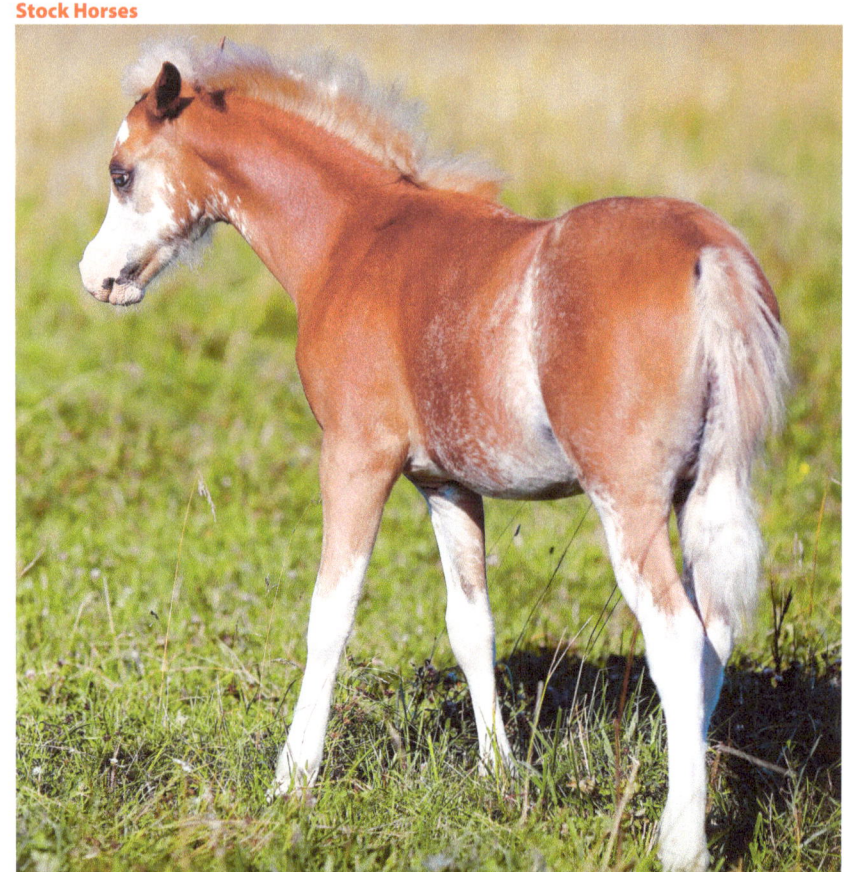

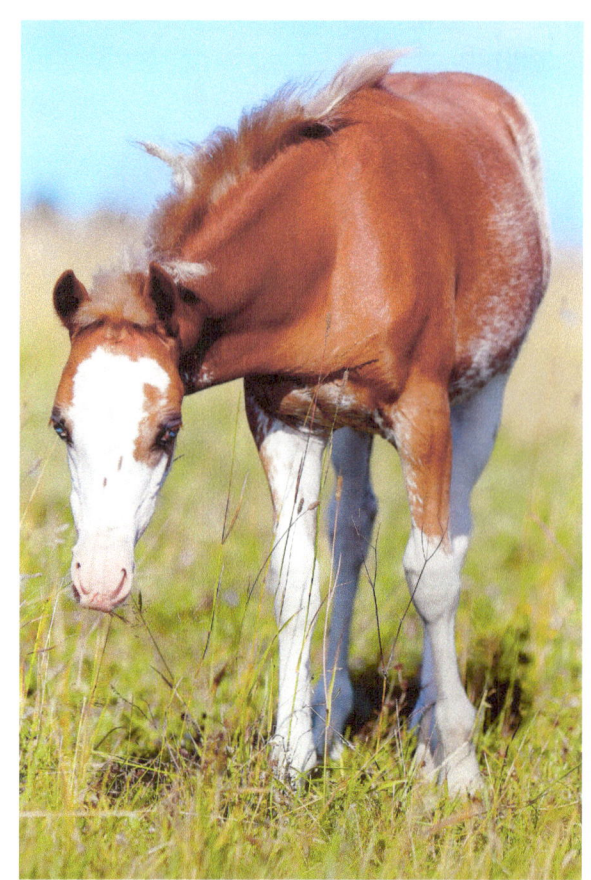

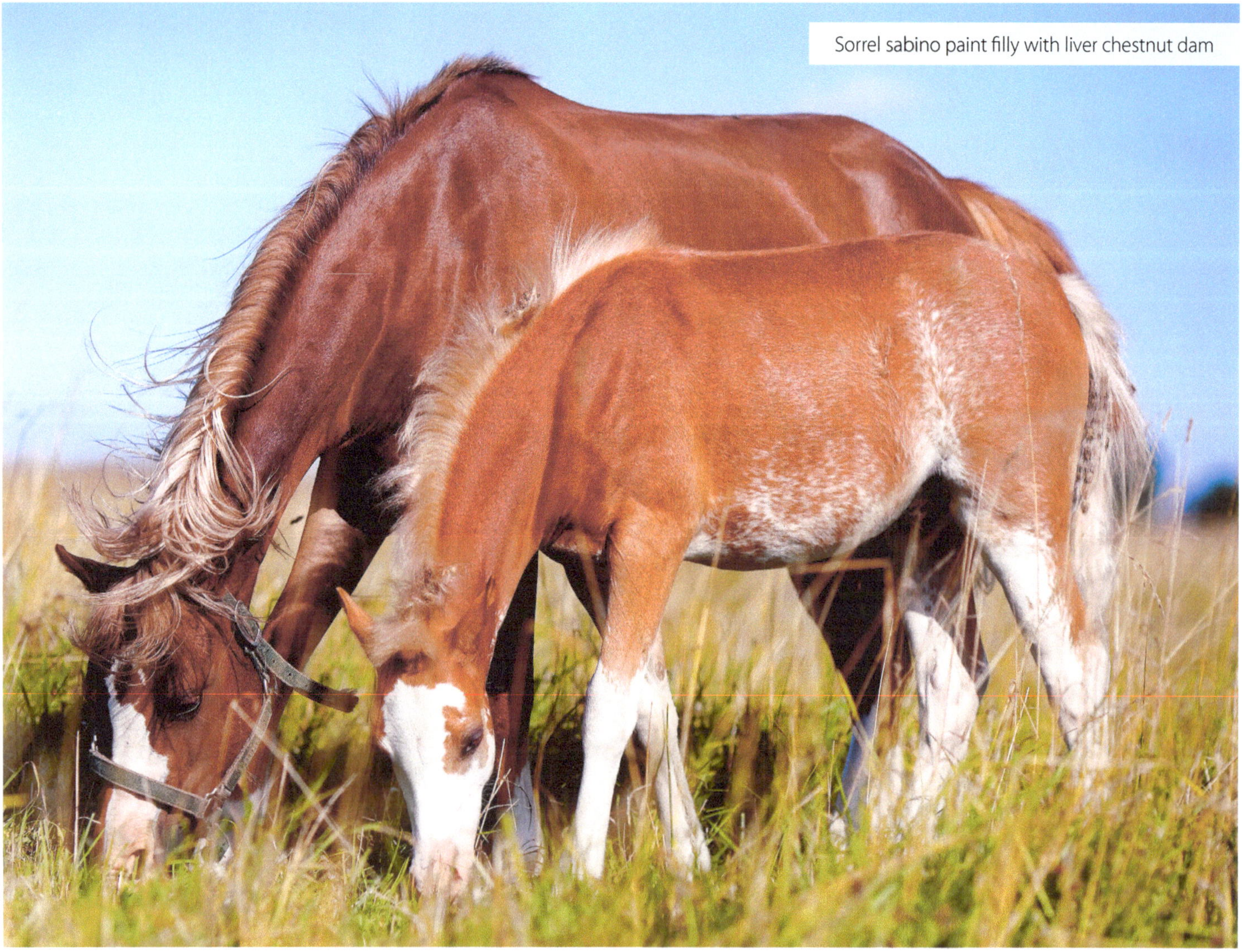

Sorrel sabino paint filly with liver chestnut dam

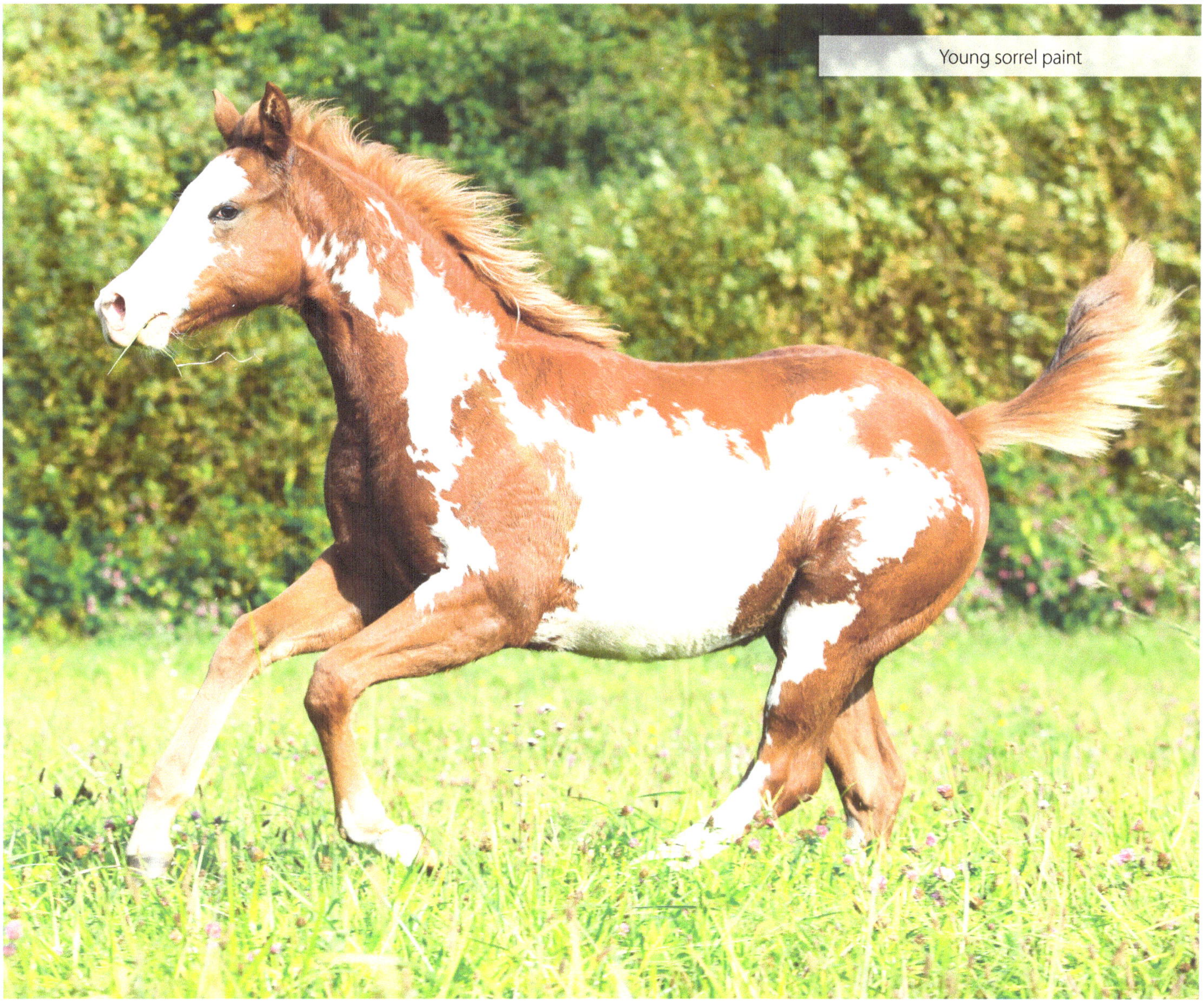

Young sorrel paint

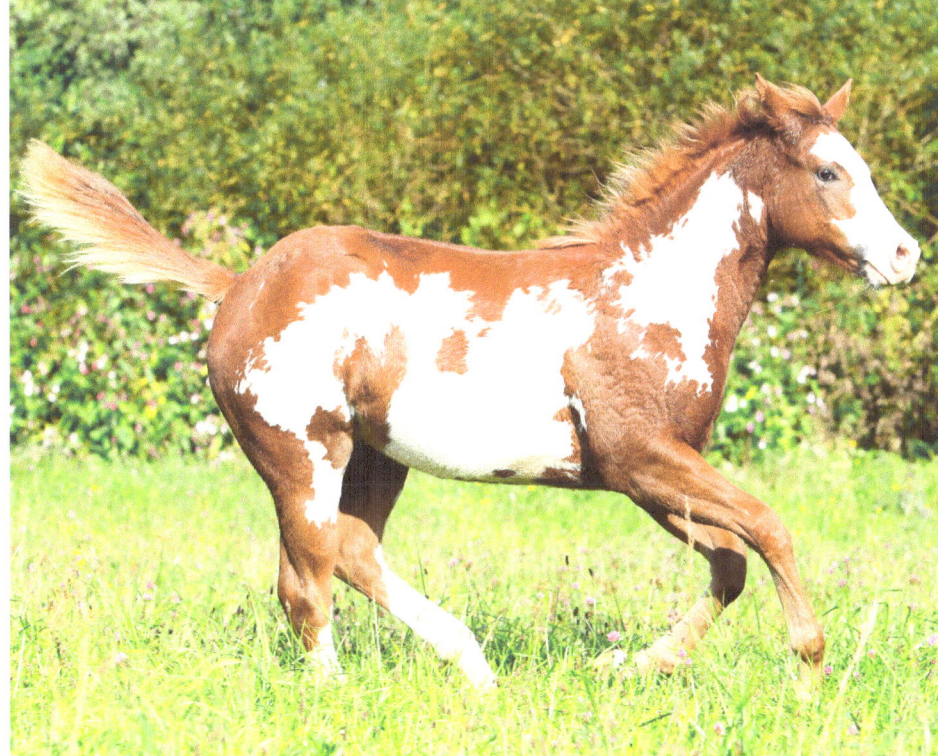

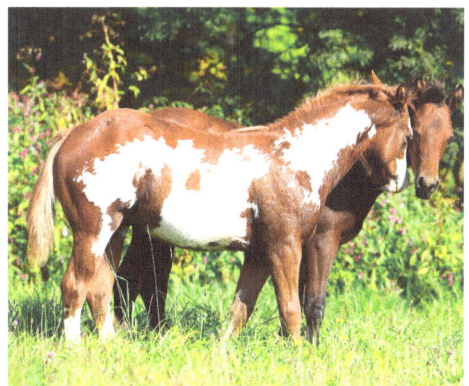

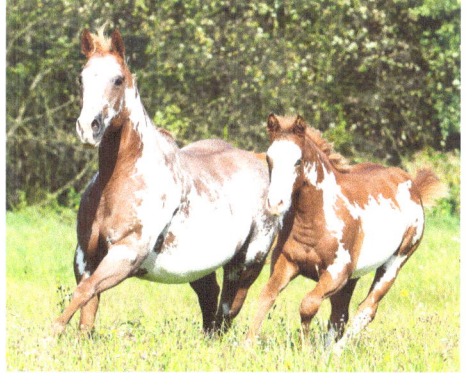

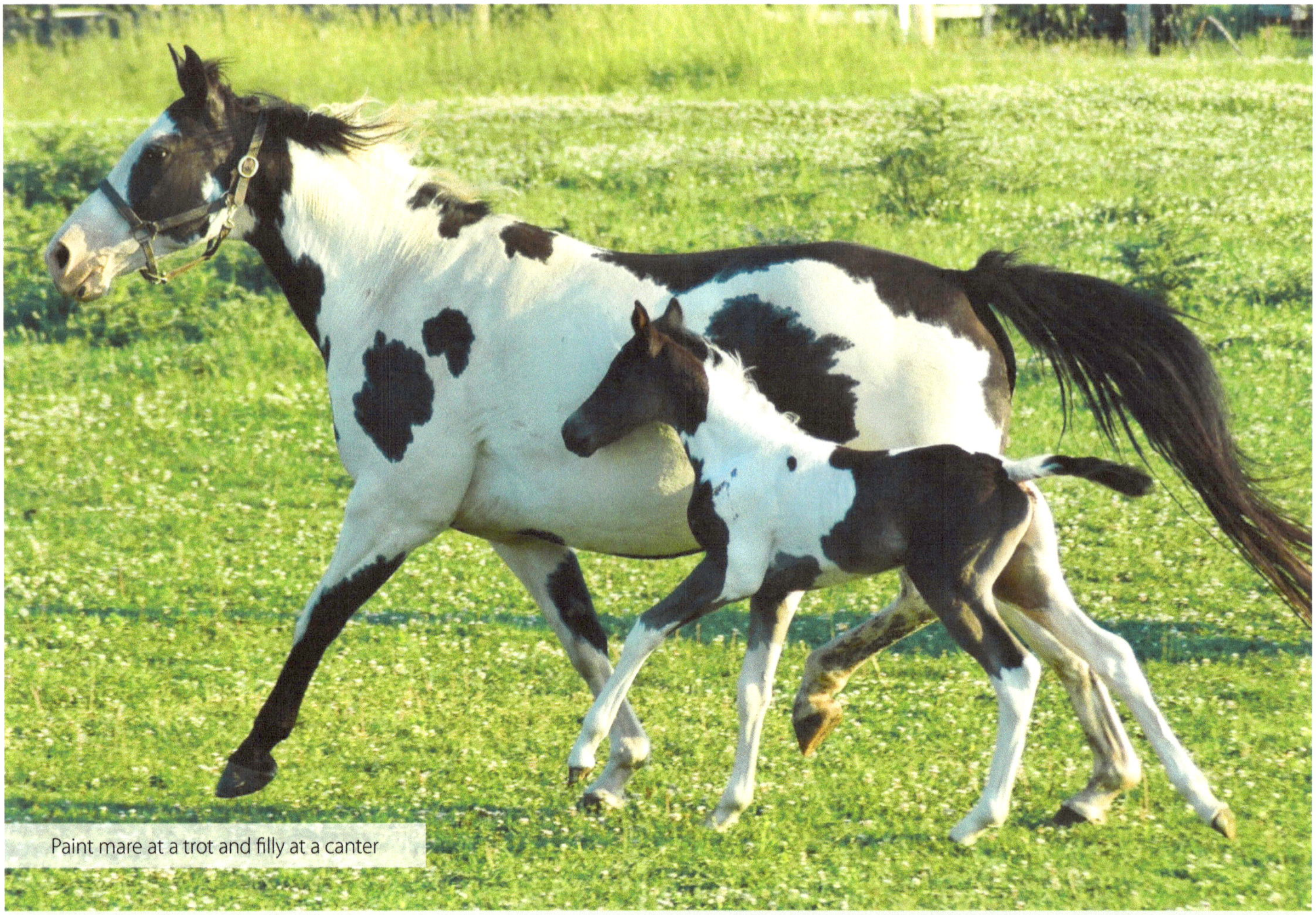

Paint mare at a trot and filly at a canter

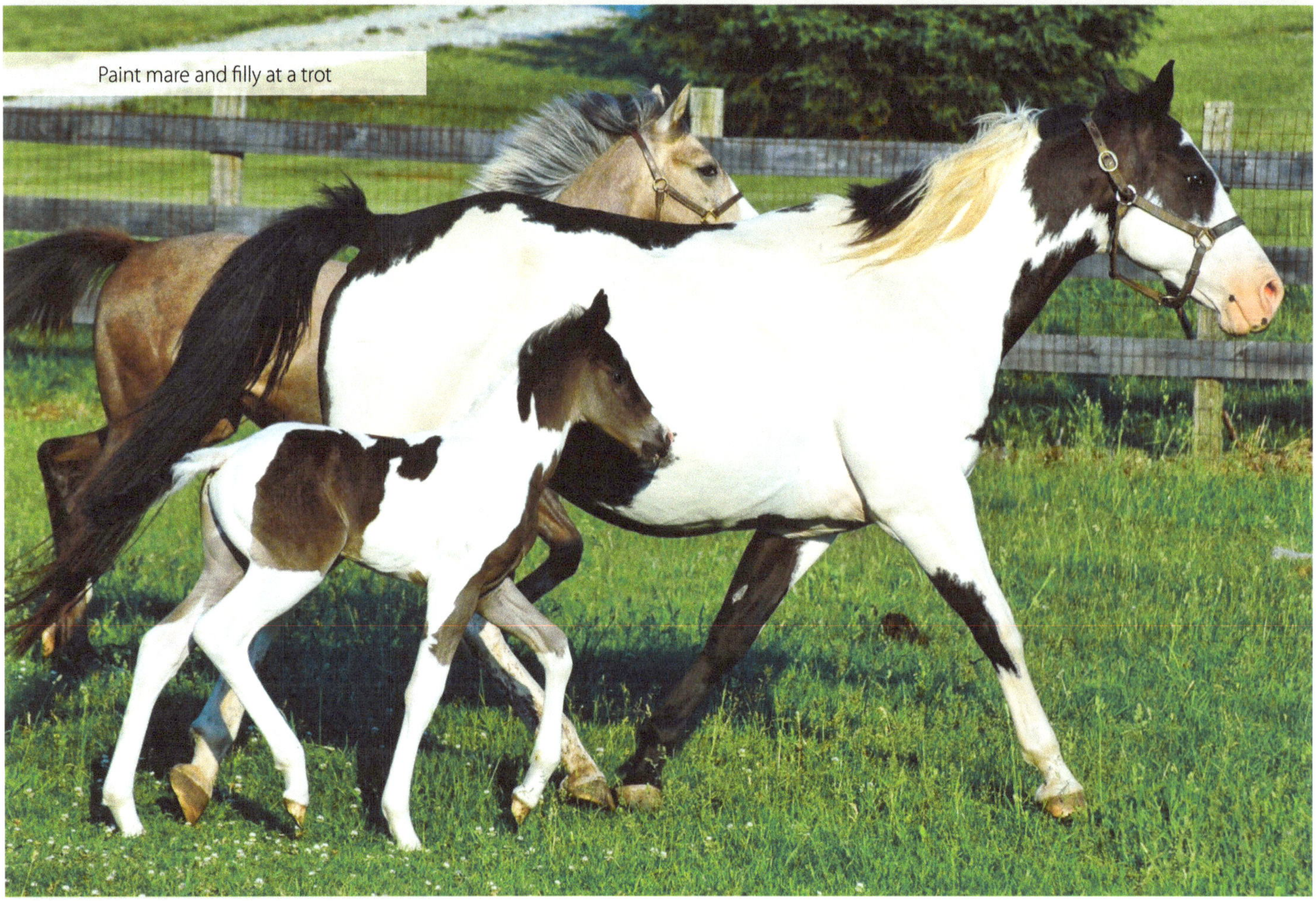

Paint mare and filly at a trot

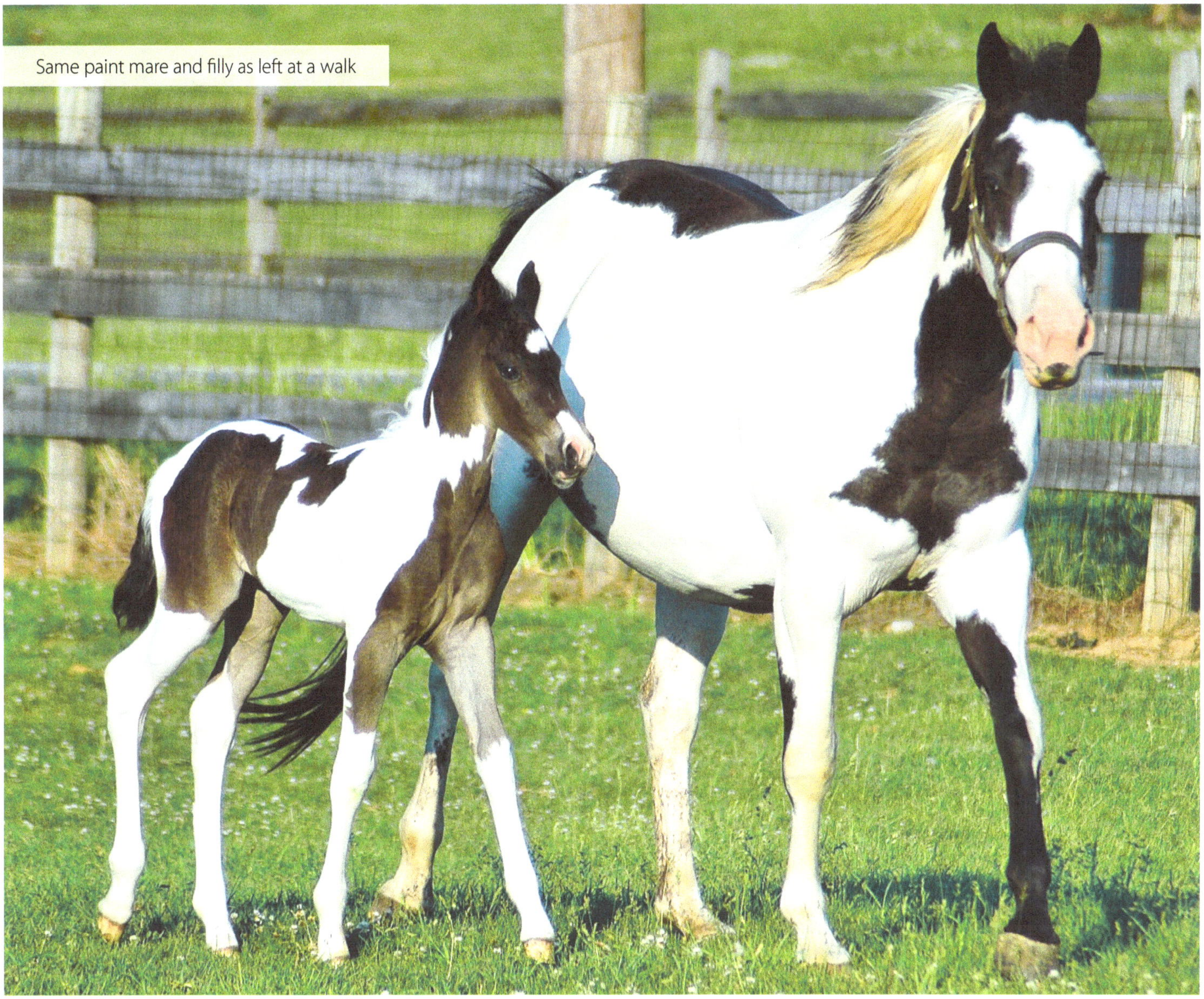

Same paint mare and filly as left at a walk

Cantering bay paint foal

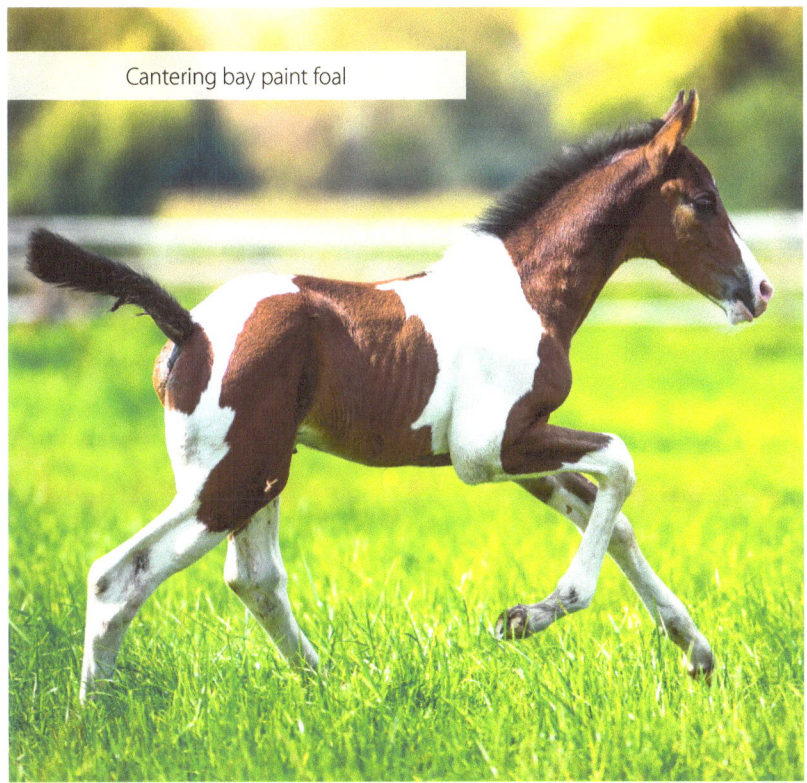

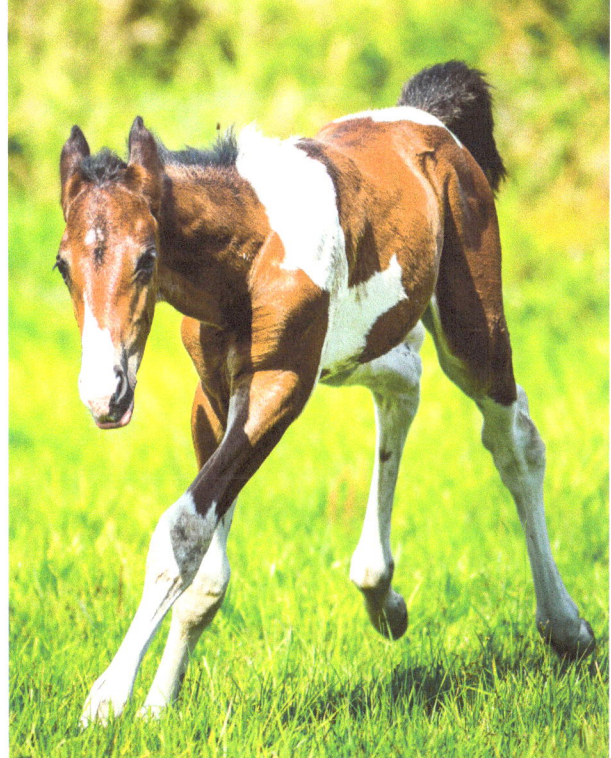

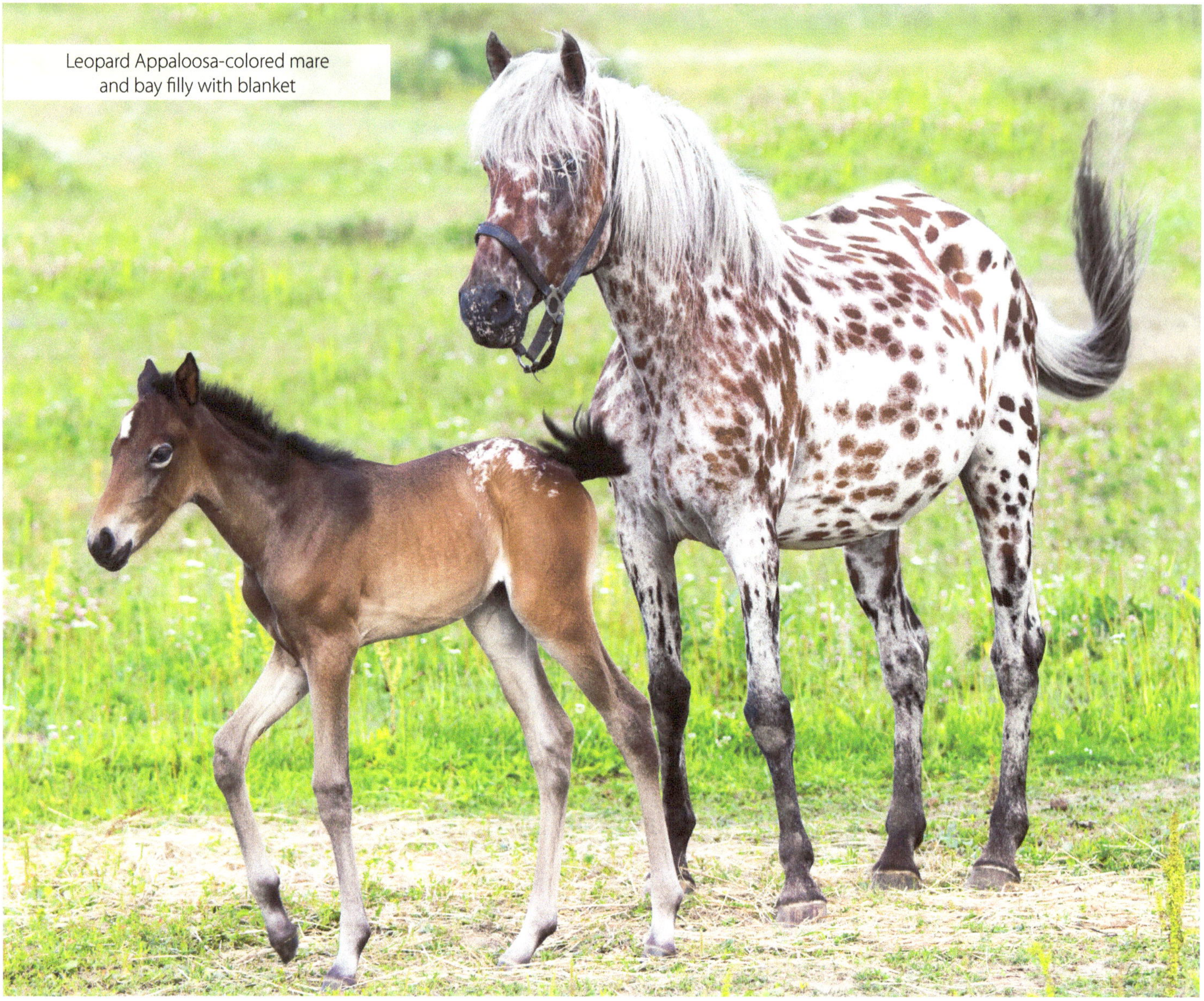

Leopard Appaloosa-colored mare
and bay filly with blanket

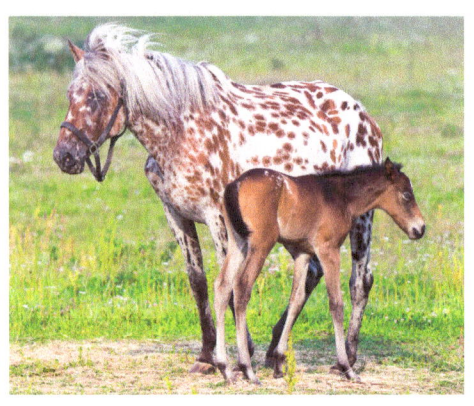

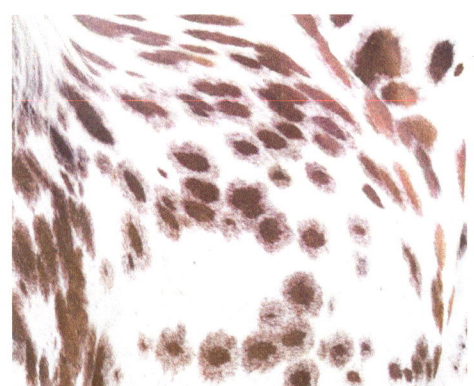

Filly at a canter

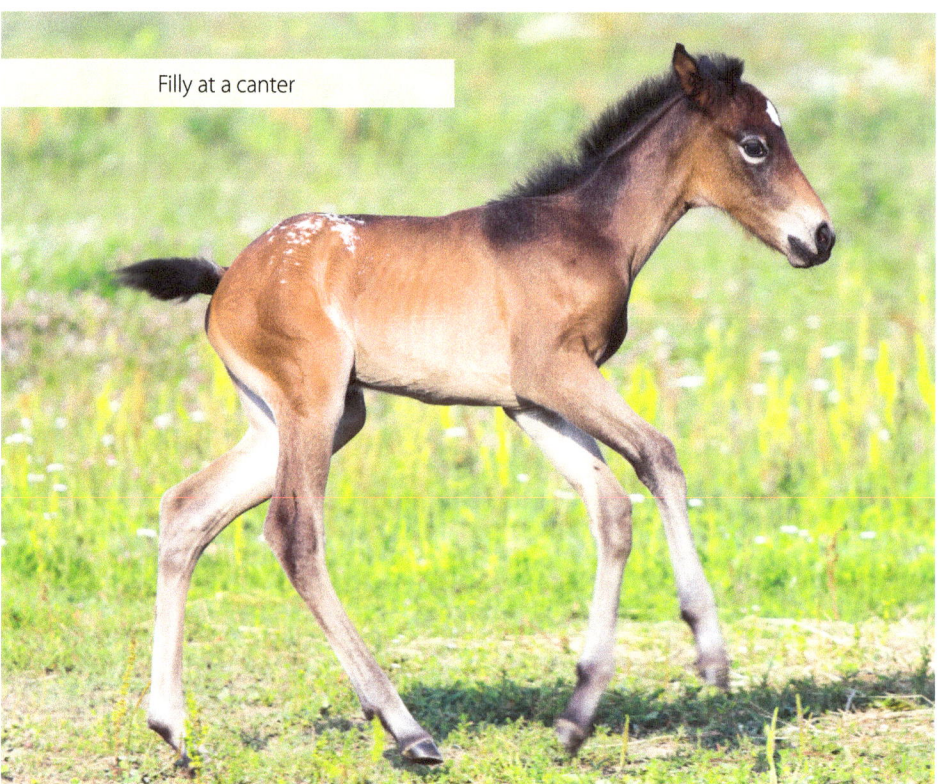

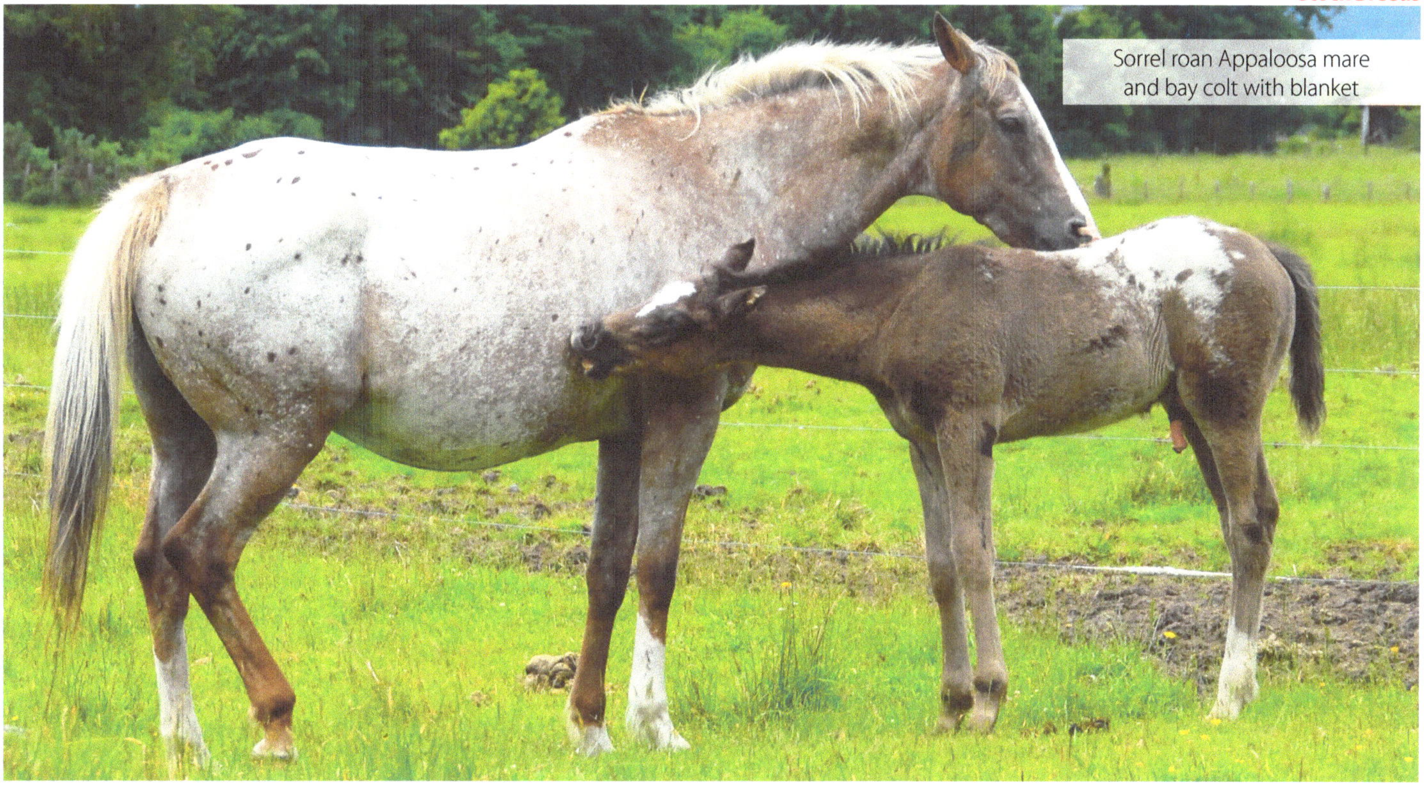

Sorrel roan Appaloosa mare and bay colt with blanket

Bay roan Appaloosa with blanket filly at a canter

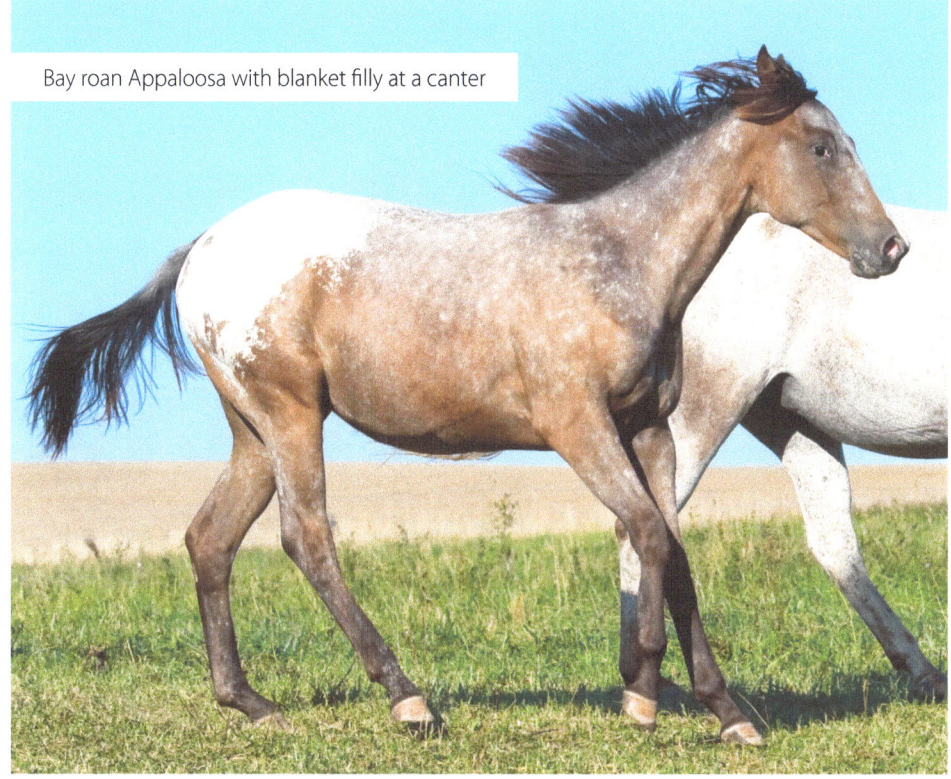

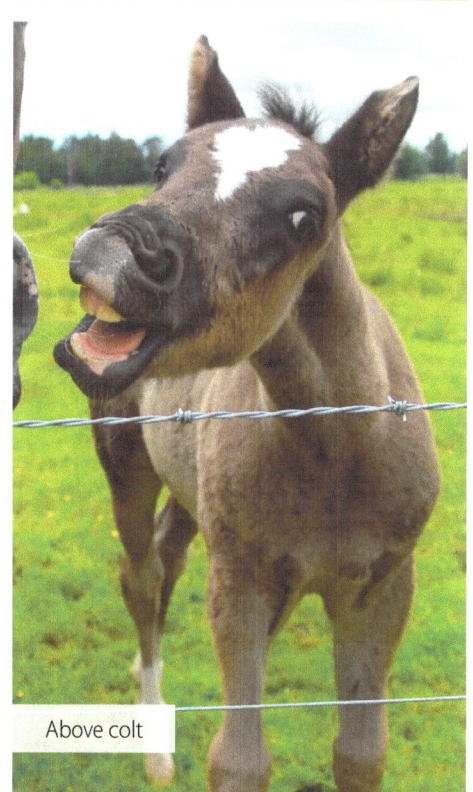

Above colt

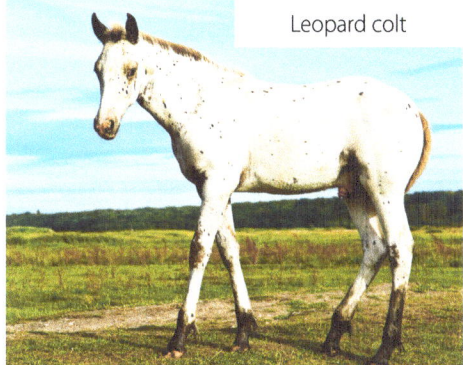

Leopard colt

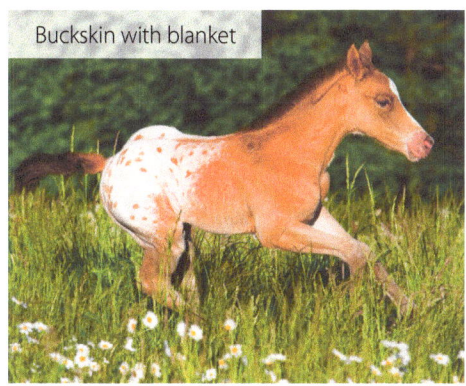

Buckskin with blanket

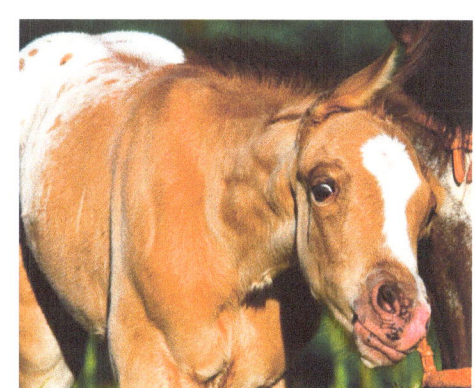

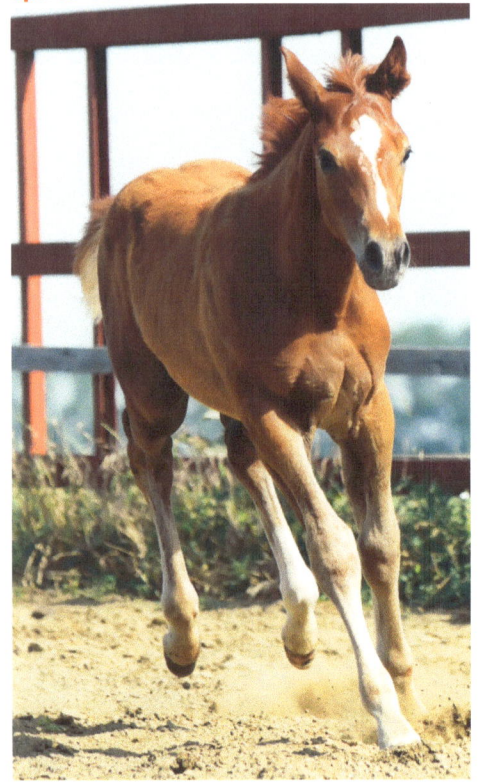

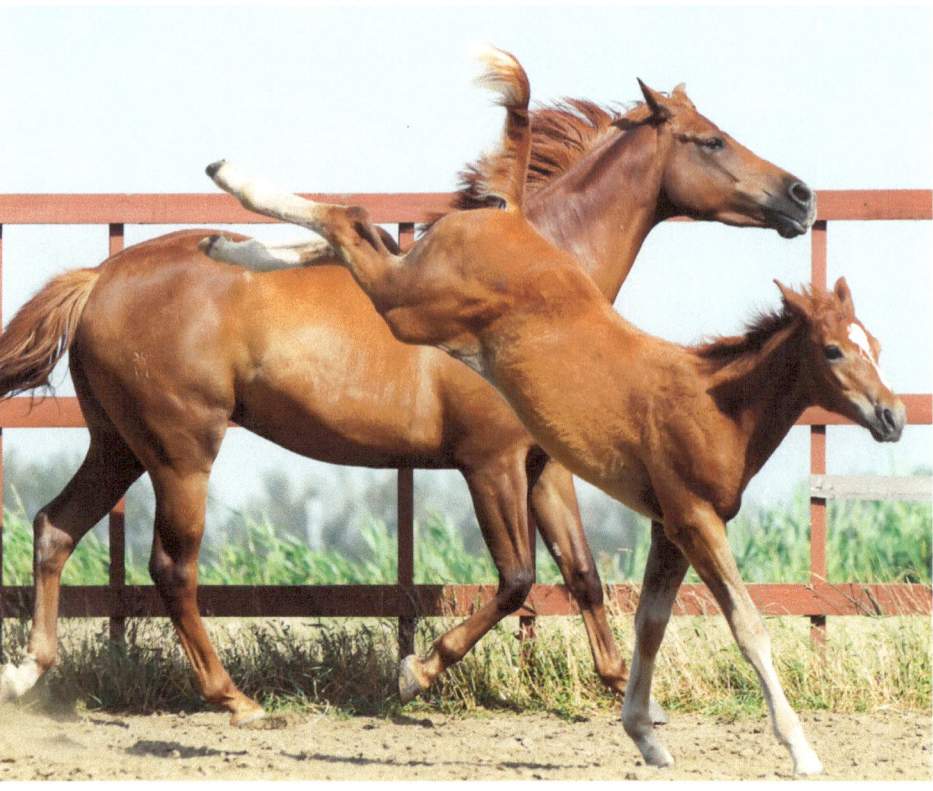

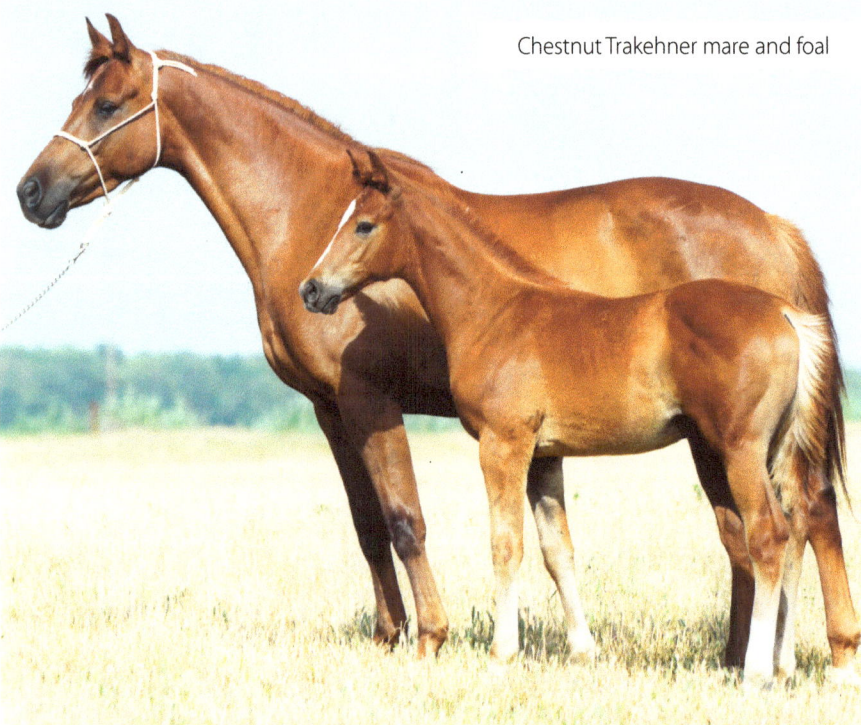

Chestnut Trakehner mare and foal

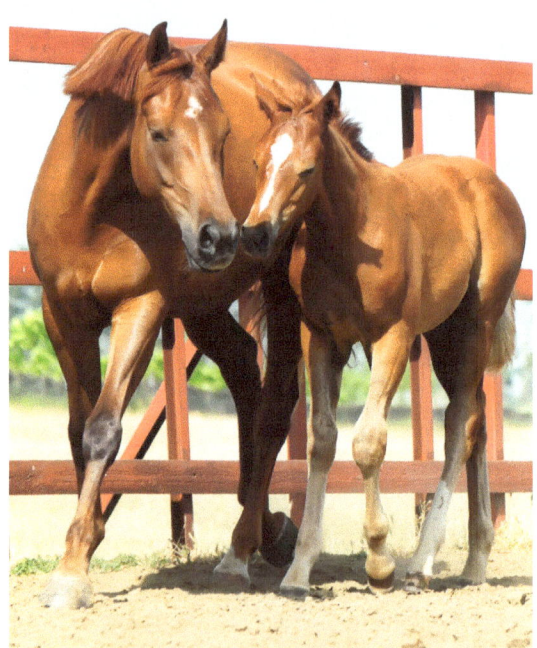

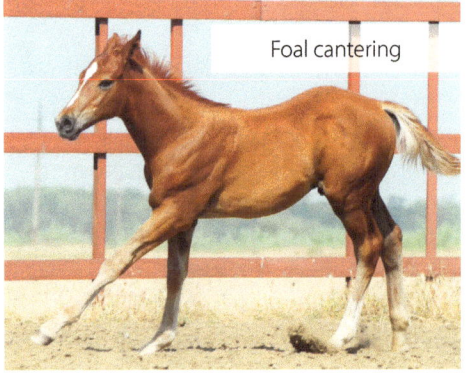

Foal cantering

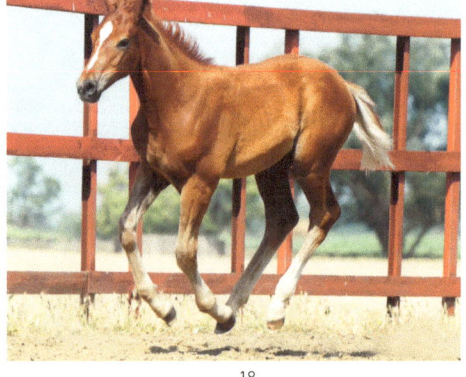

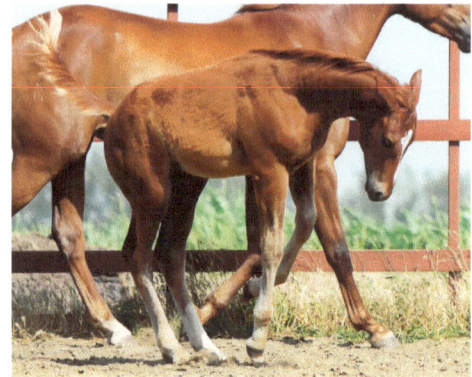

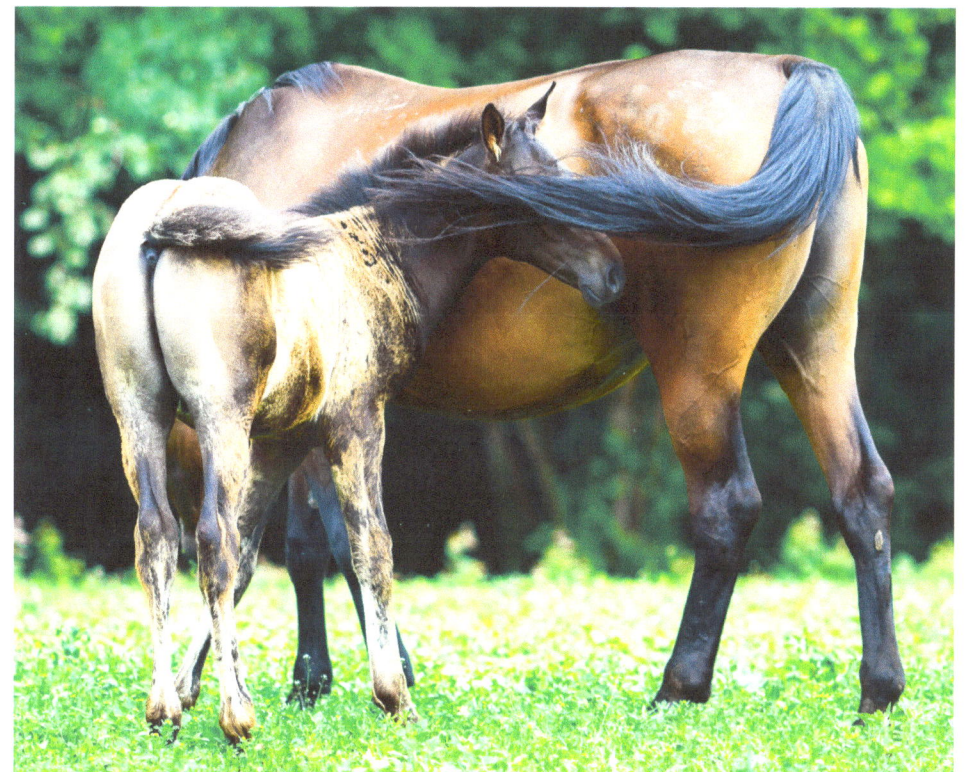

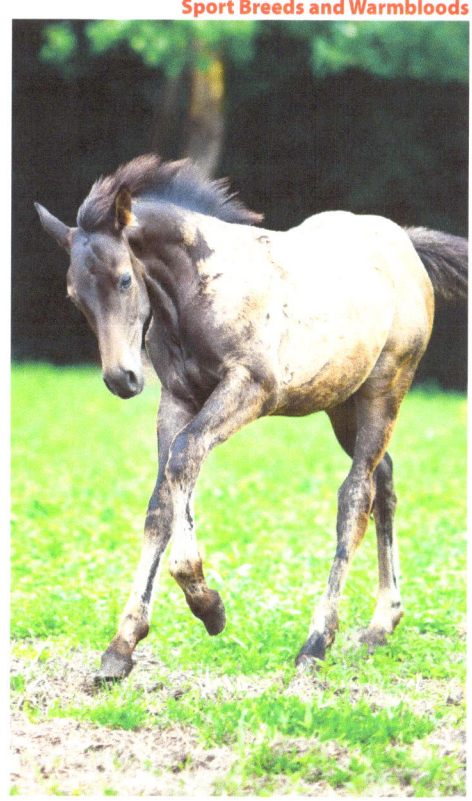

Bay Warmblood Mare and colt

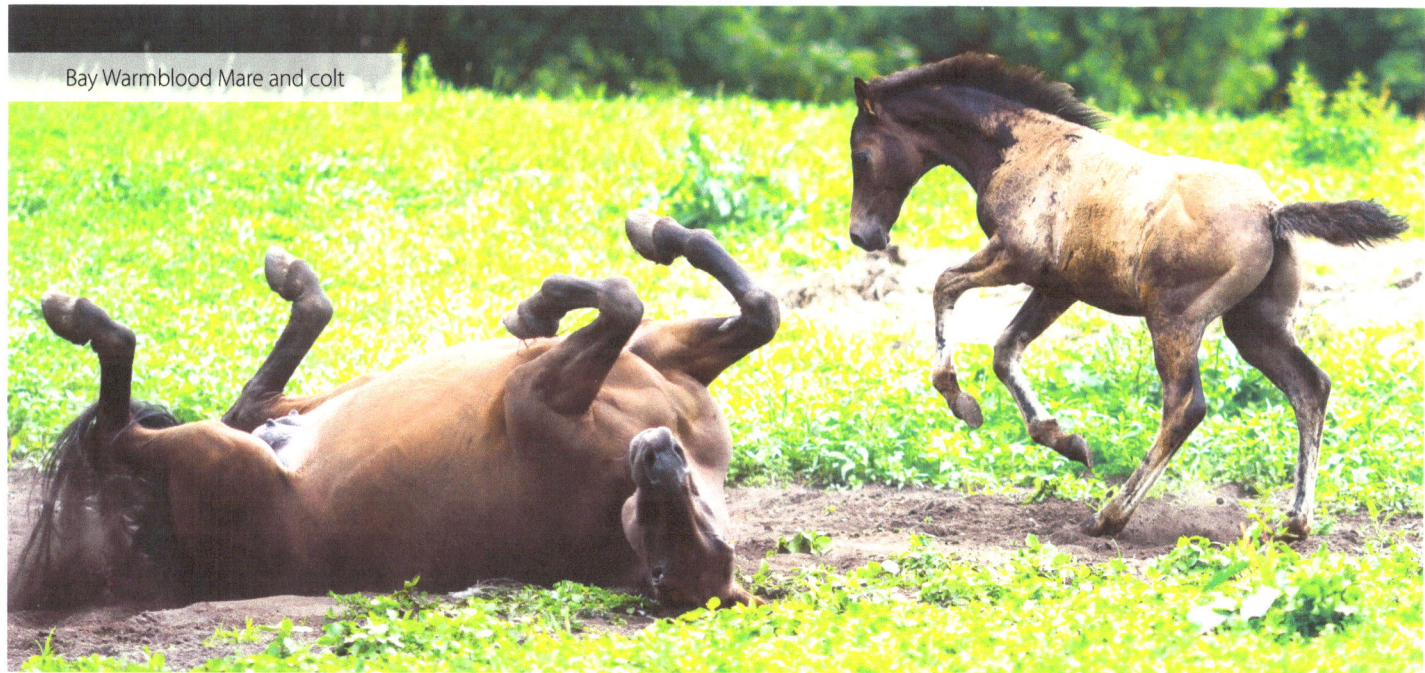

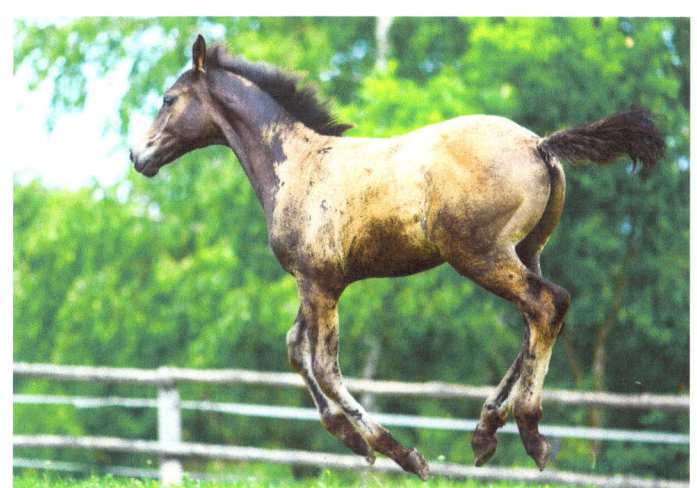

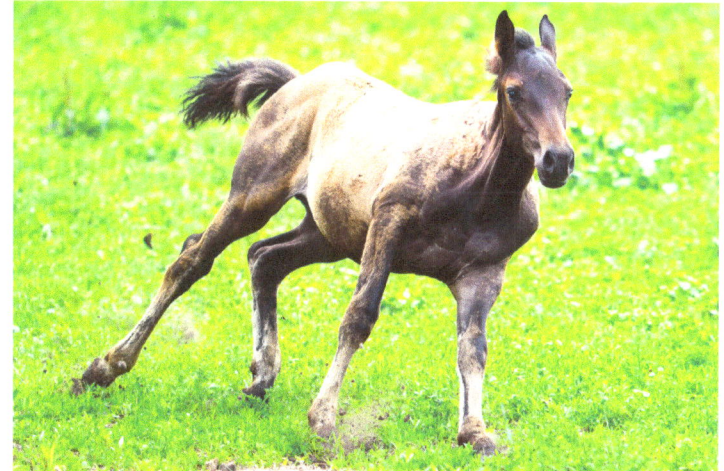

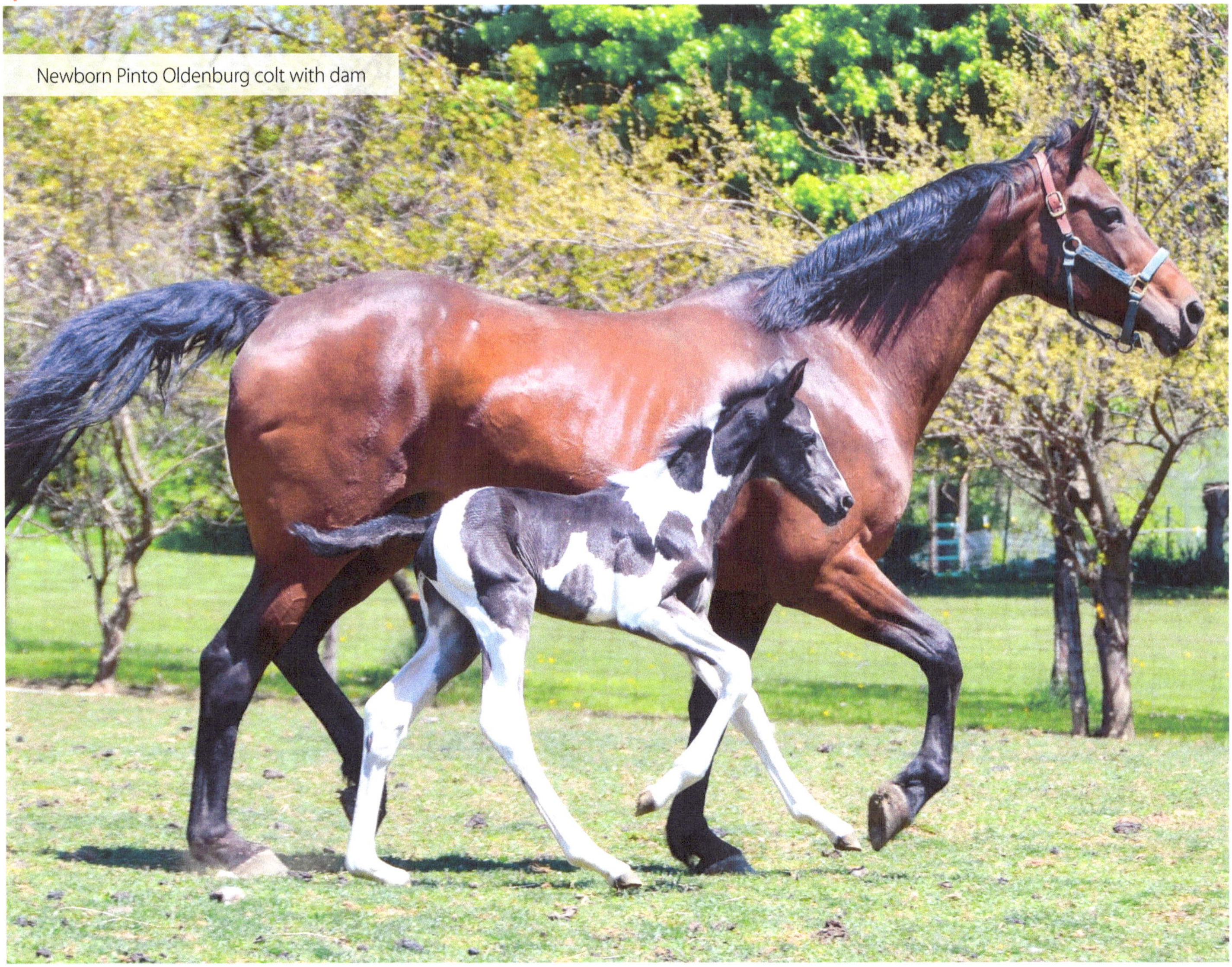

Newborn Pinto Oldenburg colt with dam

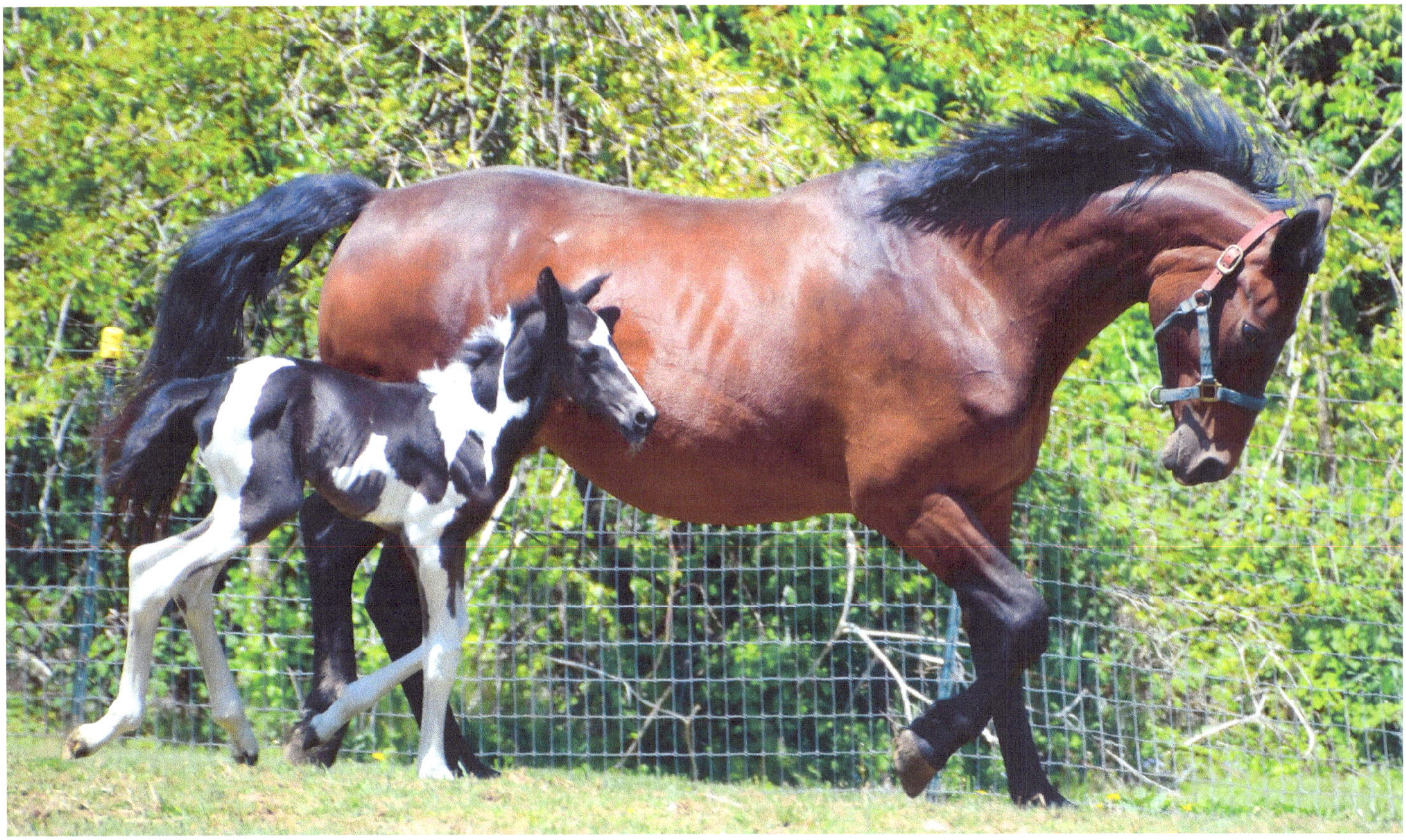

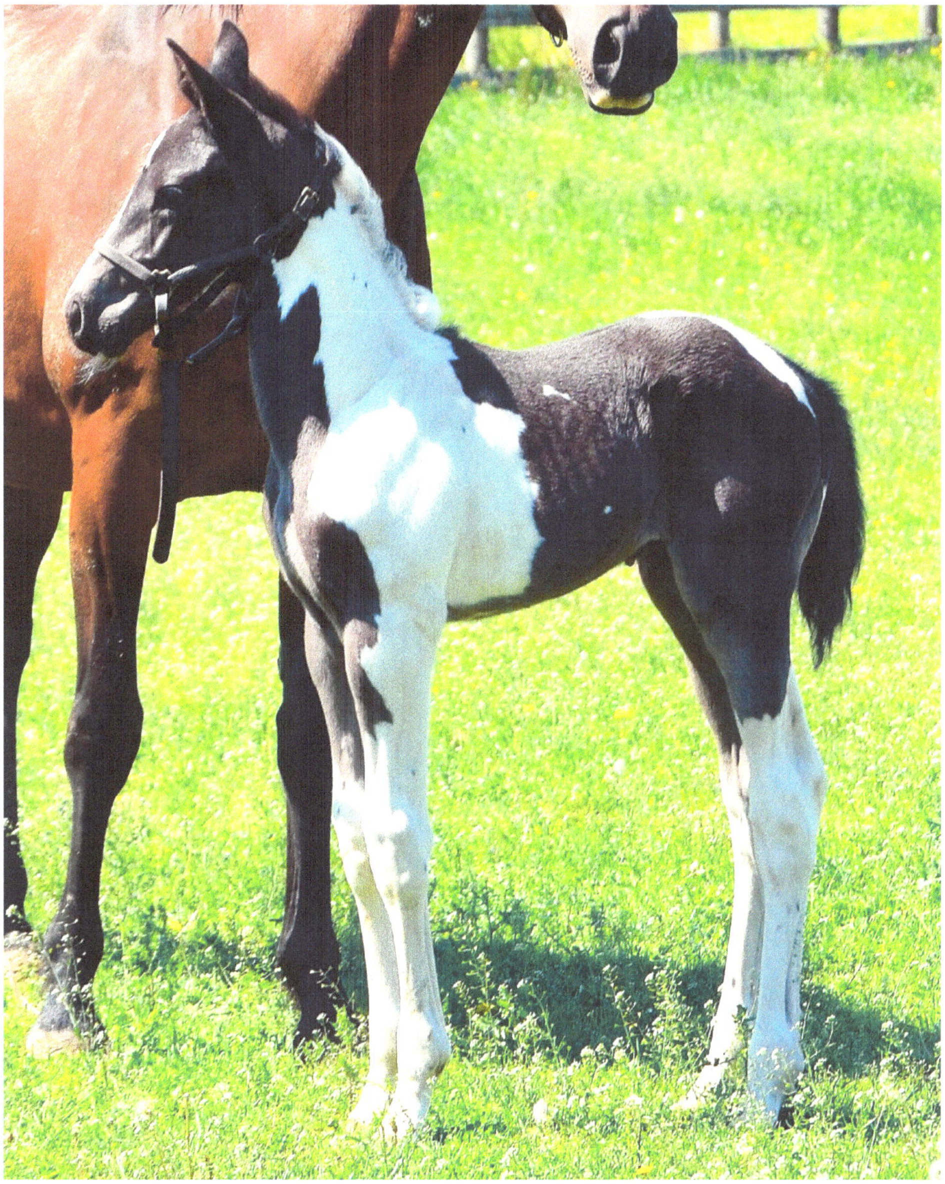

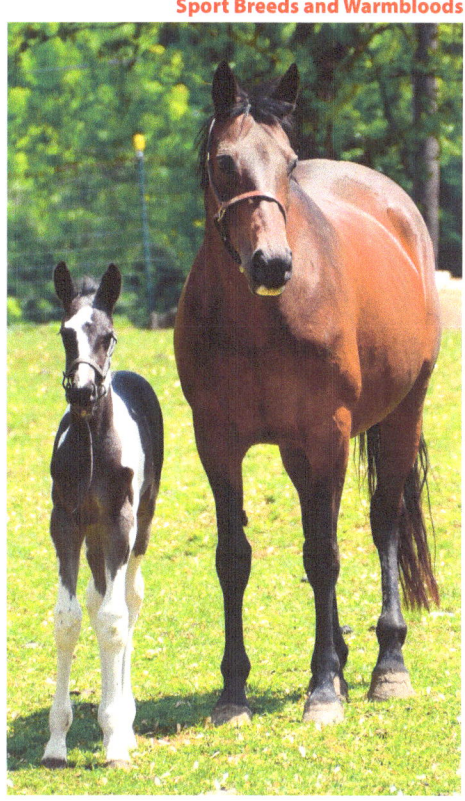

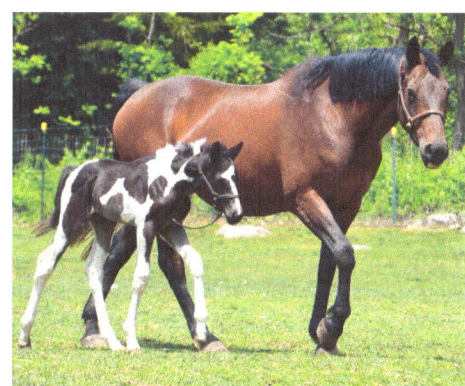

The same pinto Oldenburg colt

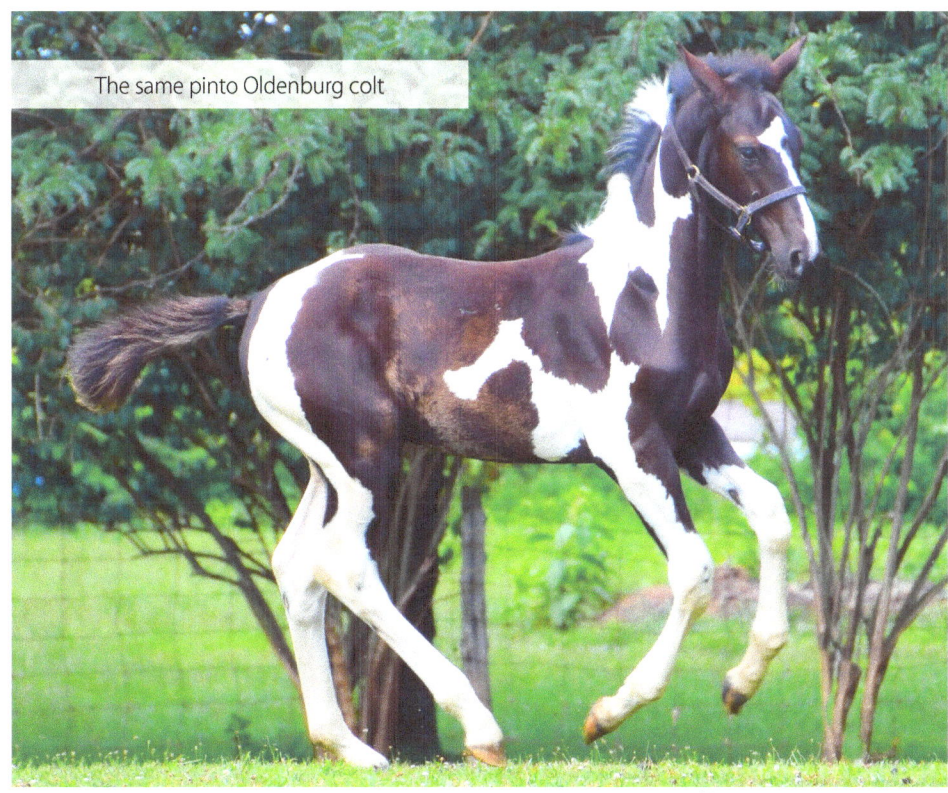

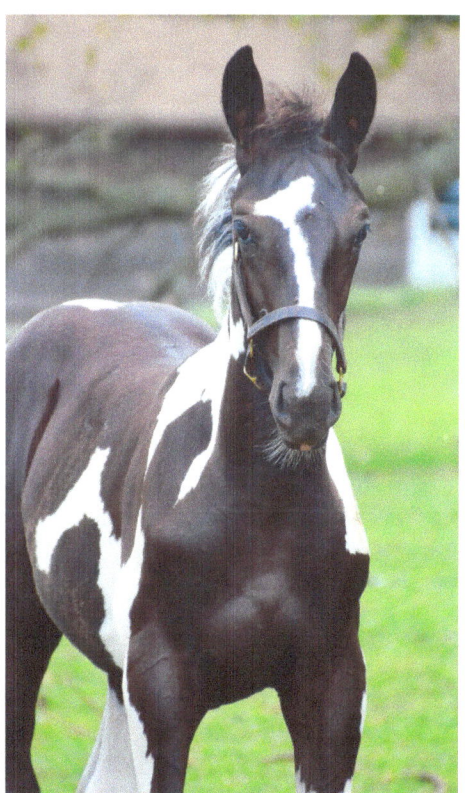

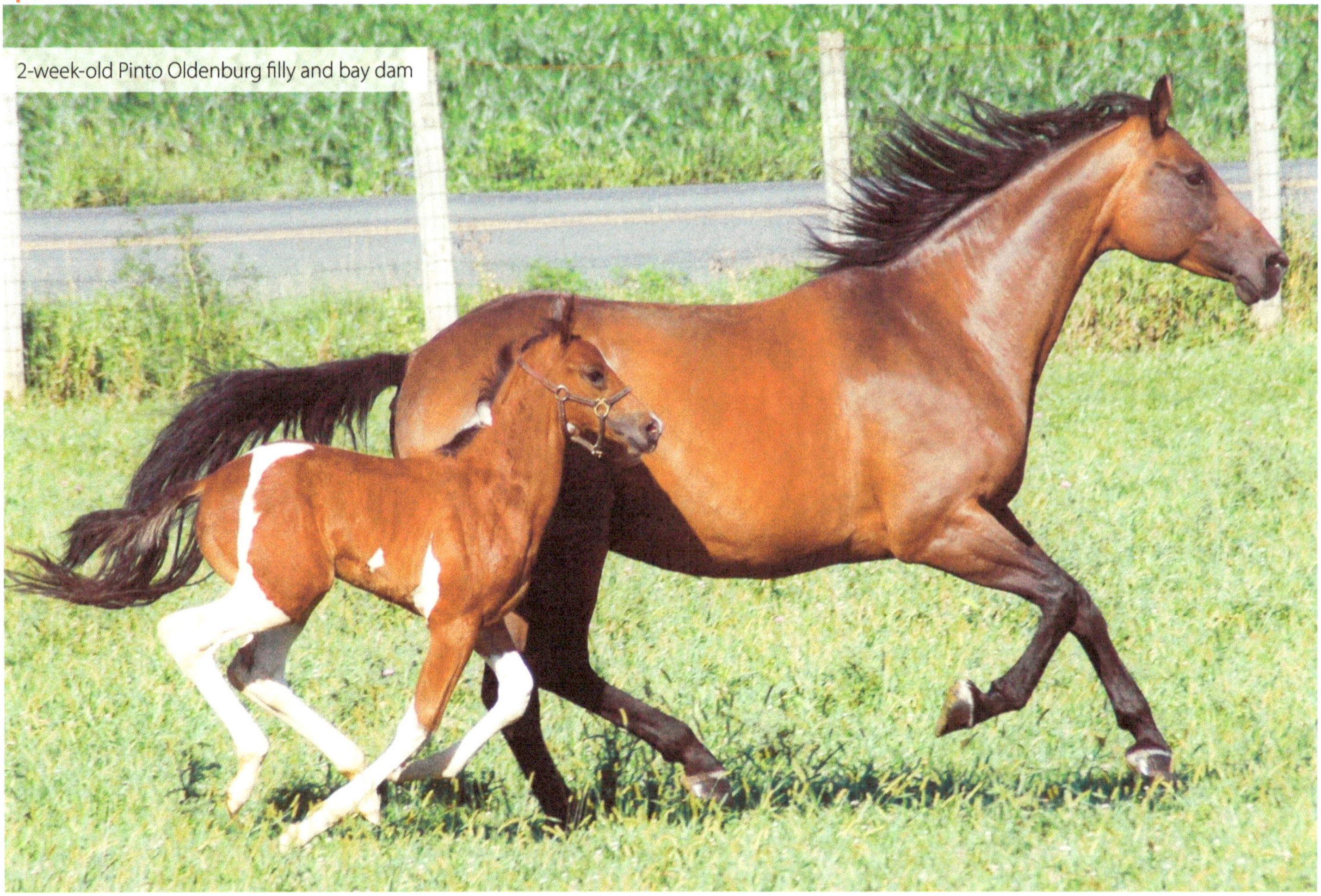

2-week-old Pinto Oldenburg filly and bay dam

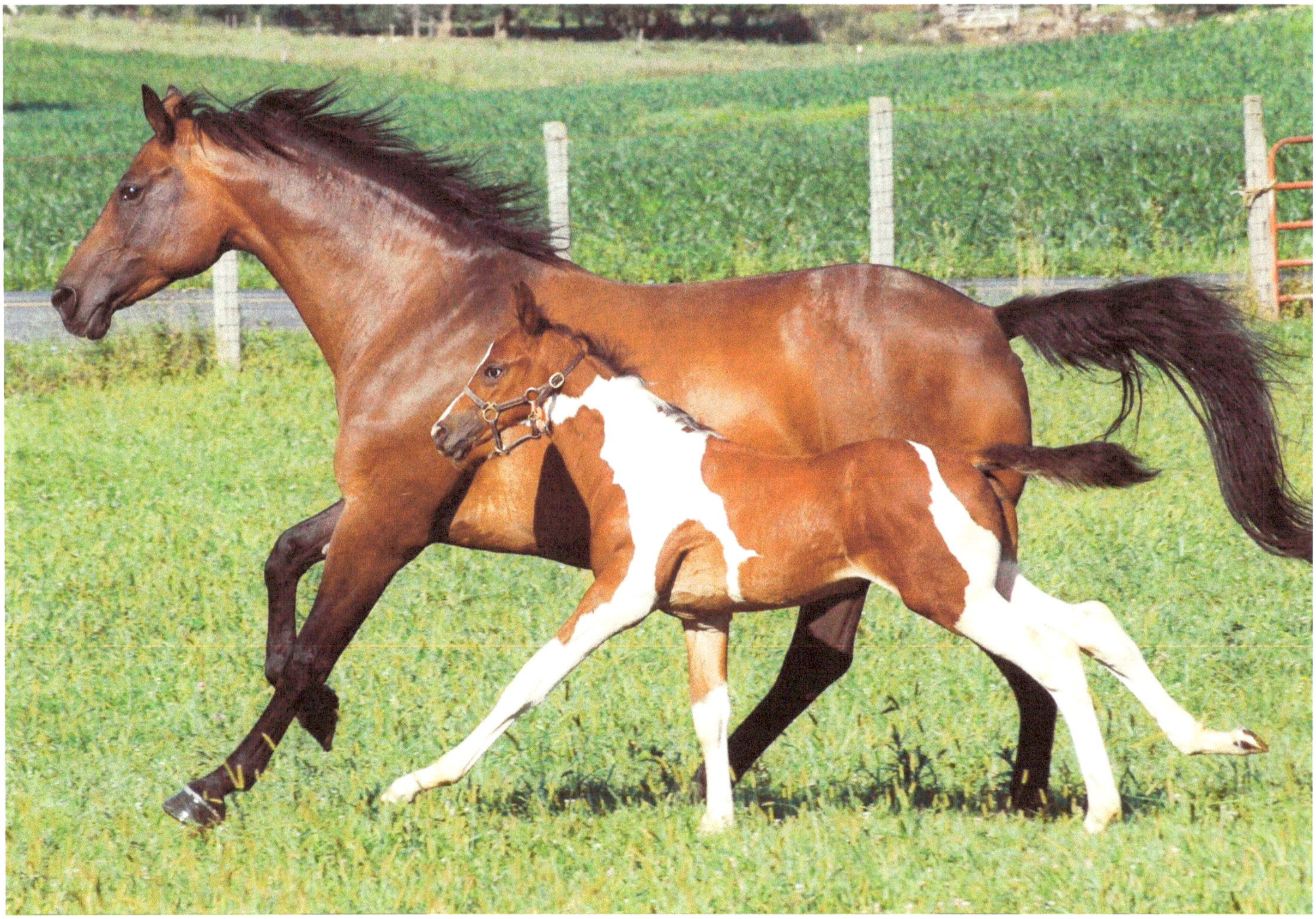

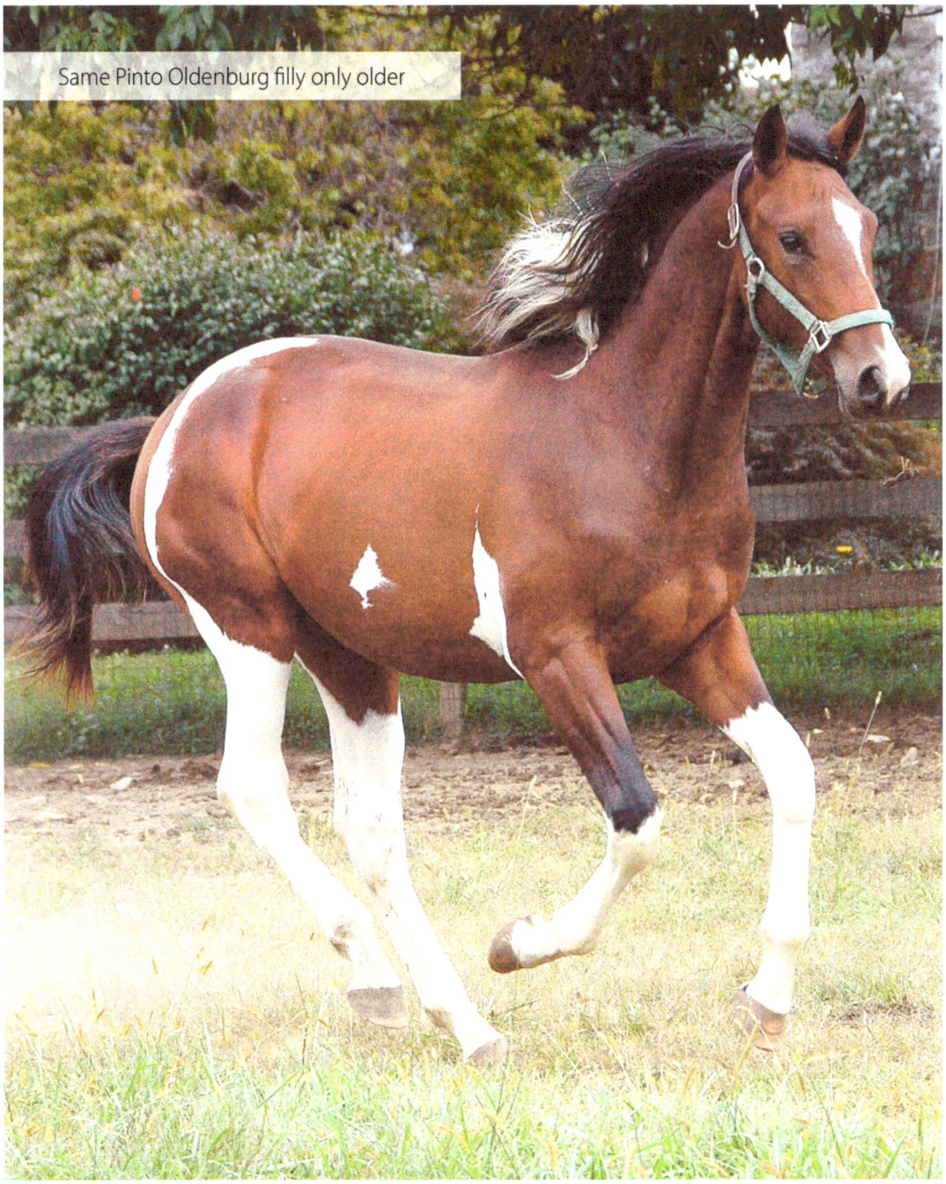

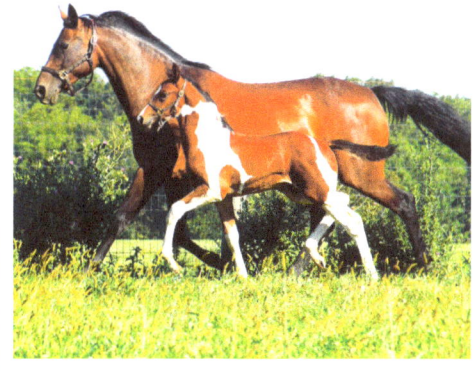

Same Pinto Oldenburg filly only older

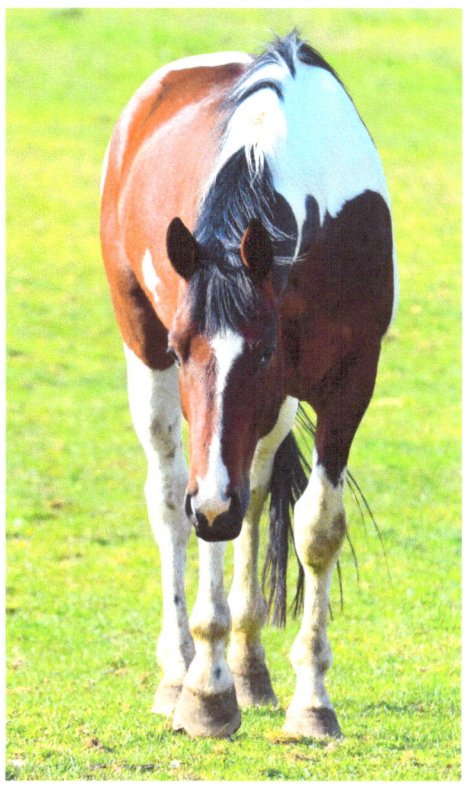

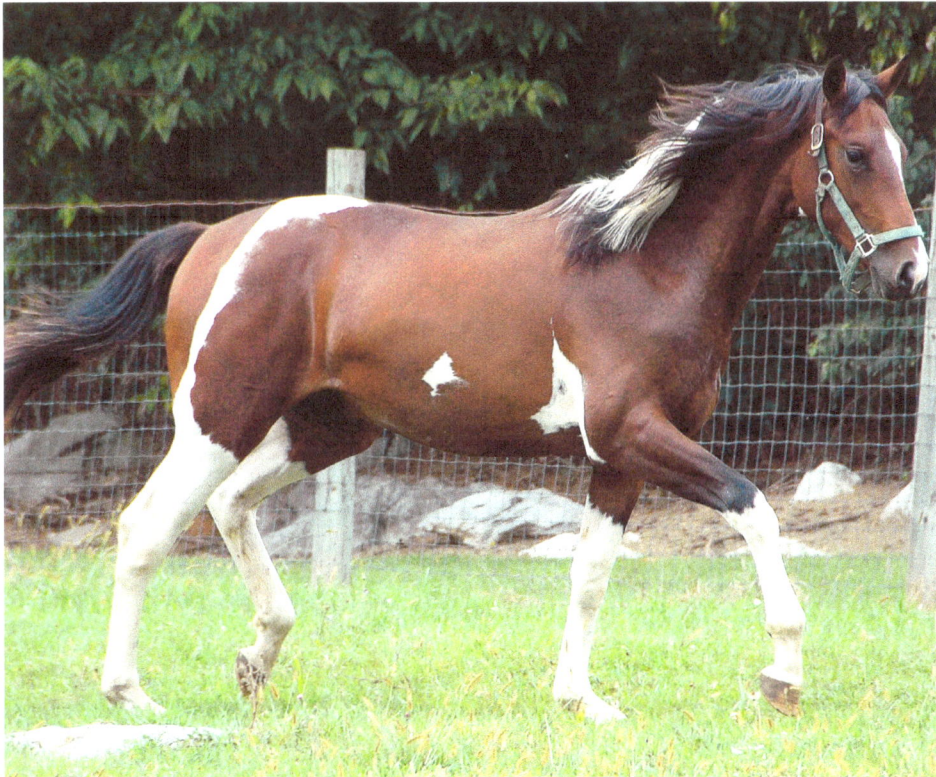

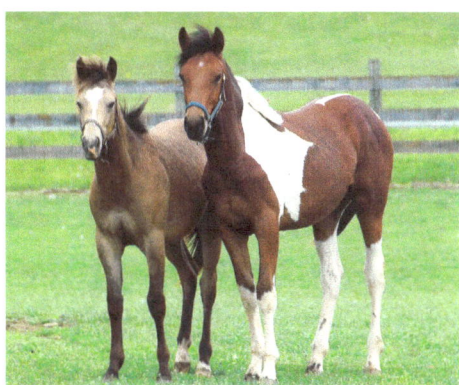

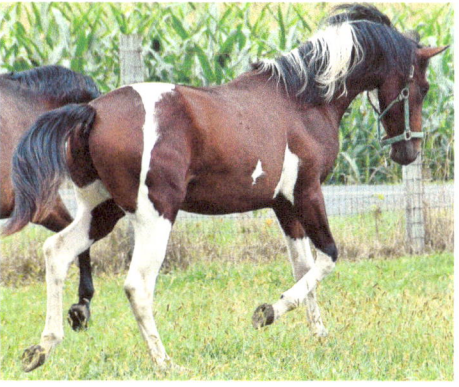

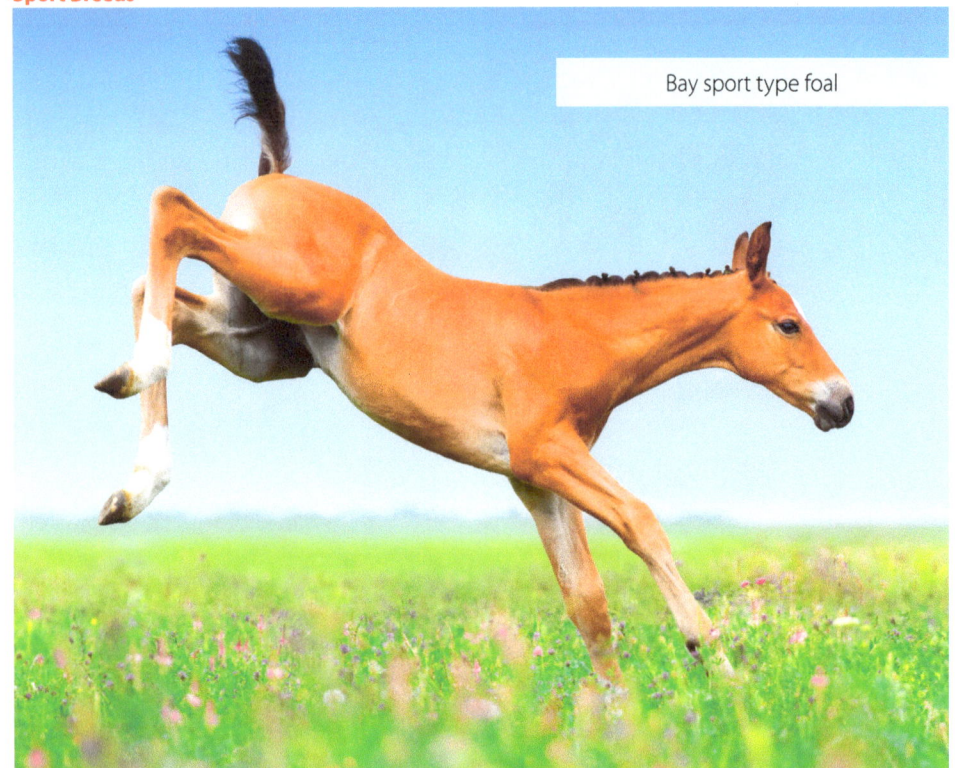

Bay sport type foal

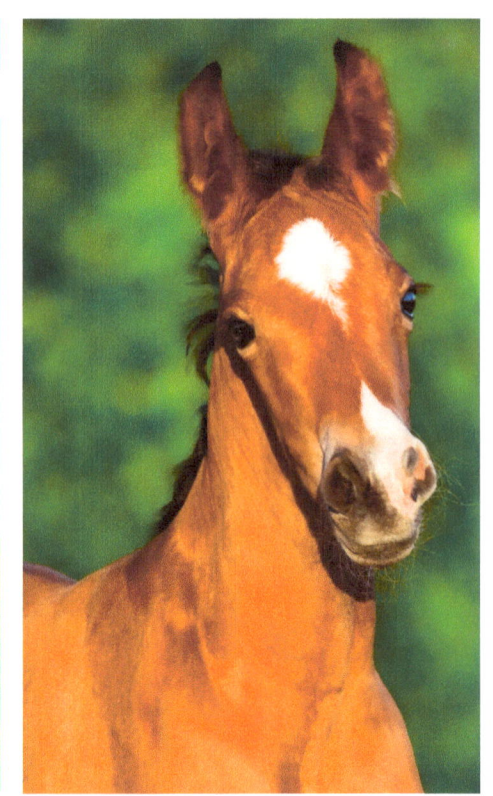

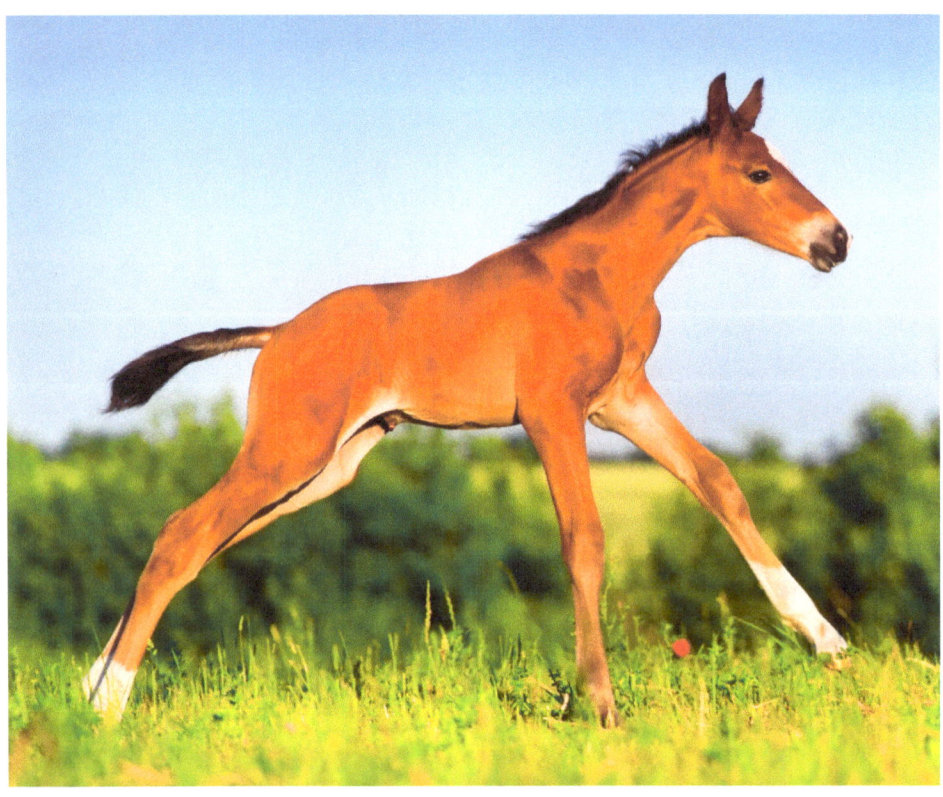

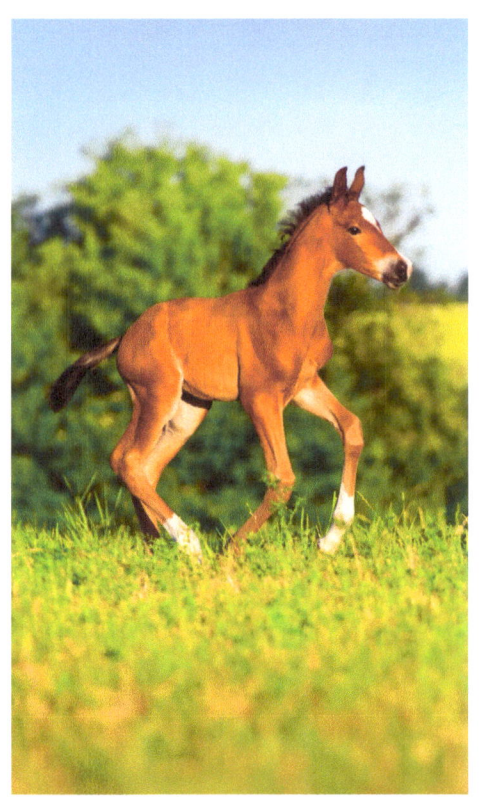

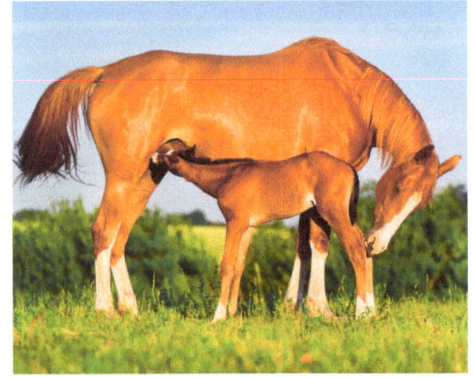

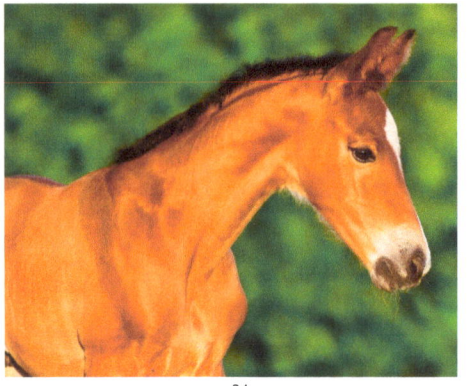

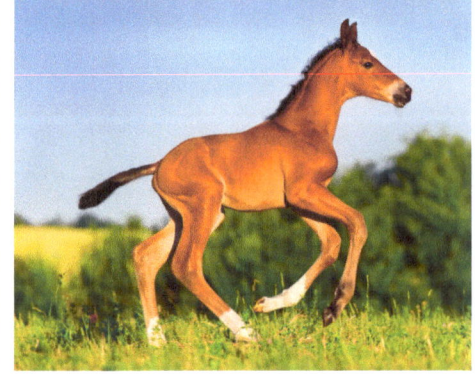

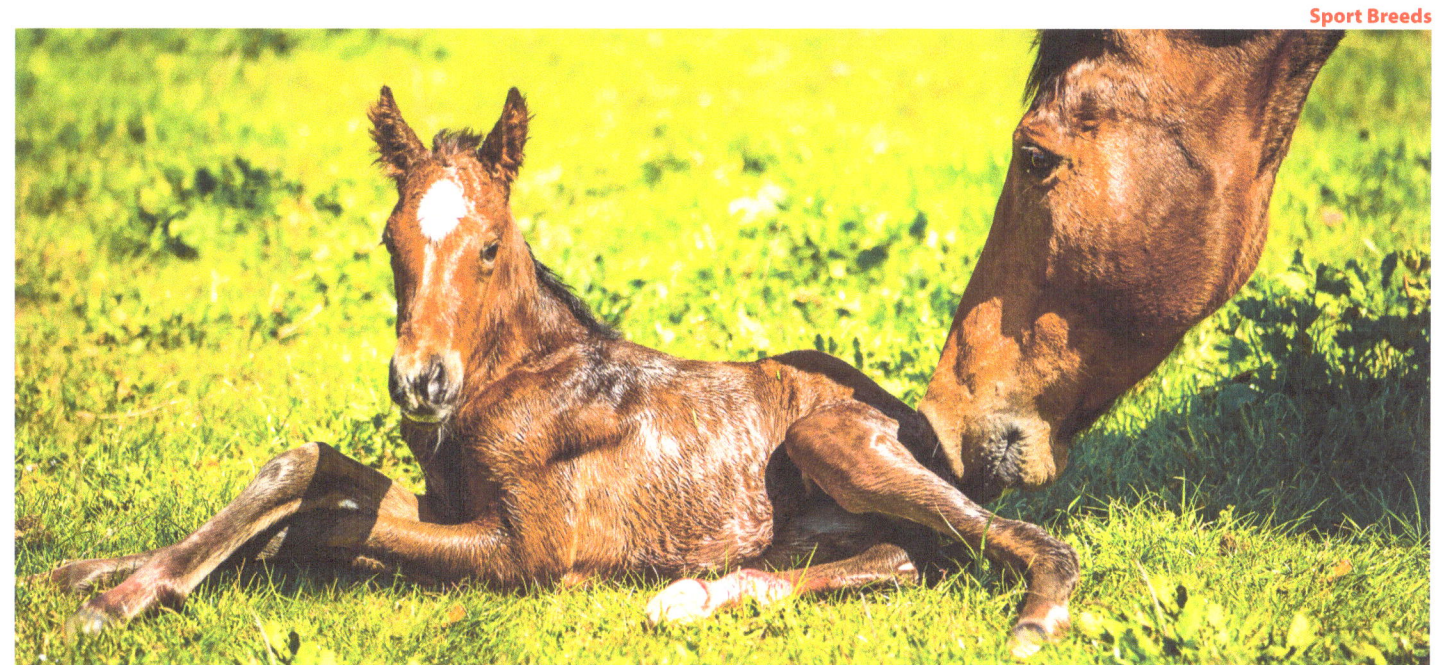

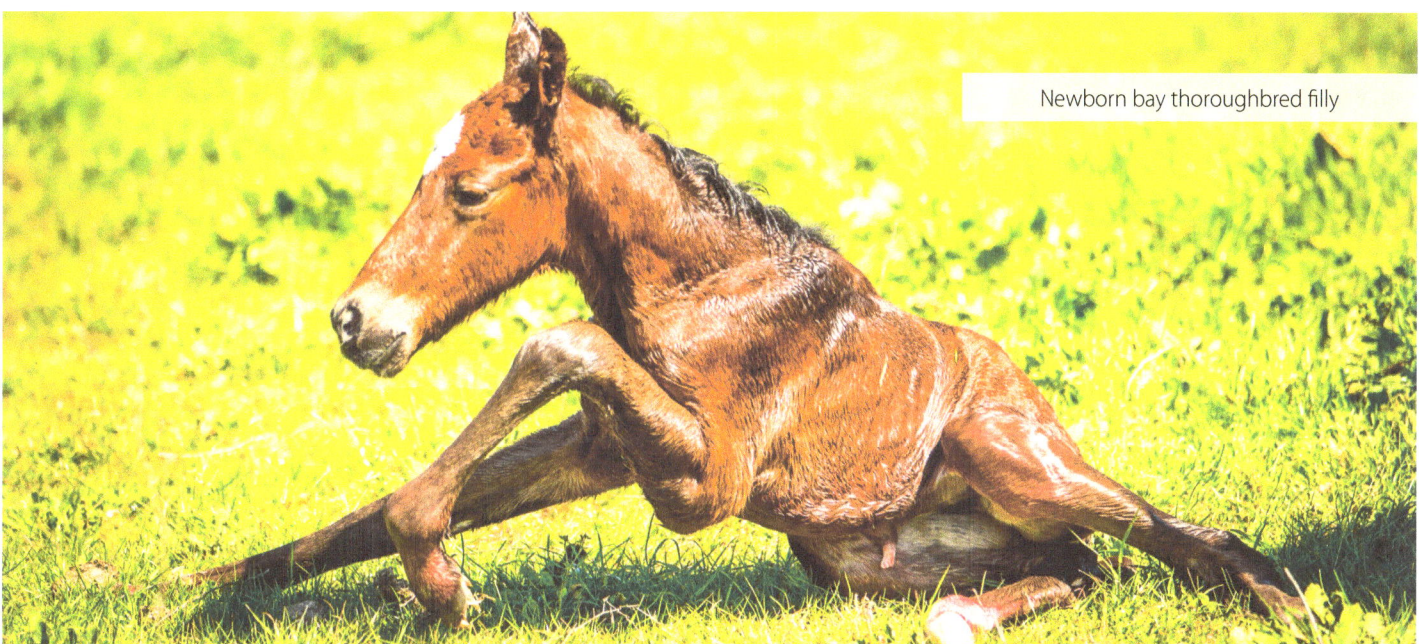

Newborn bay thoroughbred filly

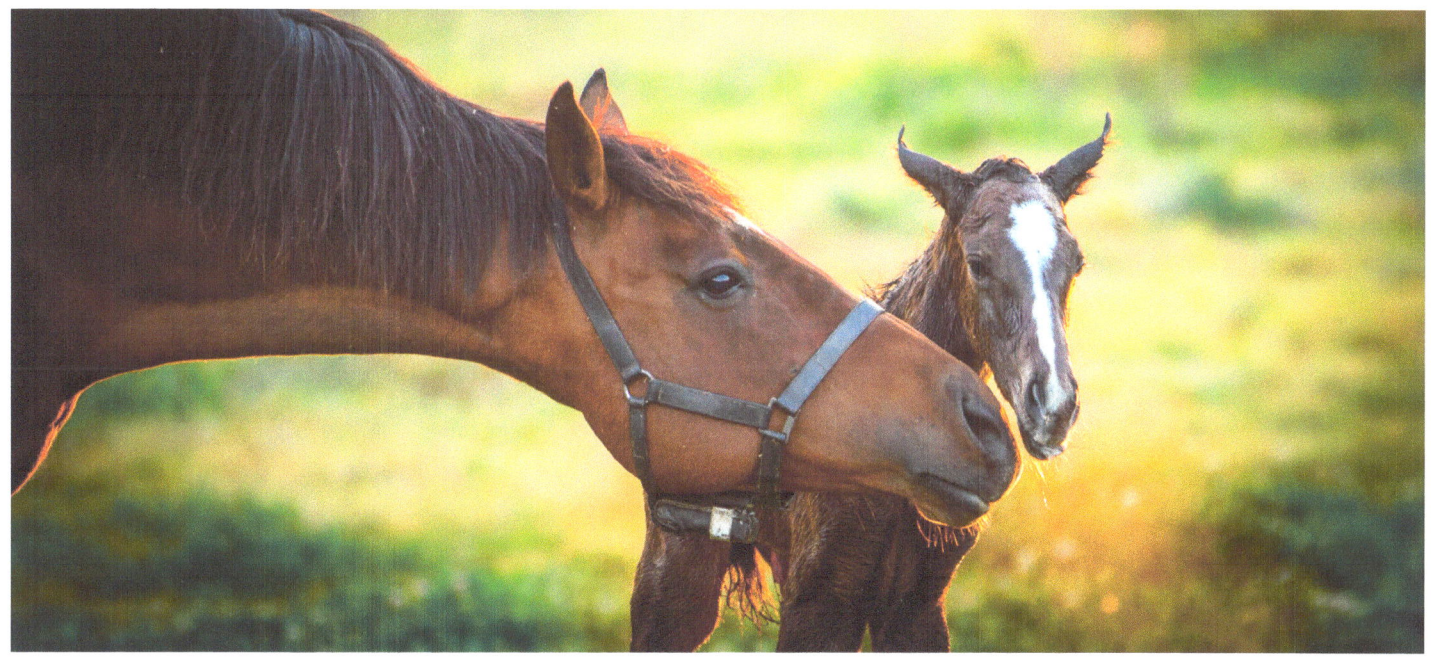

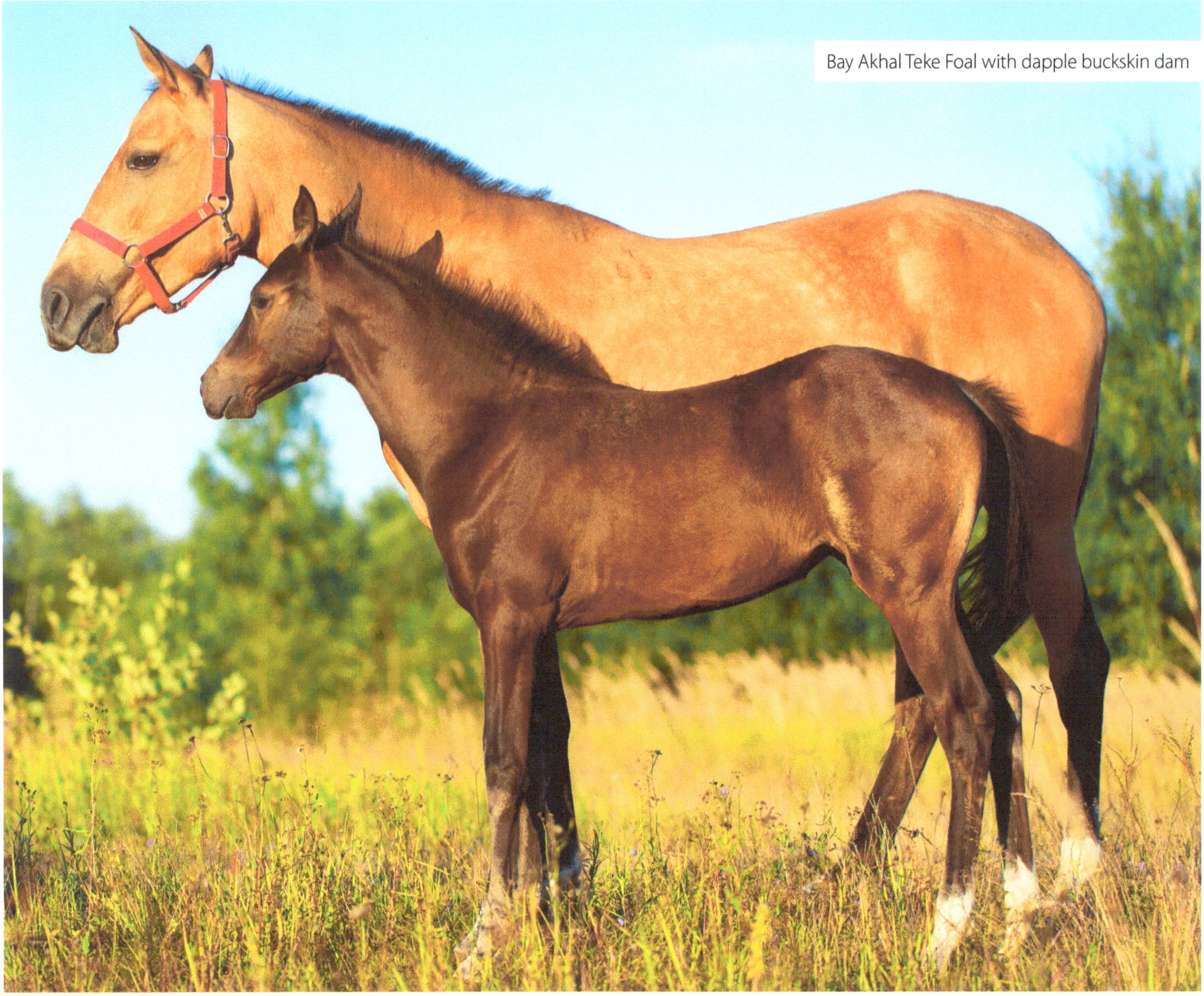

Bay Akhal Teke Foal with dapple buckskin dam

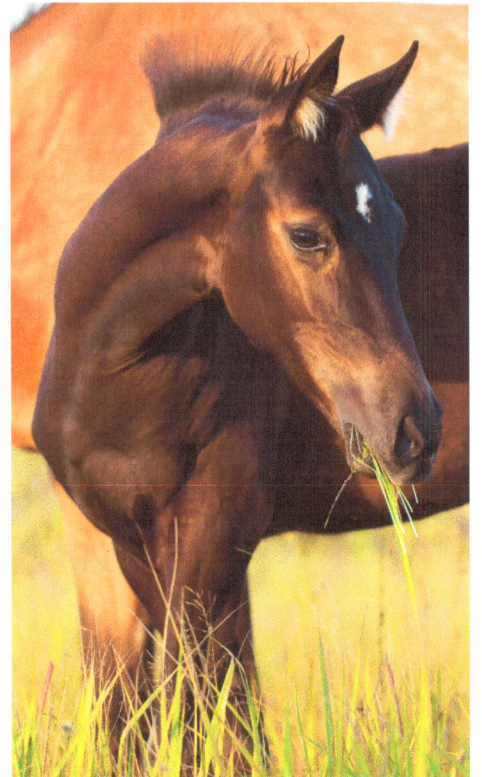

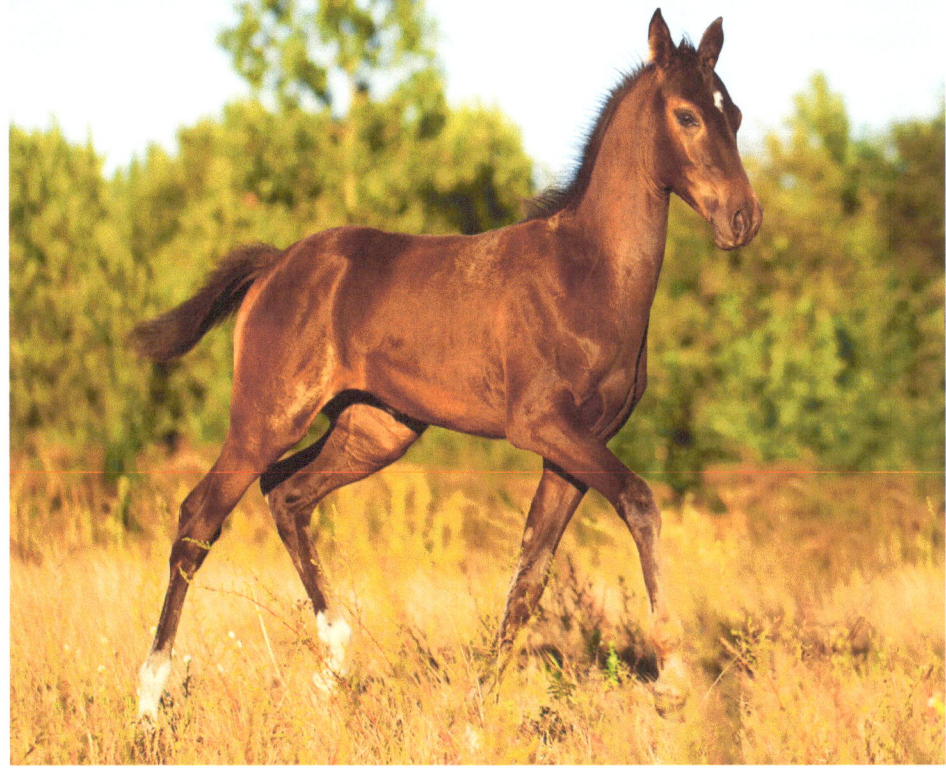

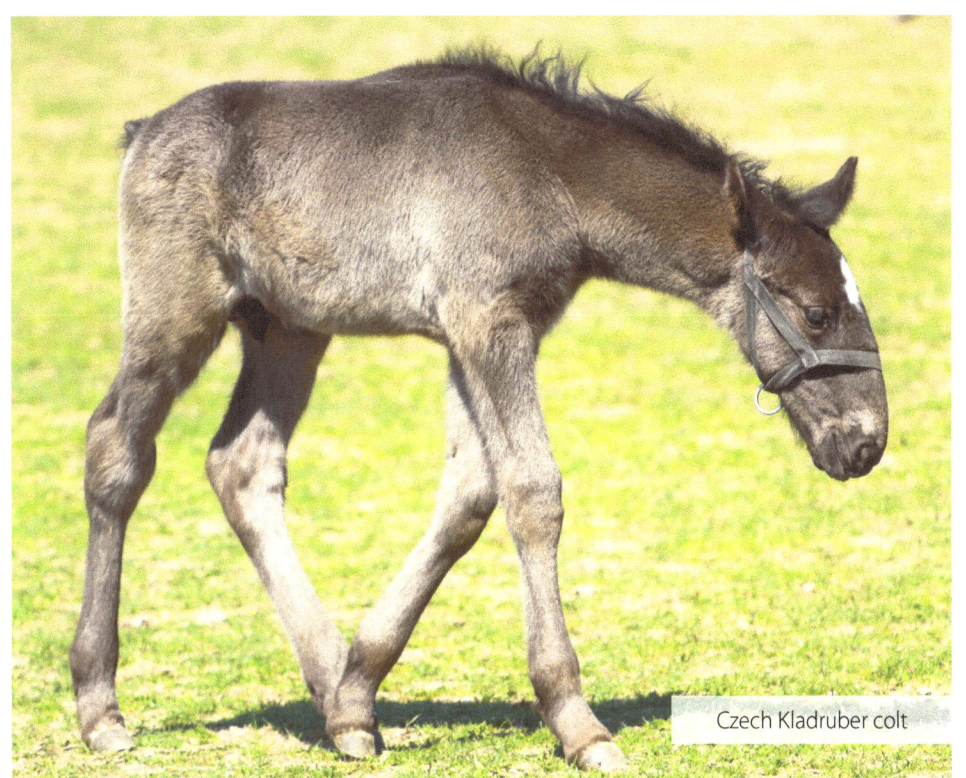

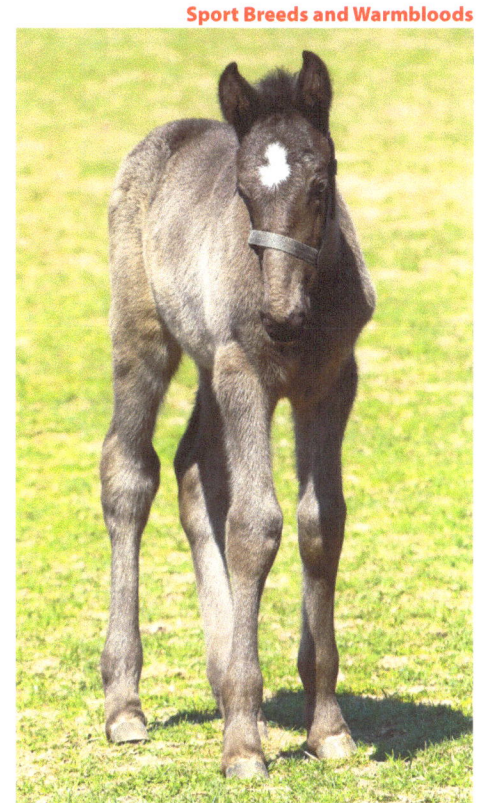

Czech Kladruber colt

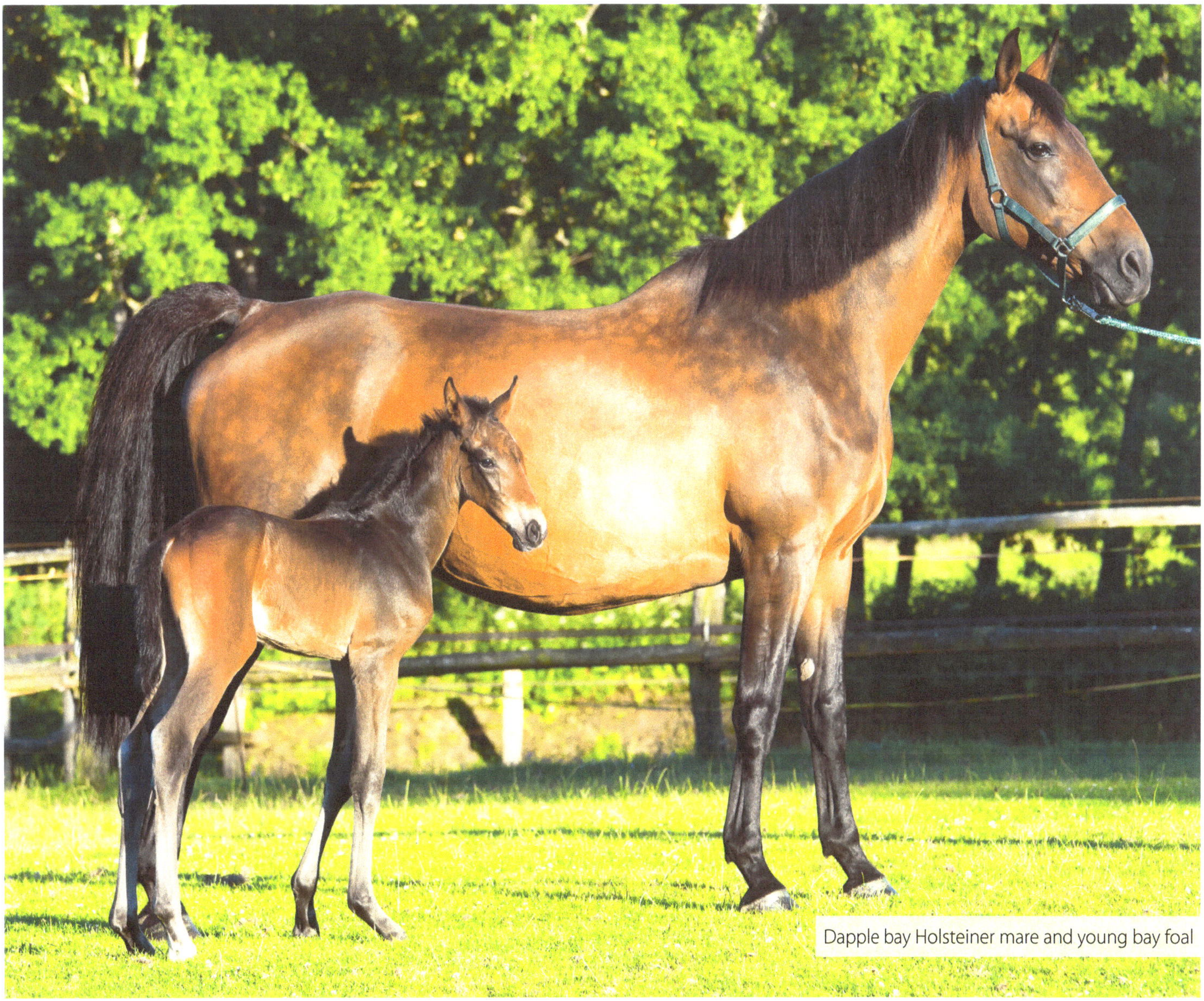

Dapple bay Holsteiner mare and young bay foal

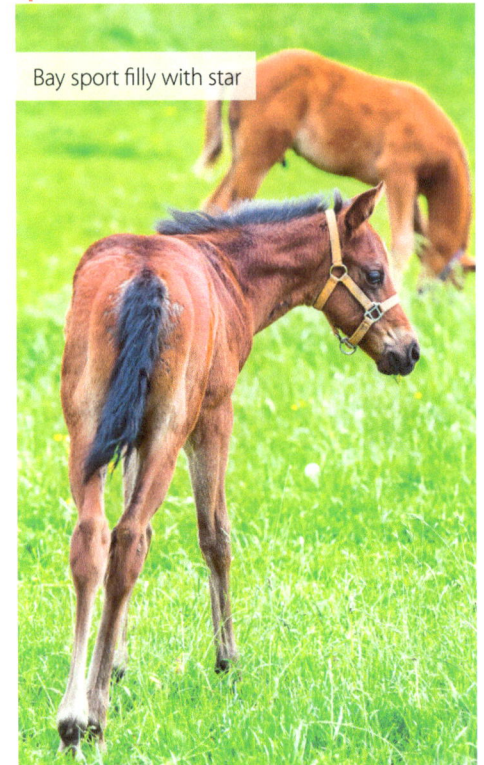

Bay sport filly with star

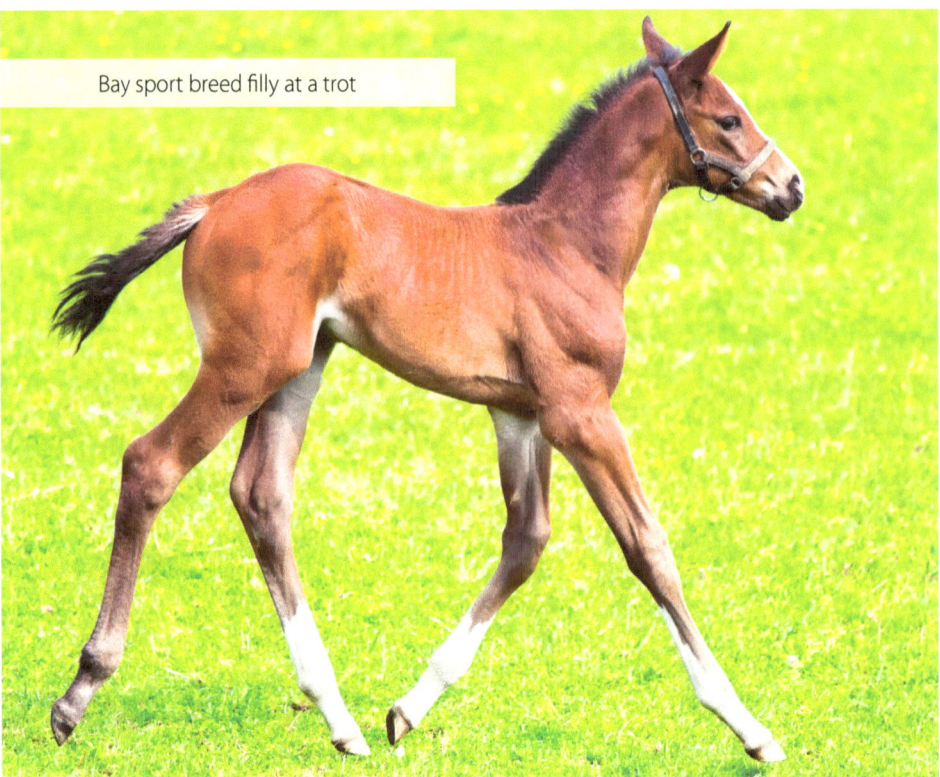

Bay sport breed filly at a trot

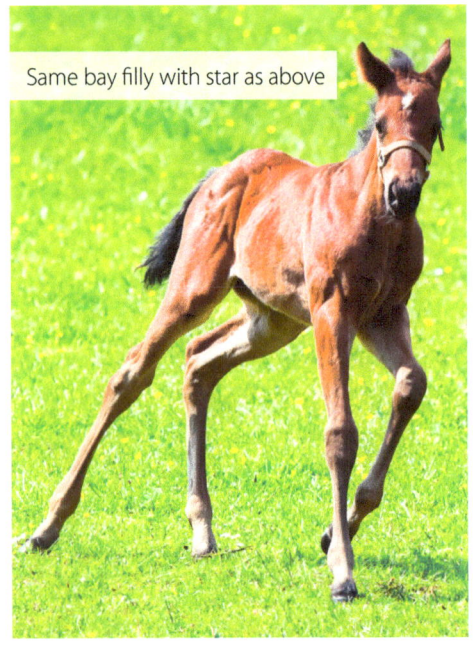

Same bay filly with star as above

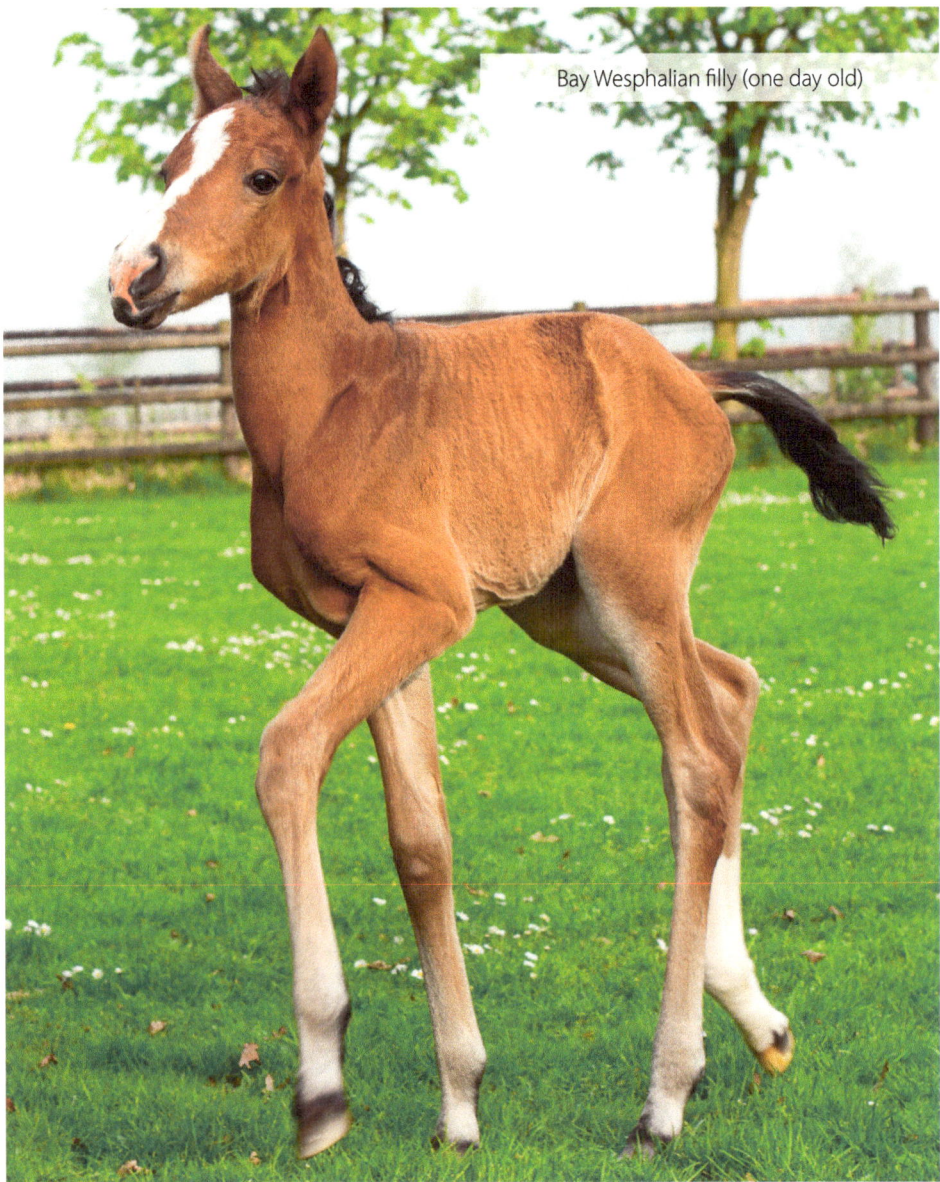

Bay Wesphalian filly (one day old)

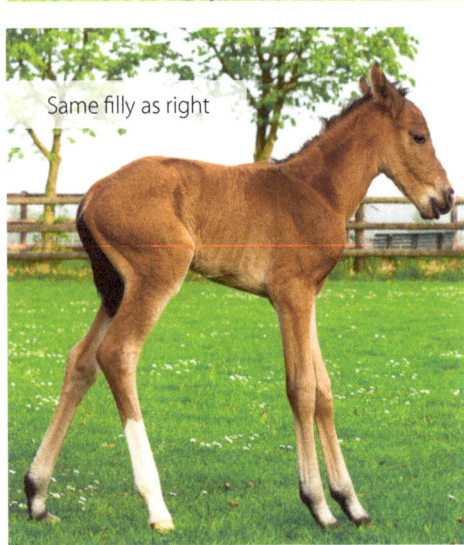

Same filly as right

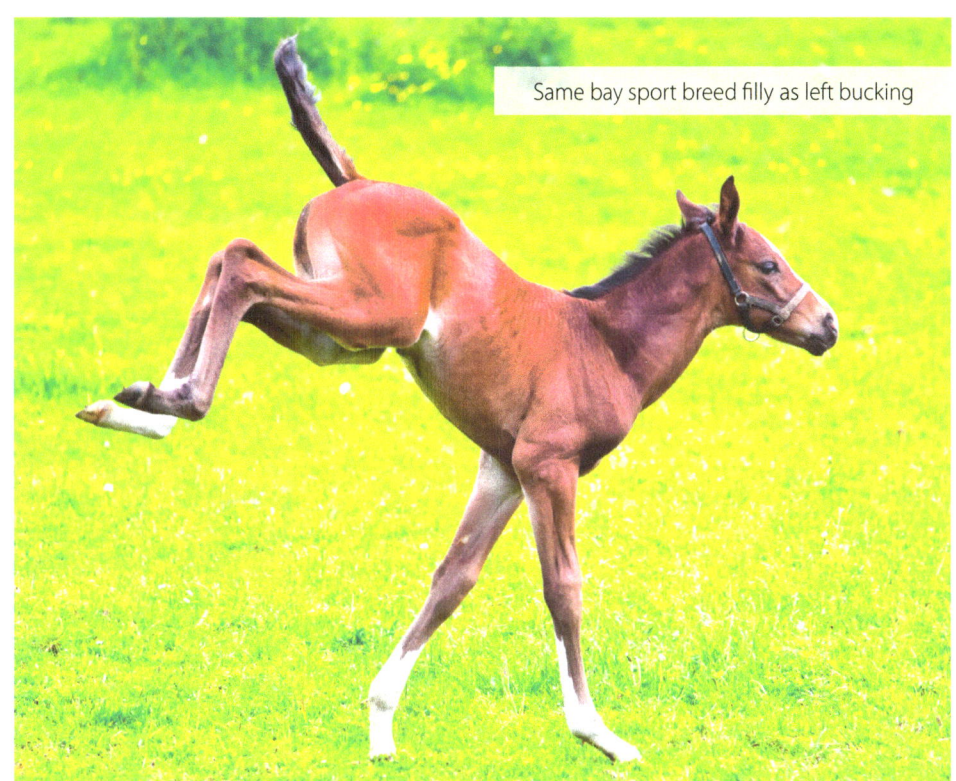

Same bay sport breed filly as left bucking

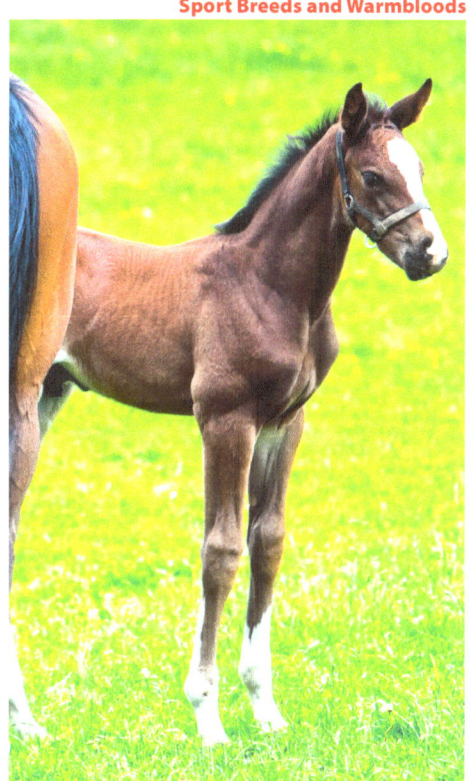

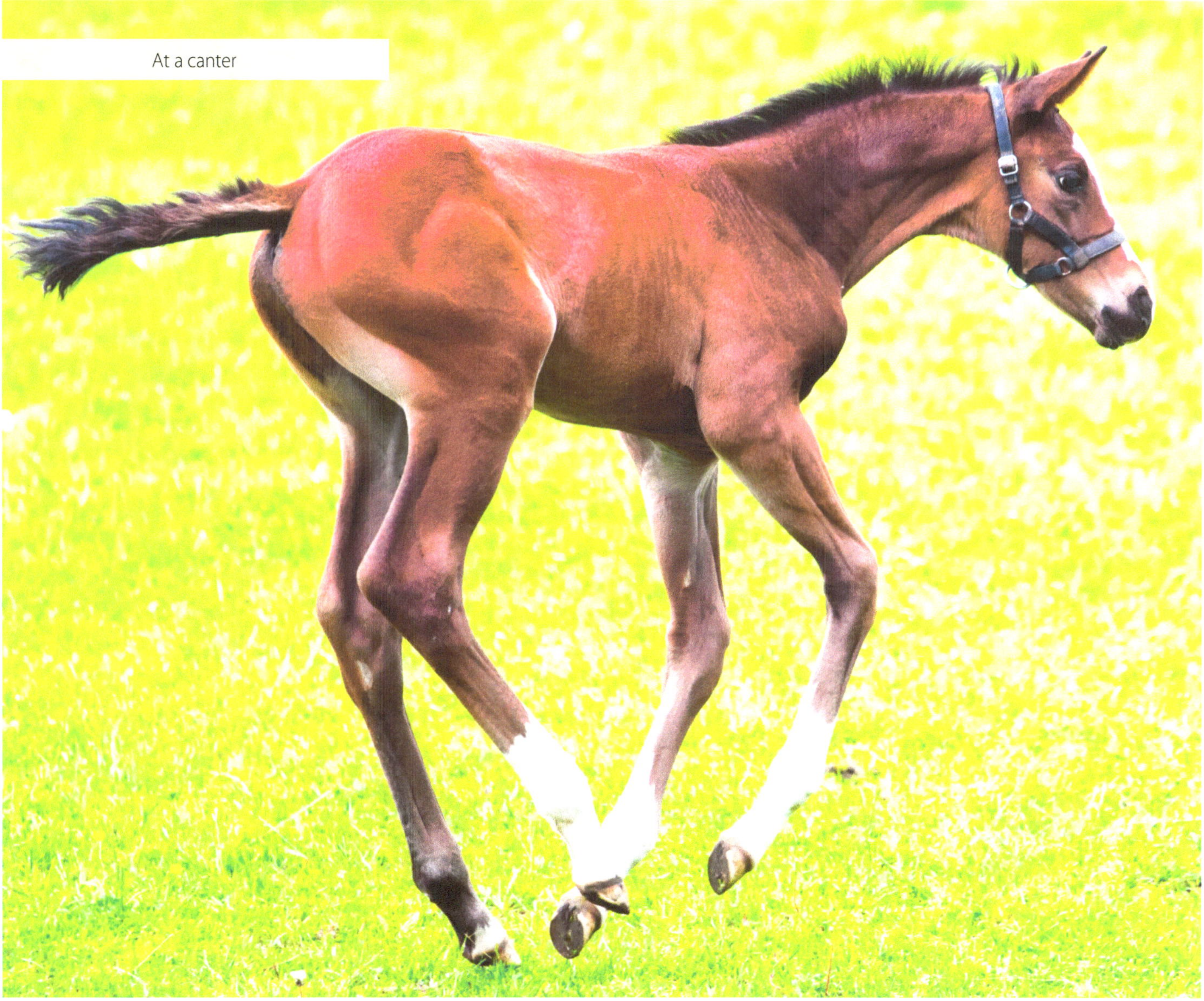

At a canter

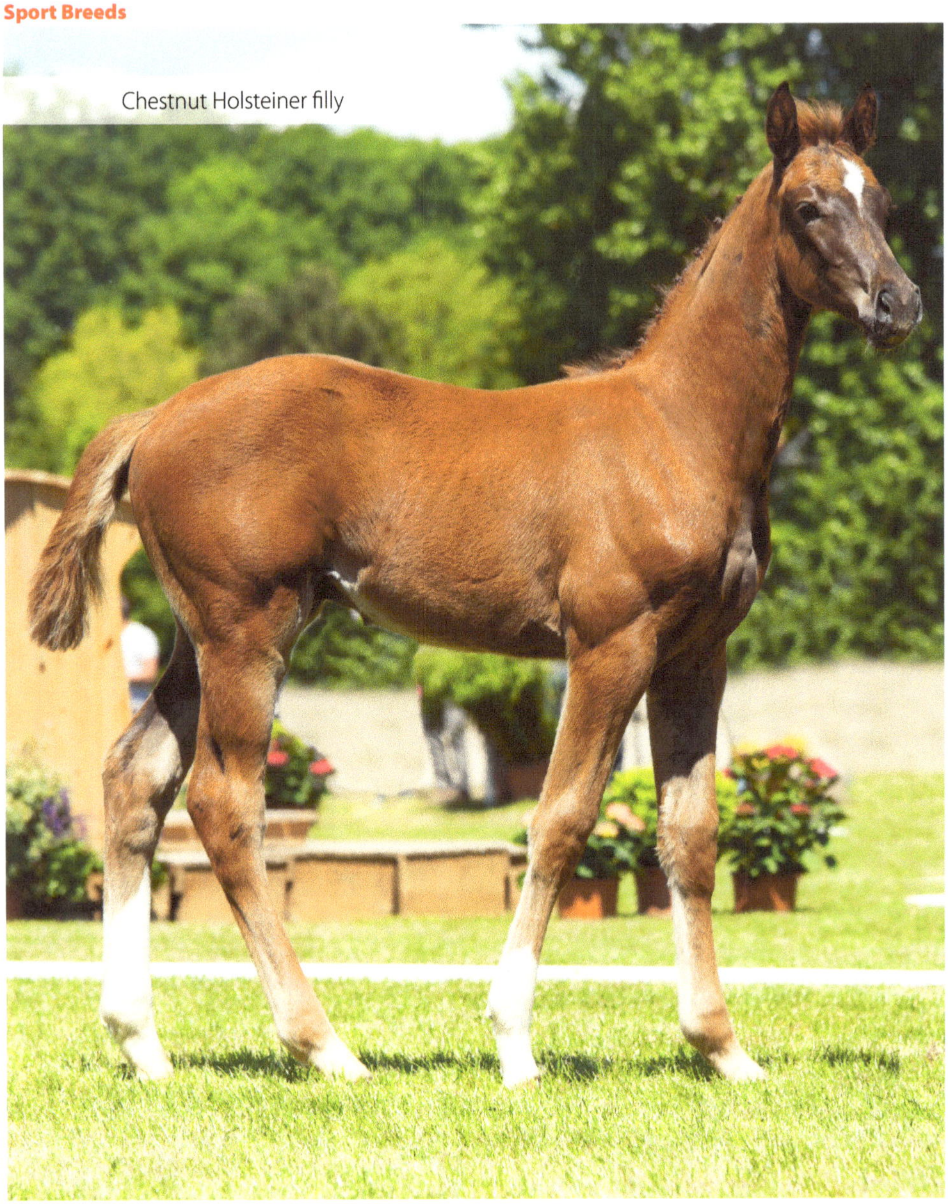

Chestnut Holsteiner filly

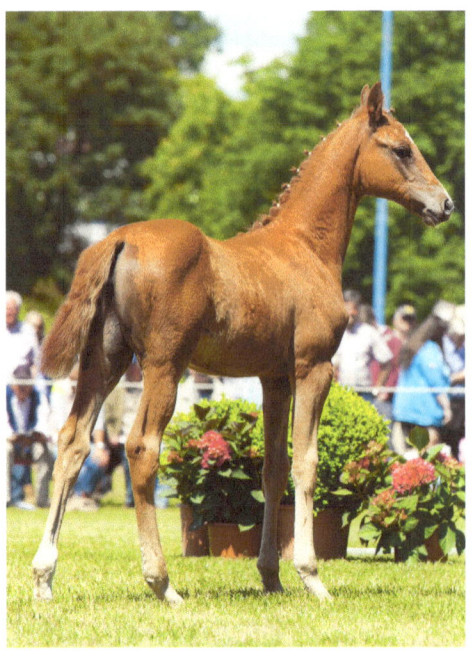

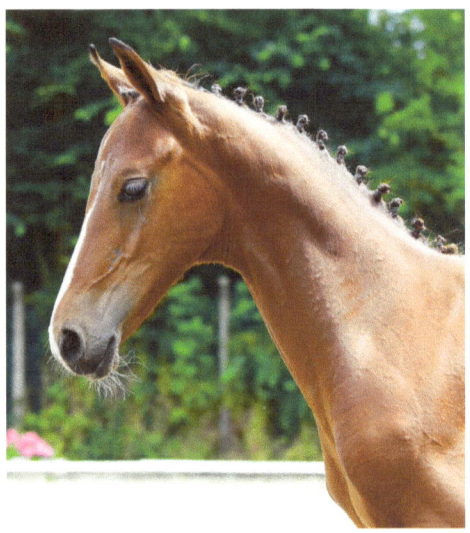

Chestnut Holsteiner filly at a trot

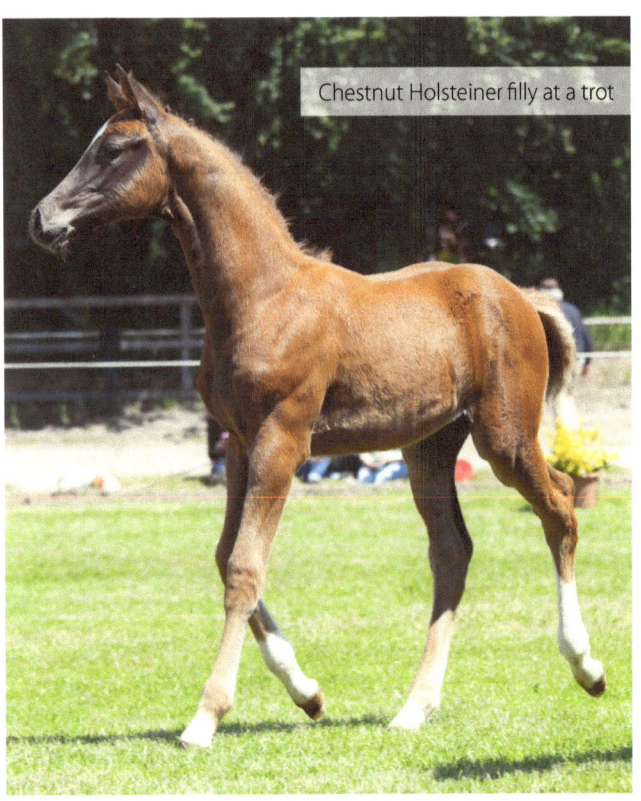

Holsteiner filly with dapple gray dam

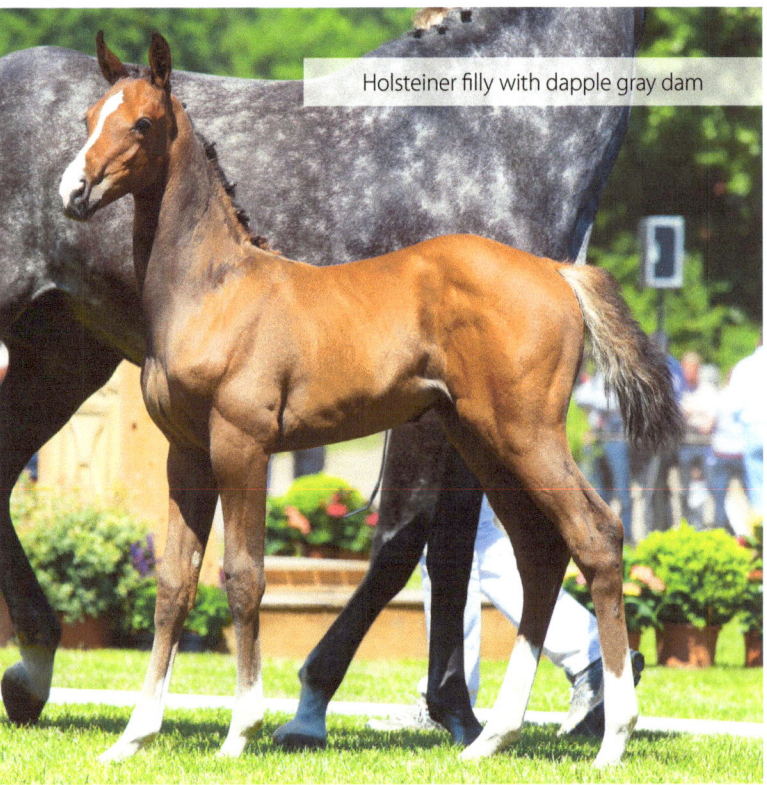

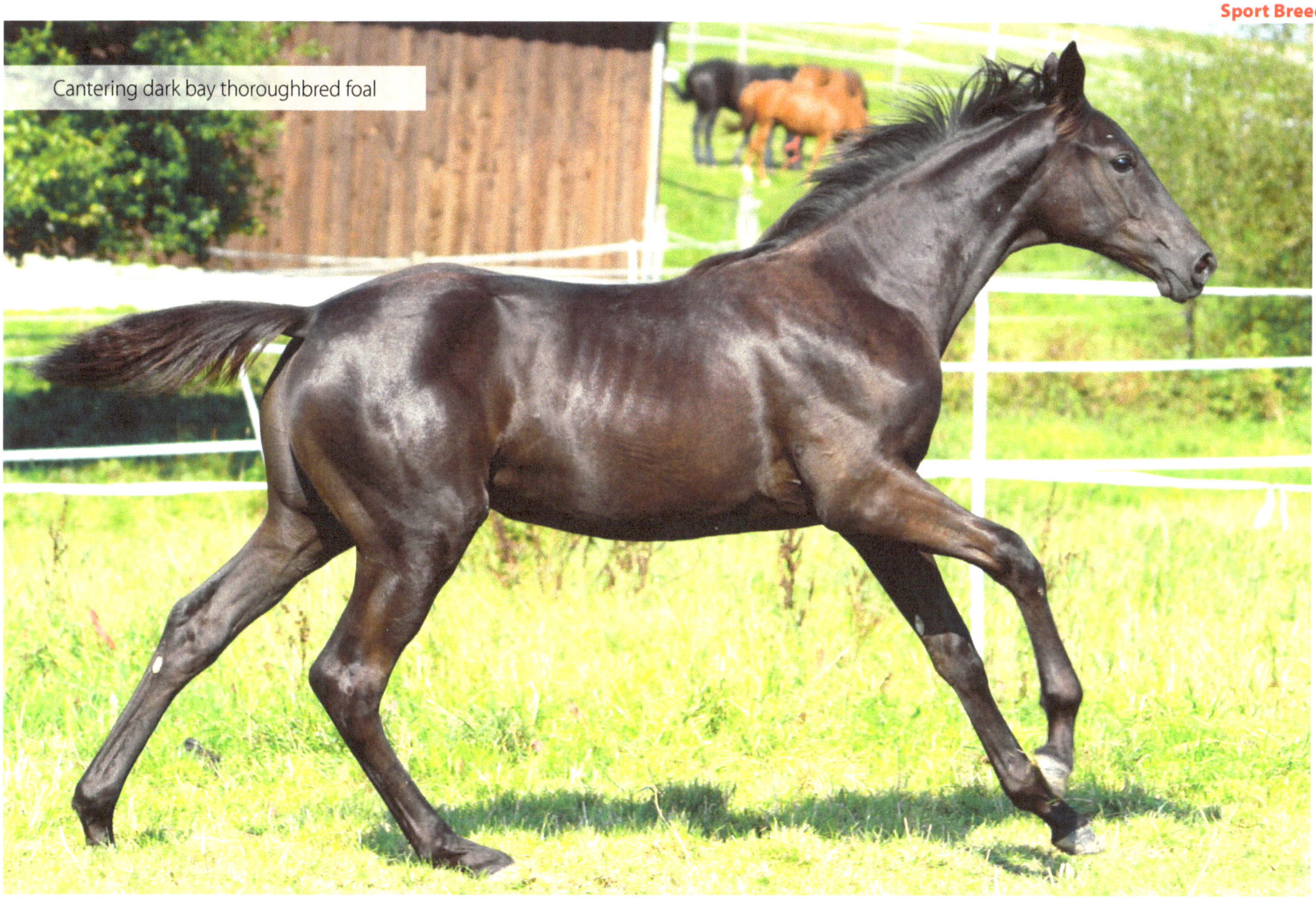

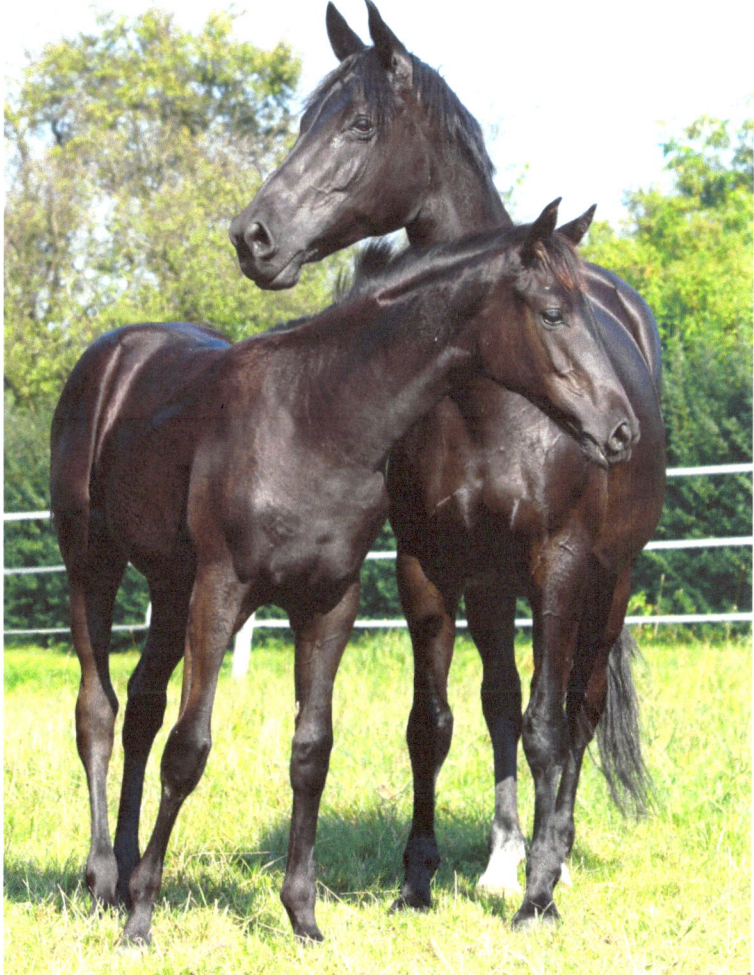

Cantering dark bay thoroughbred foal

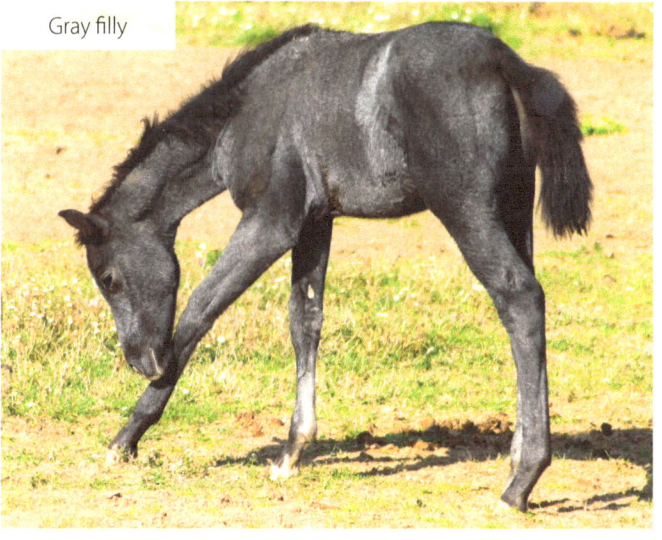

Gray filly

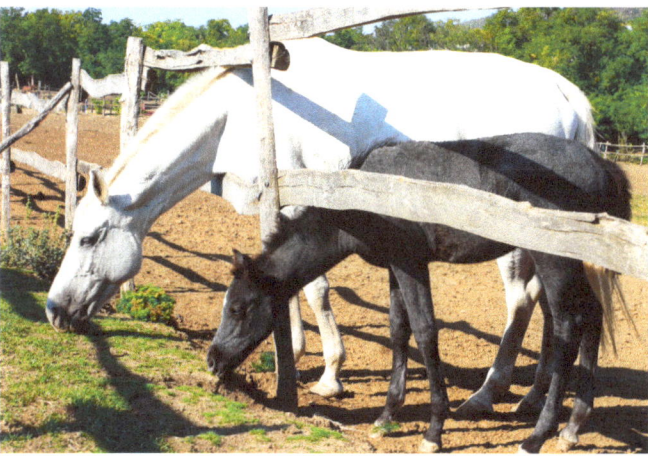

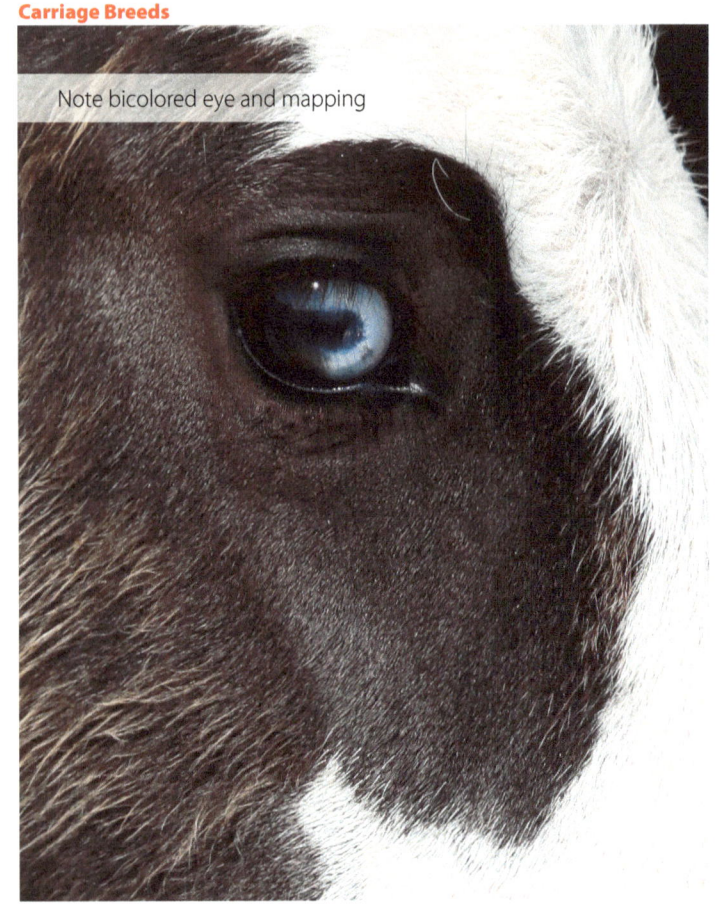

Note bicolored eye and mapping

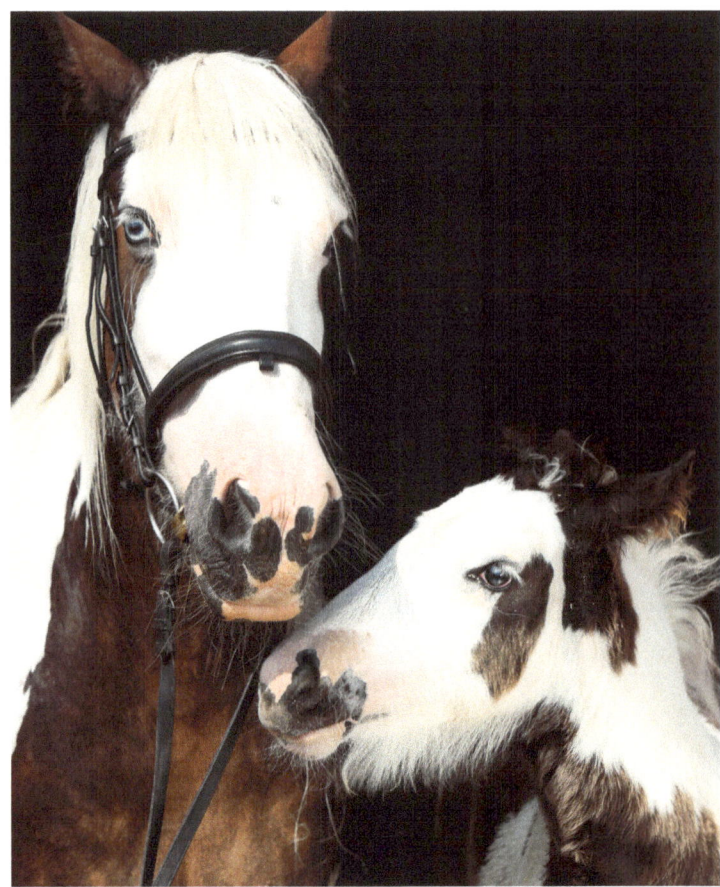

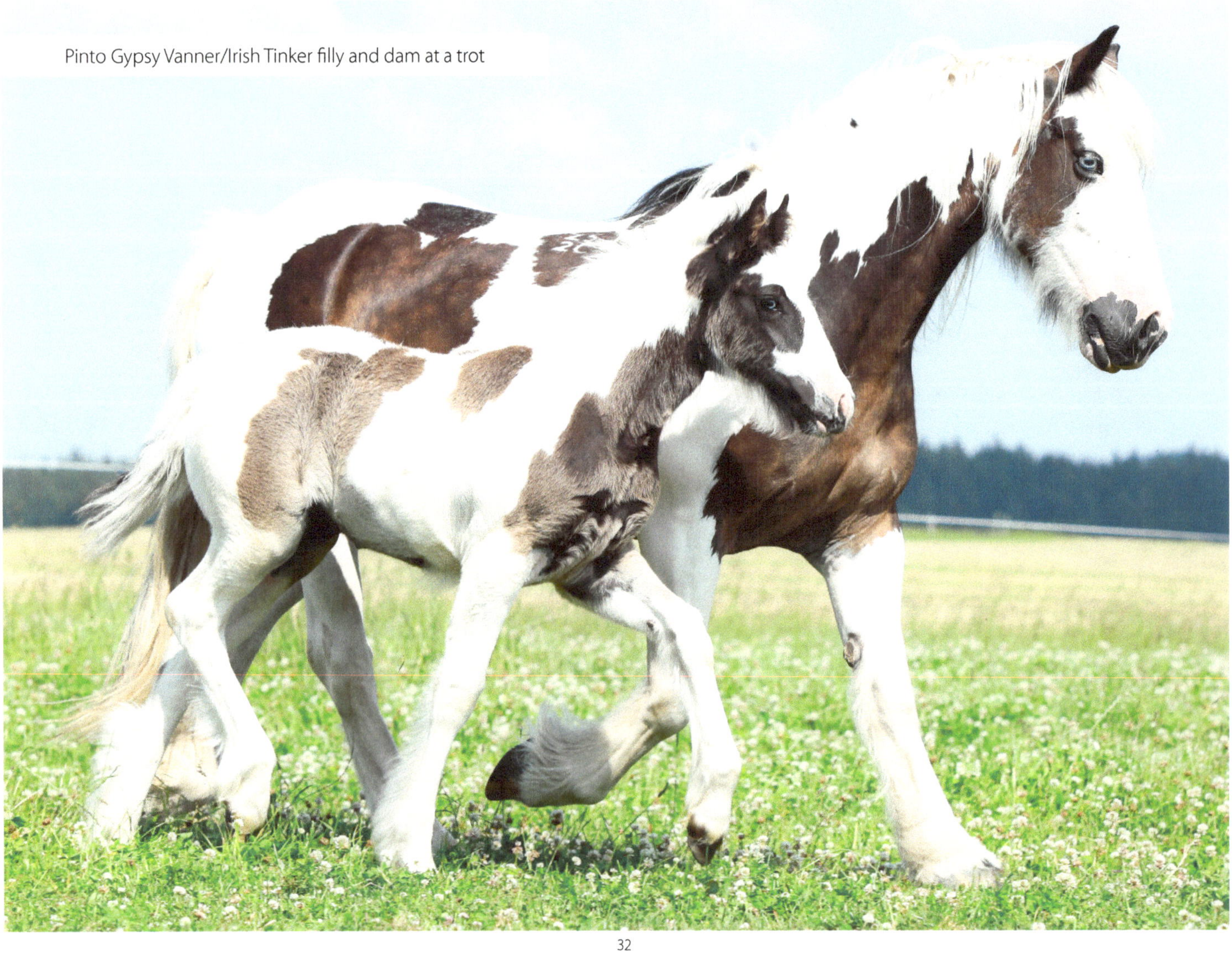

Pinto Gypsy Vanner/Irish Tinker filly and dam at a trot

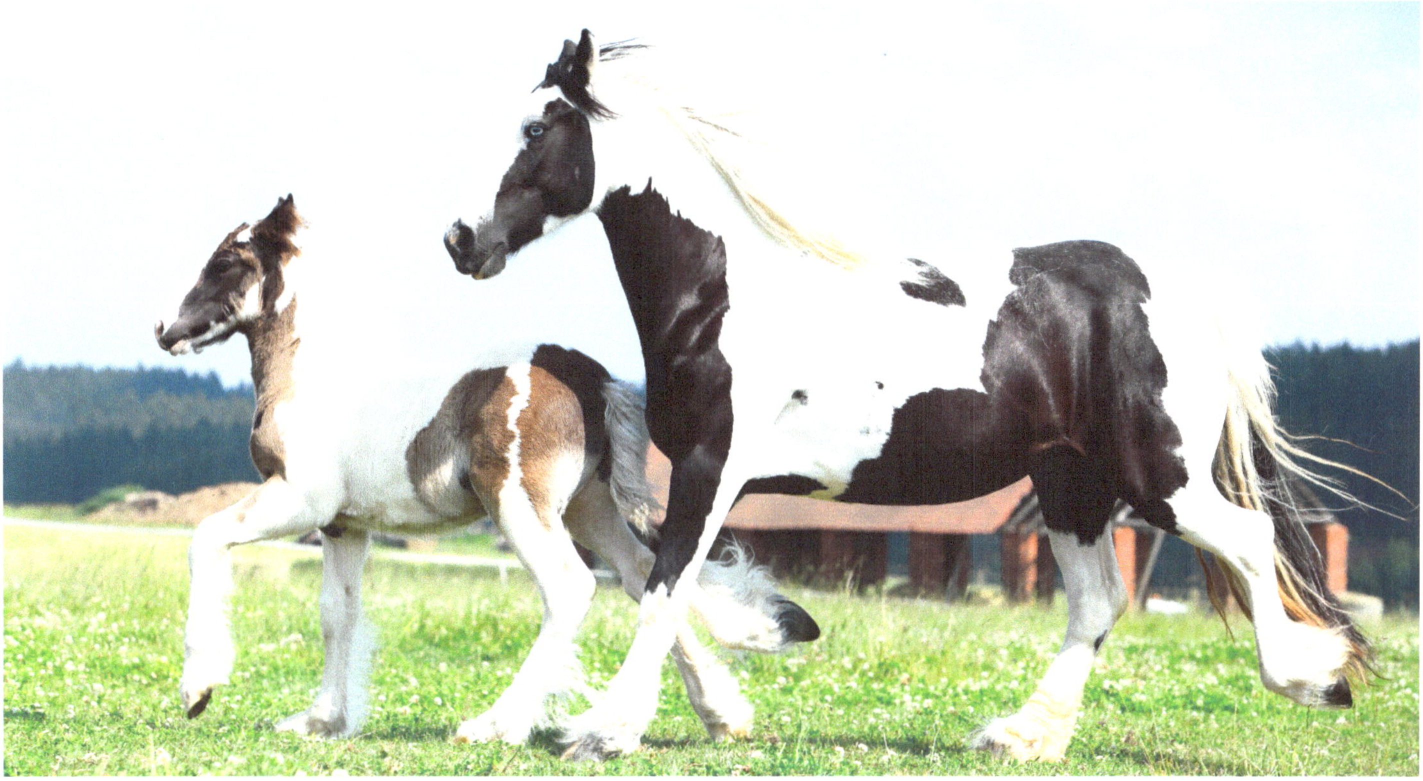

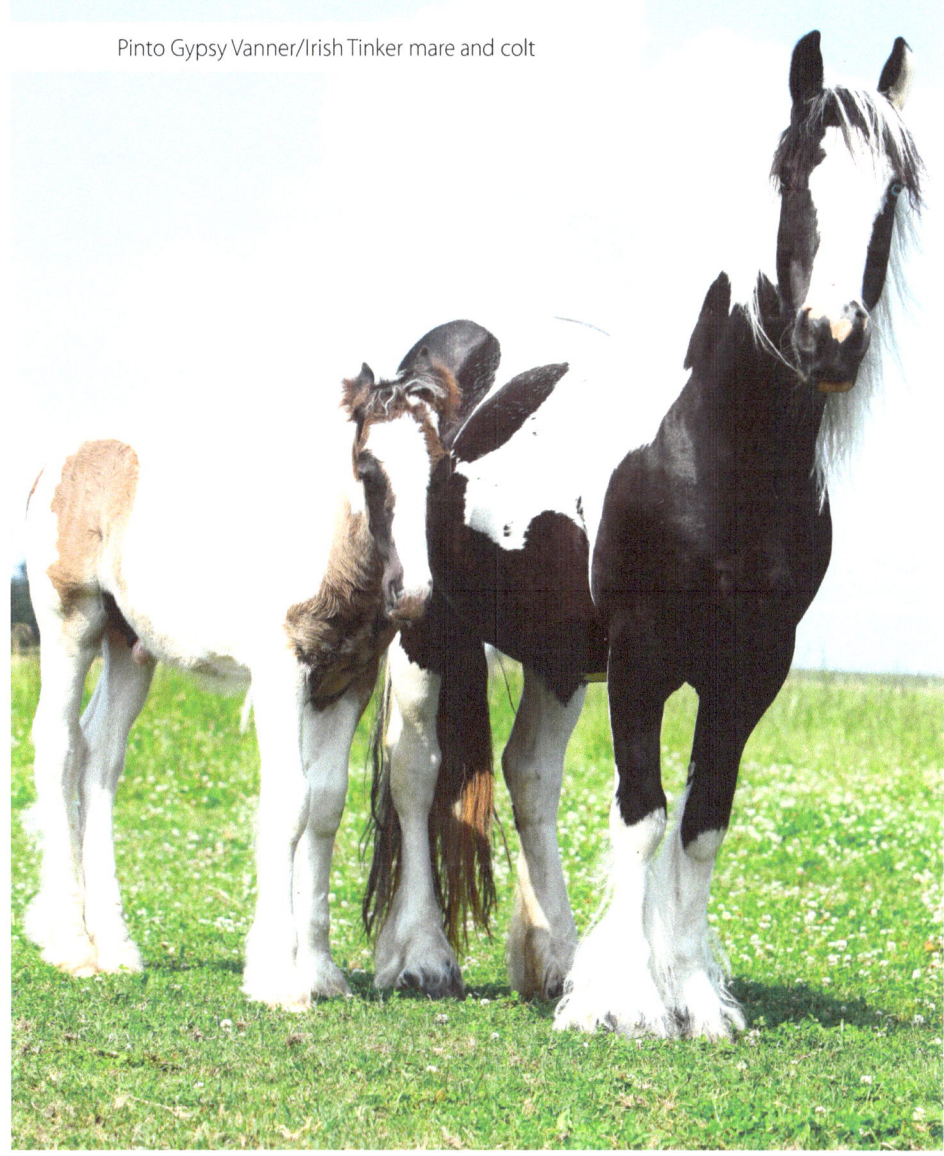

Pinto Gypsy Vanner/Irish Tinker mare and colt

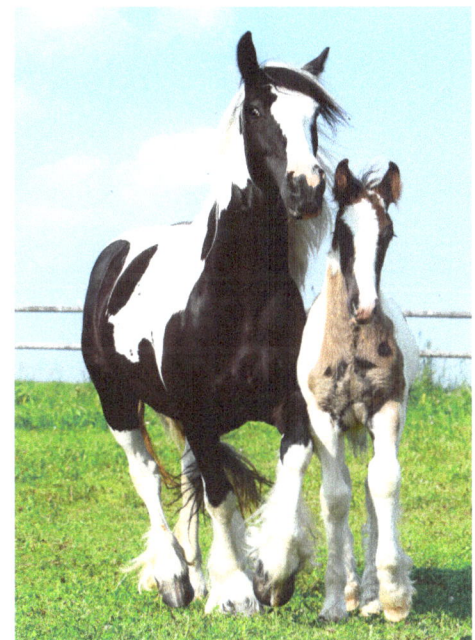

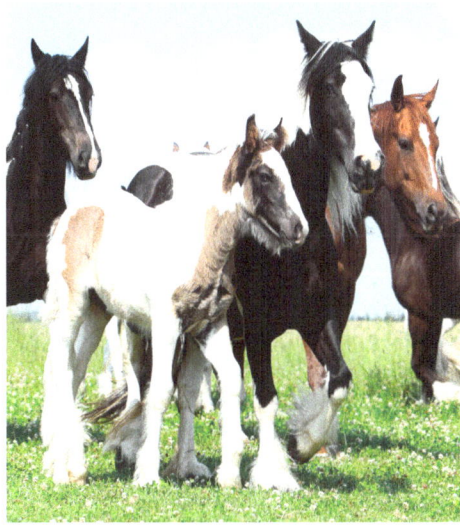

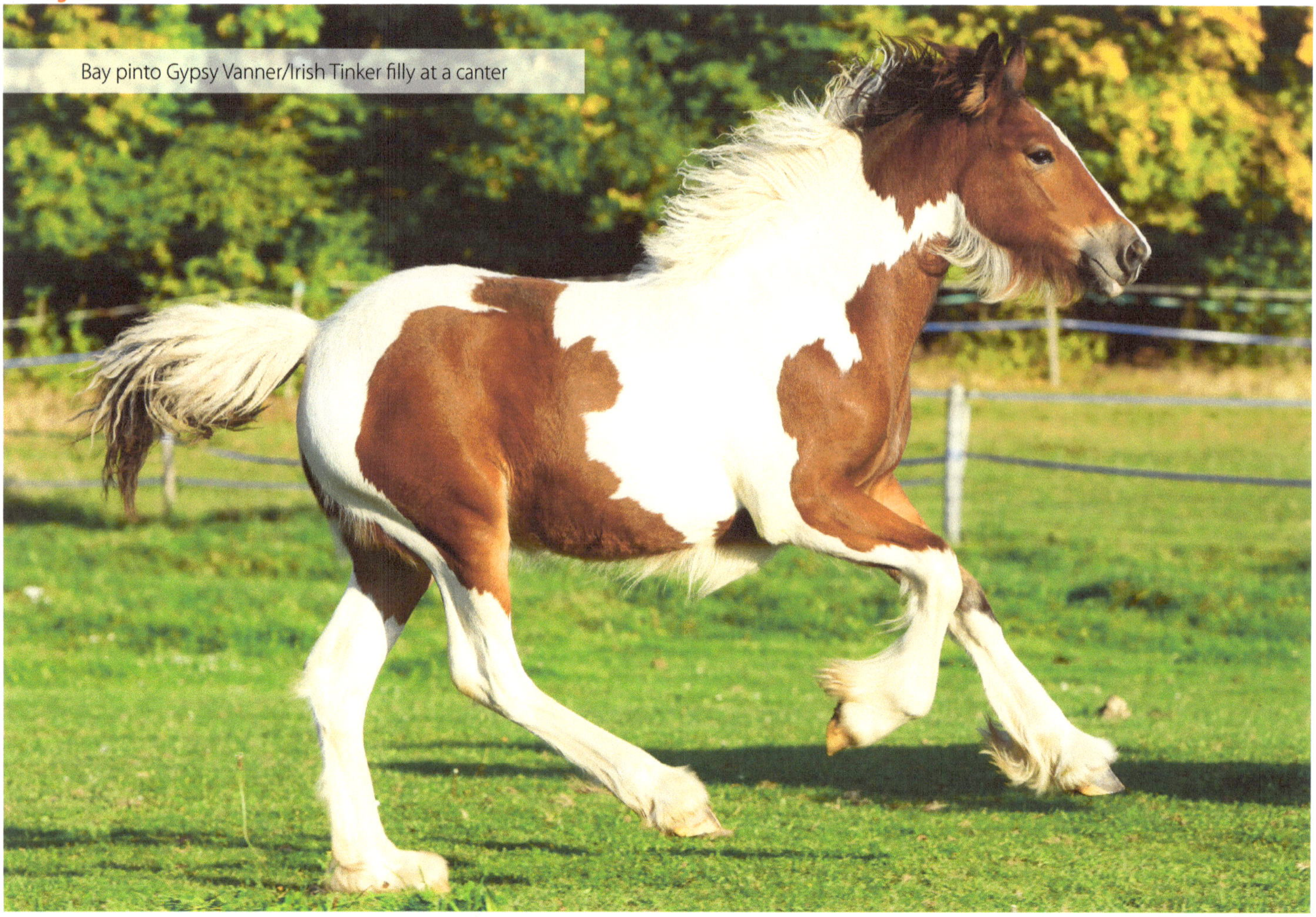

Bay pinto Gypsy Vanner/Irish Tinker filly at a canter

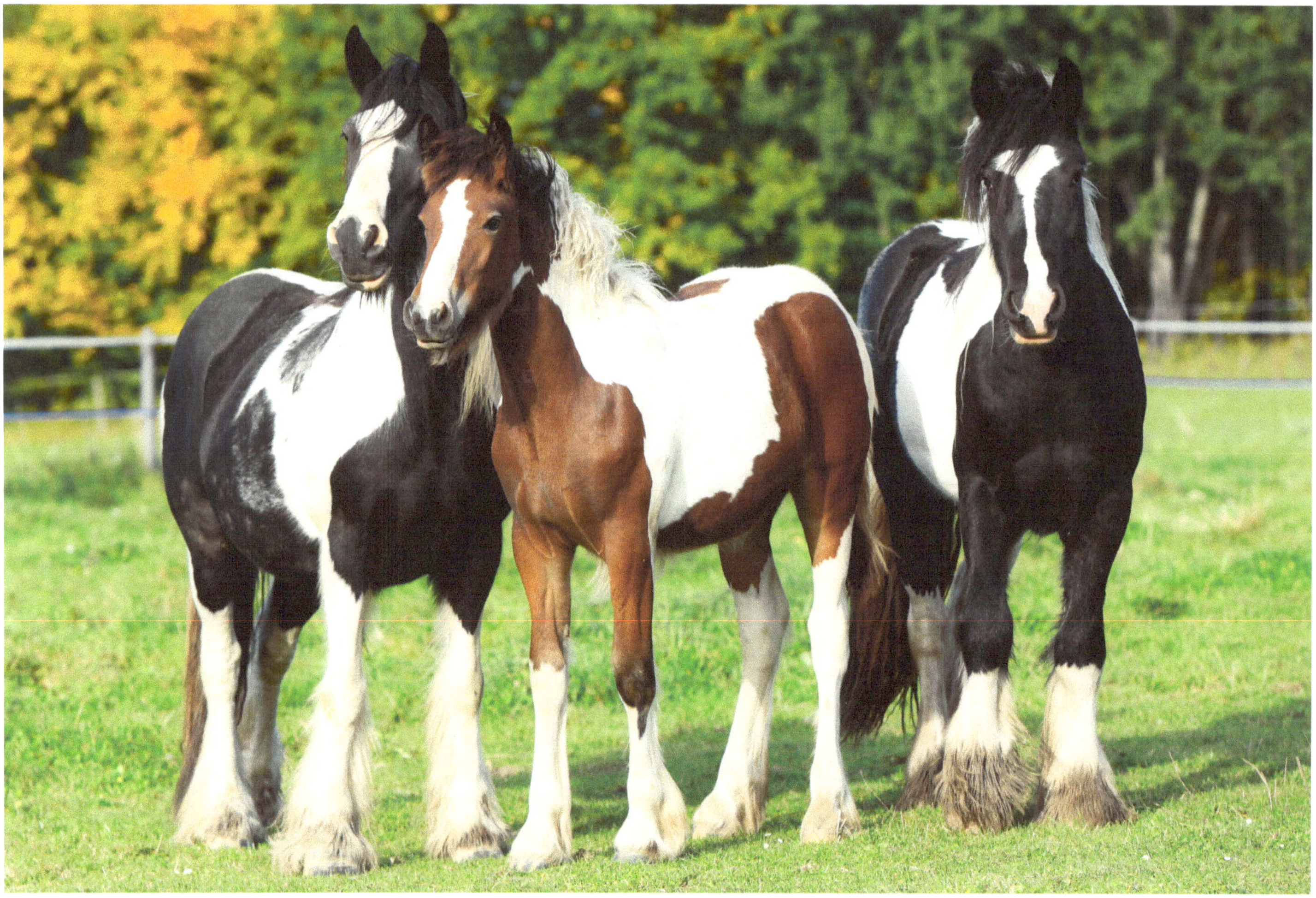

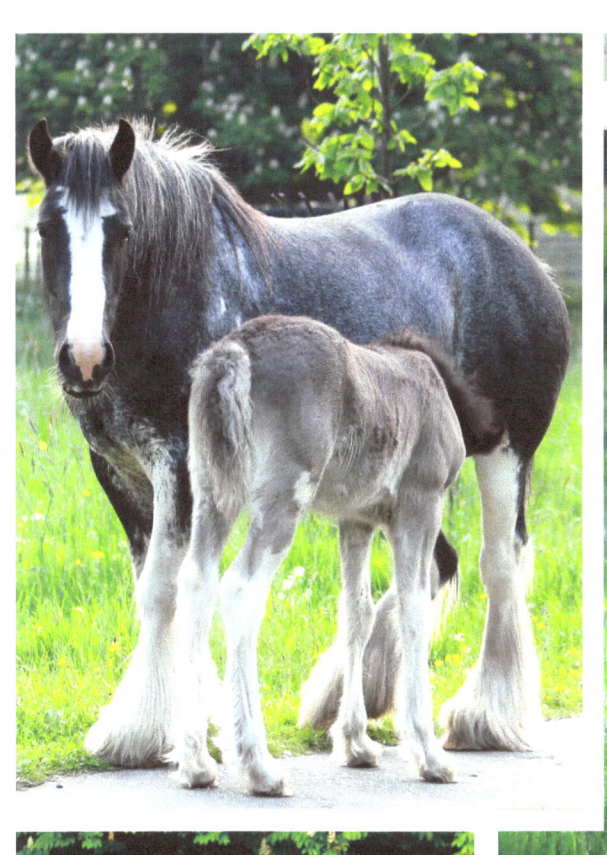

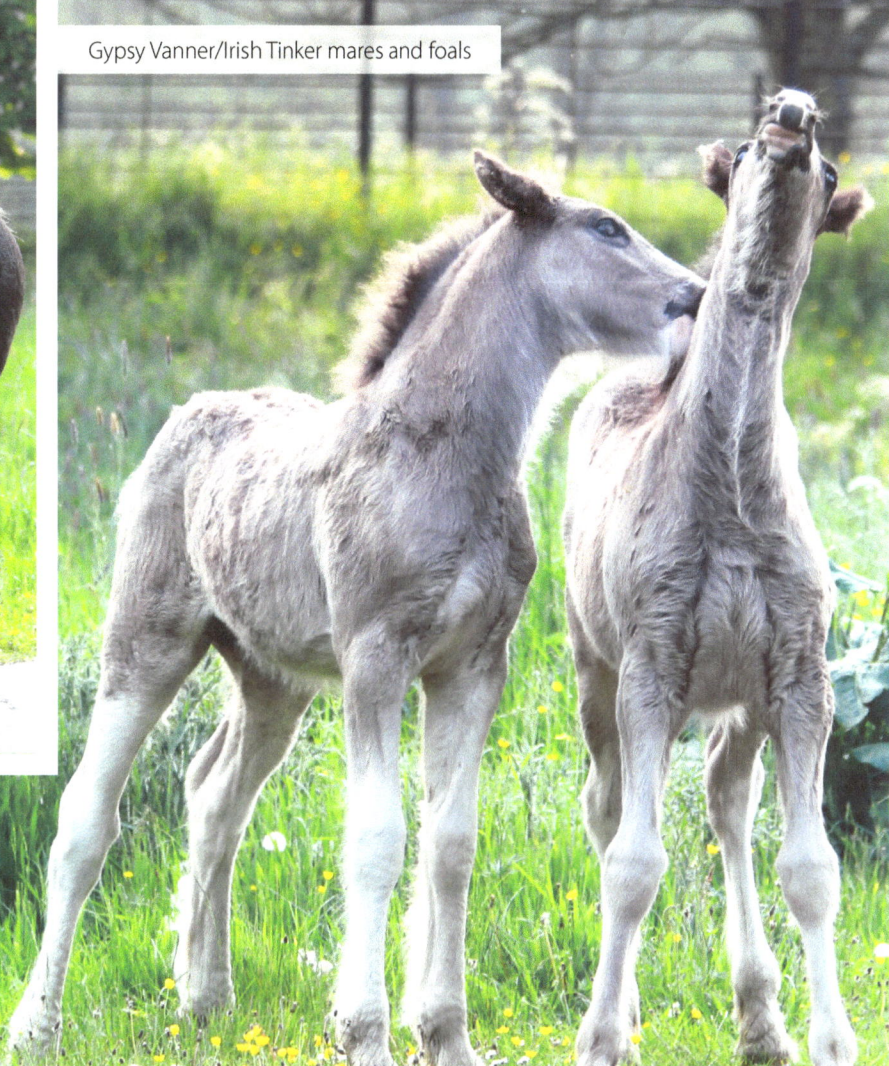

Gypsy Vanner/Irish Tinker mares and foals

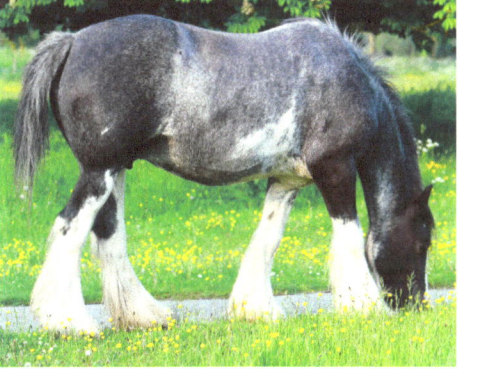

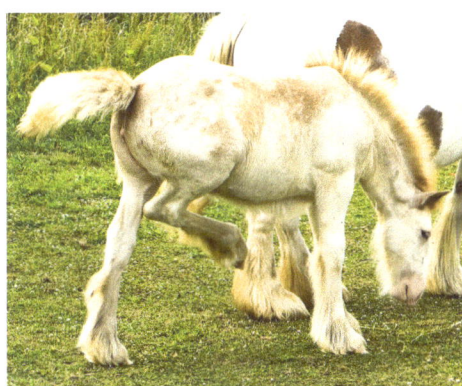

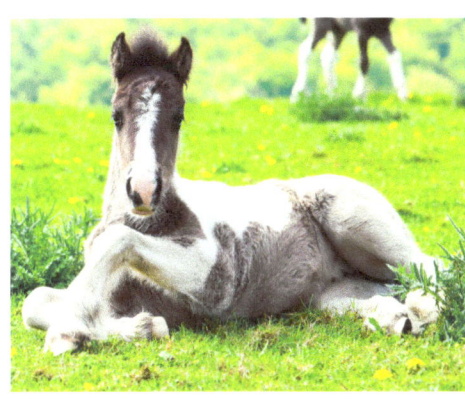

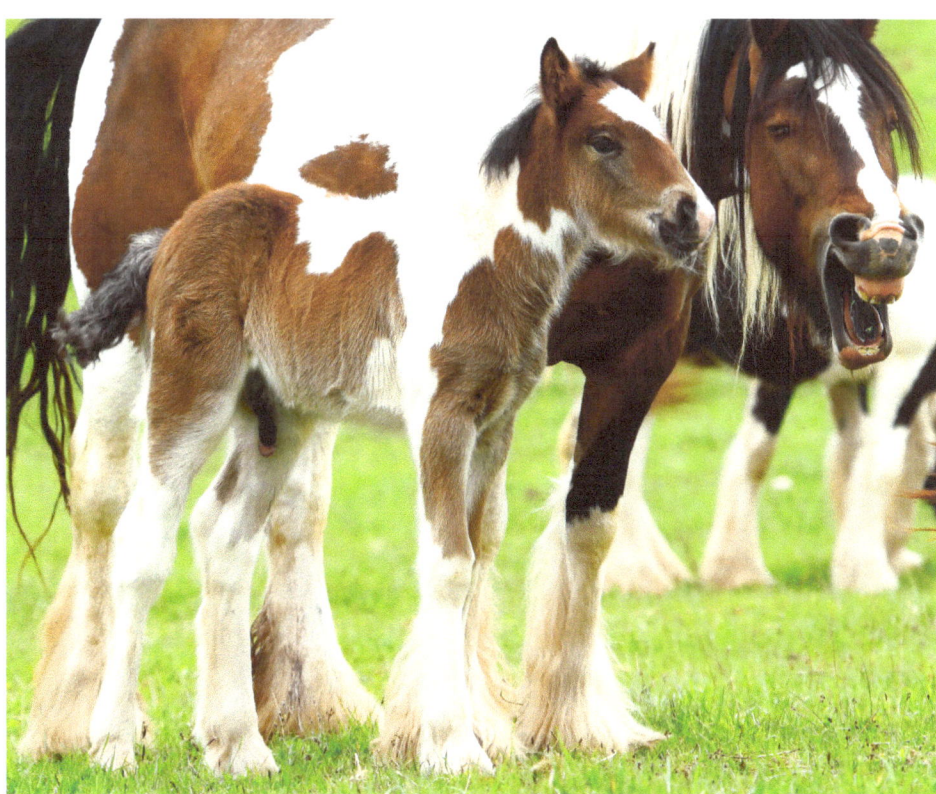

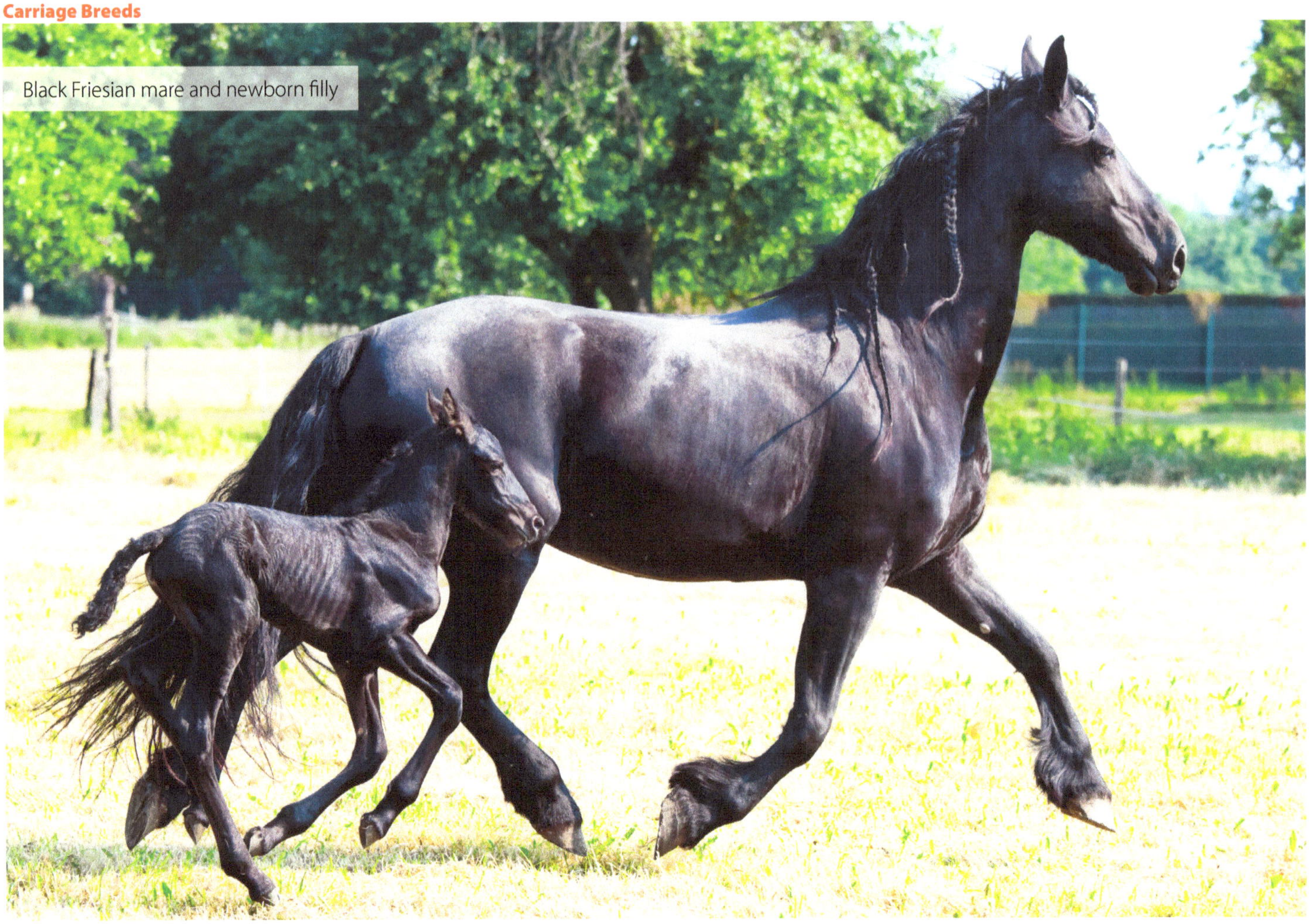

Black Friesian mare and newborn filly

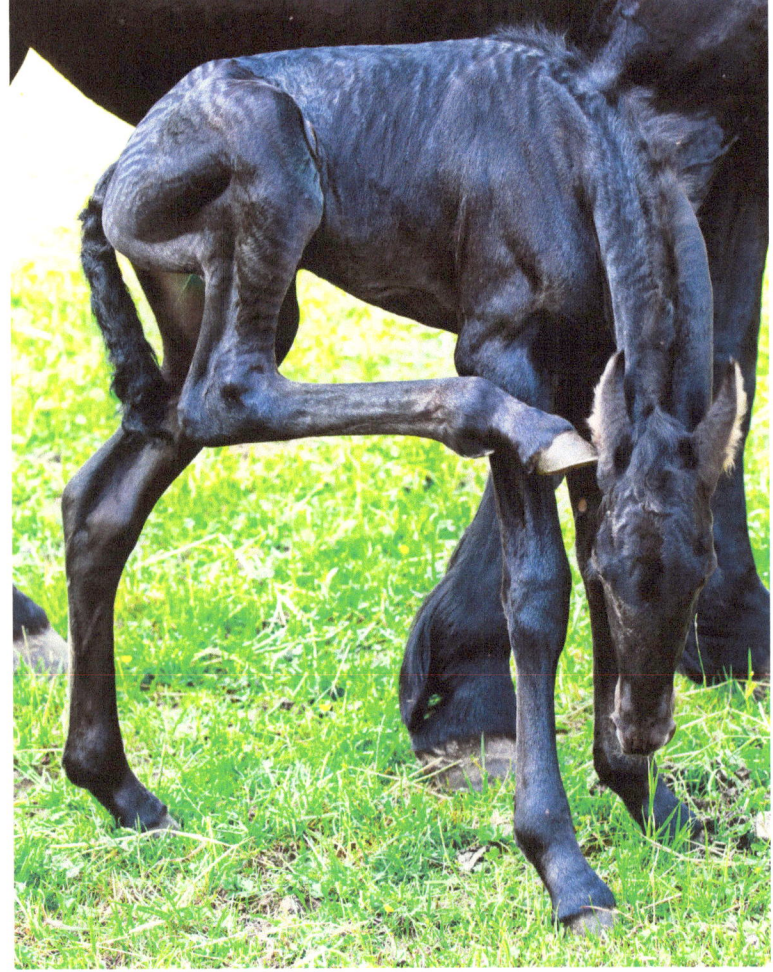
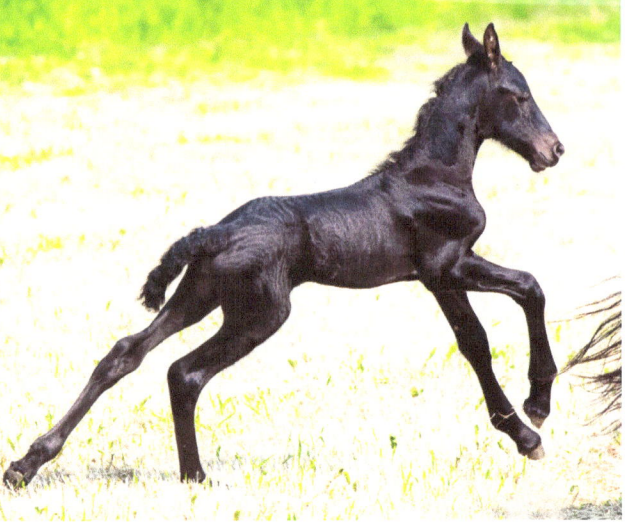
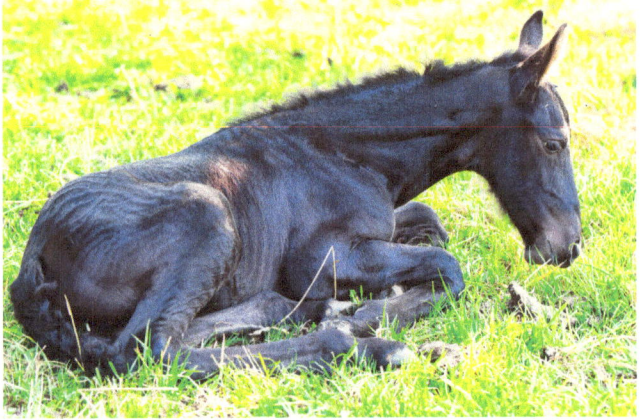

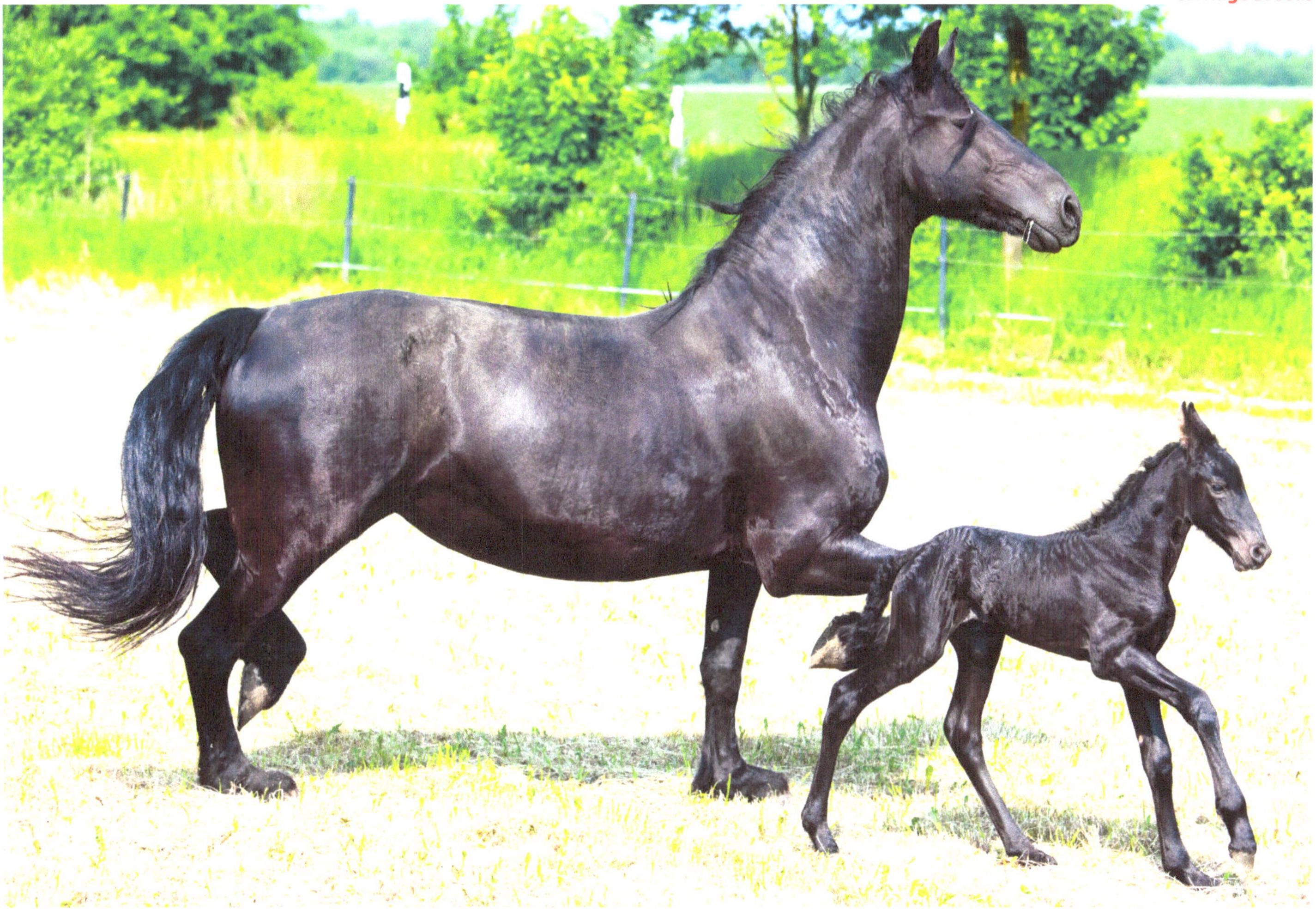

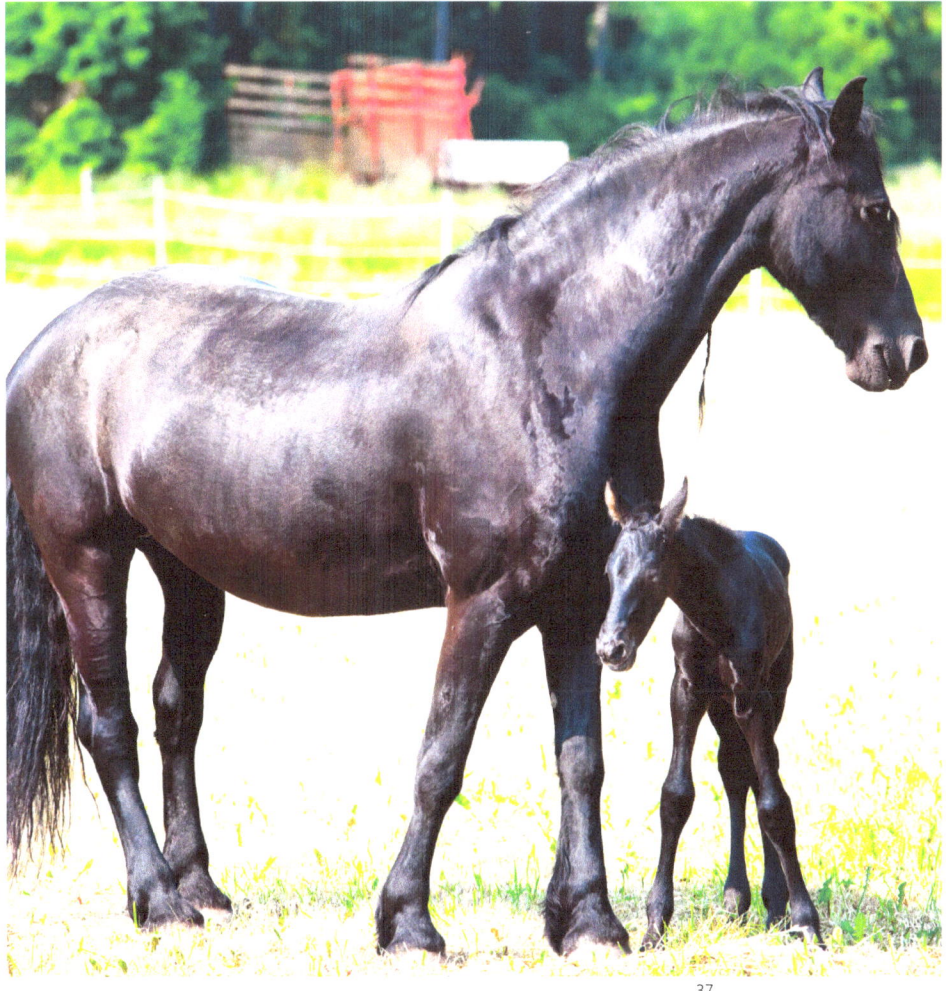

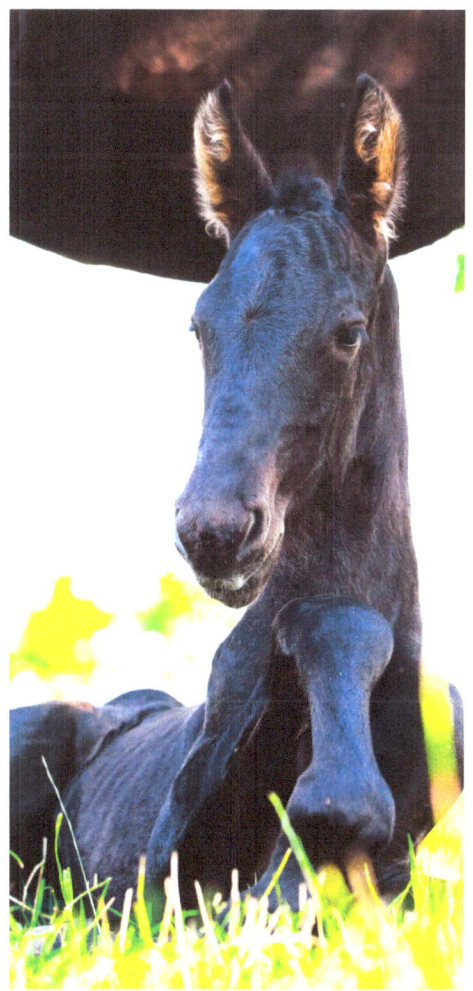

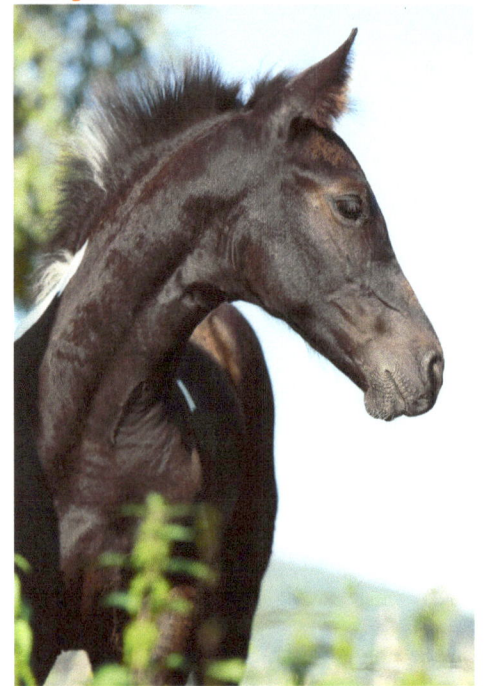

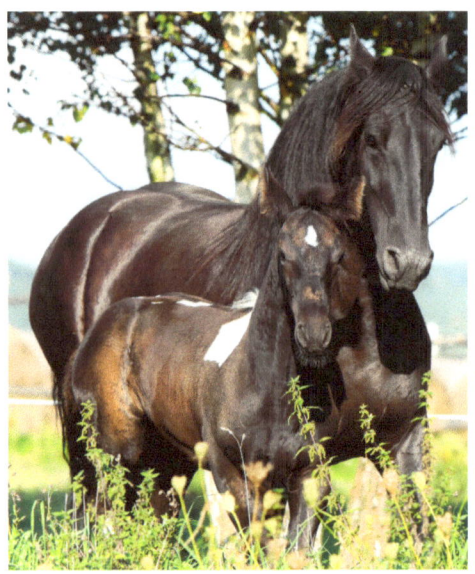

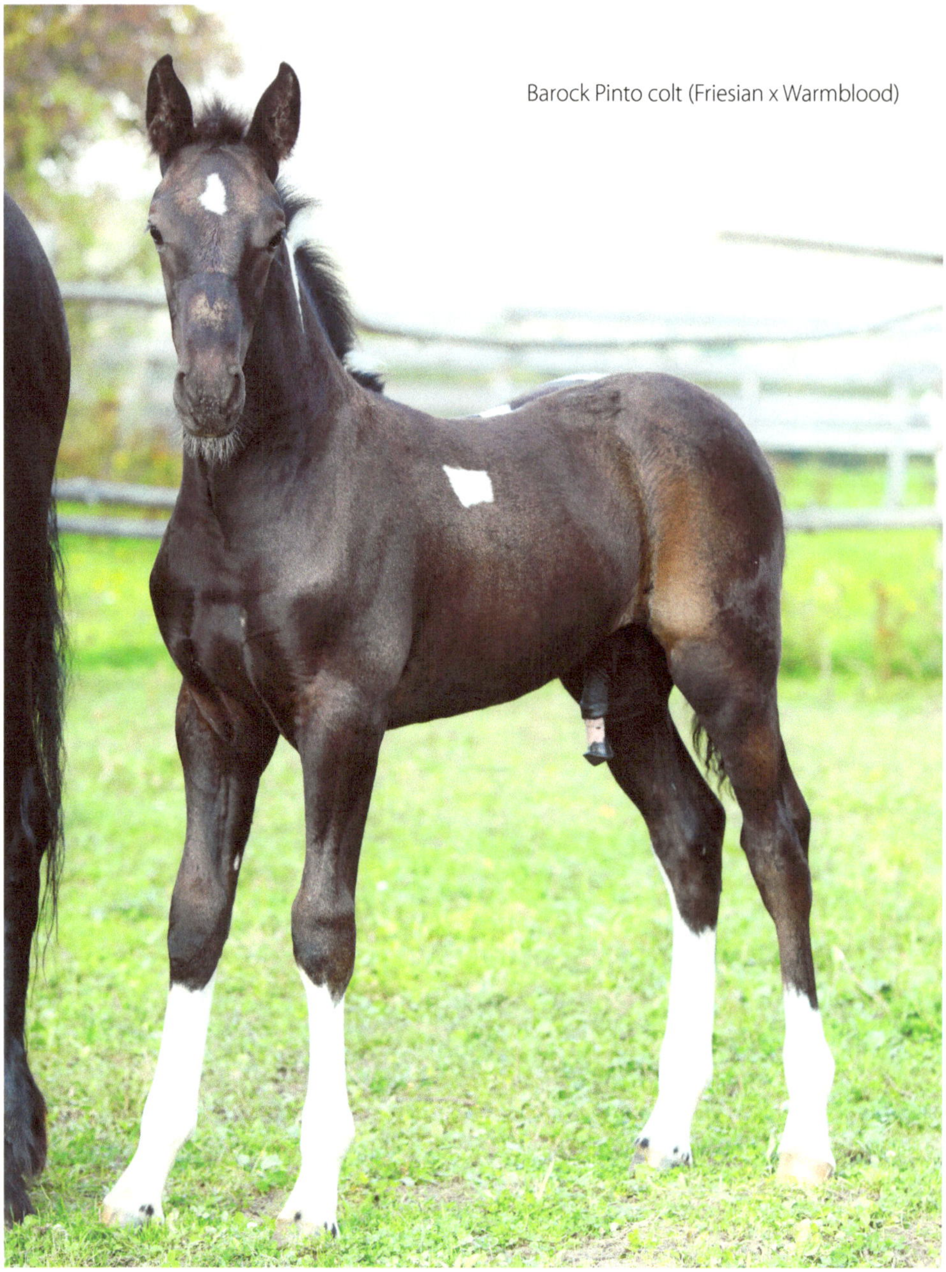

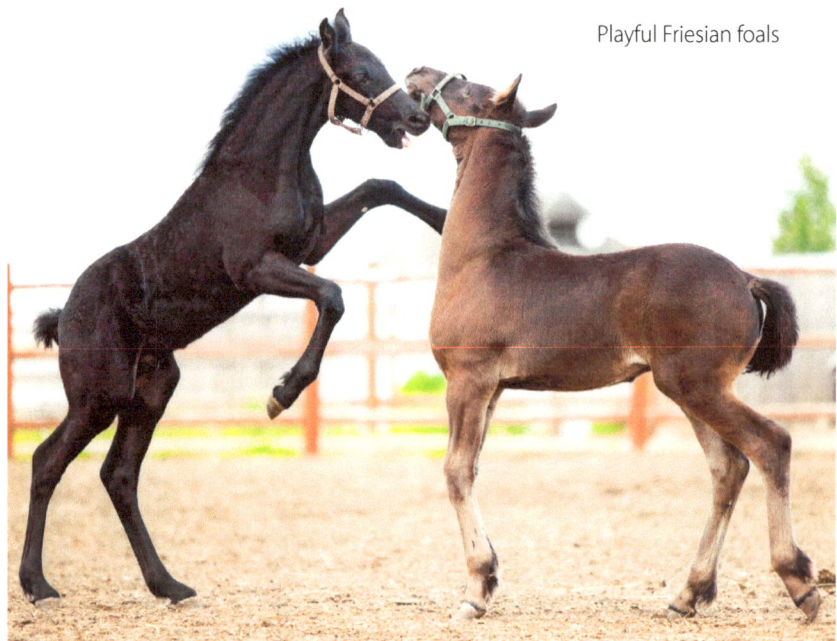

Barock Pinto colt (Friesian x Warmblood)

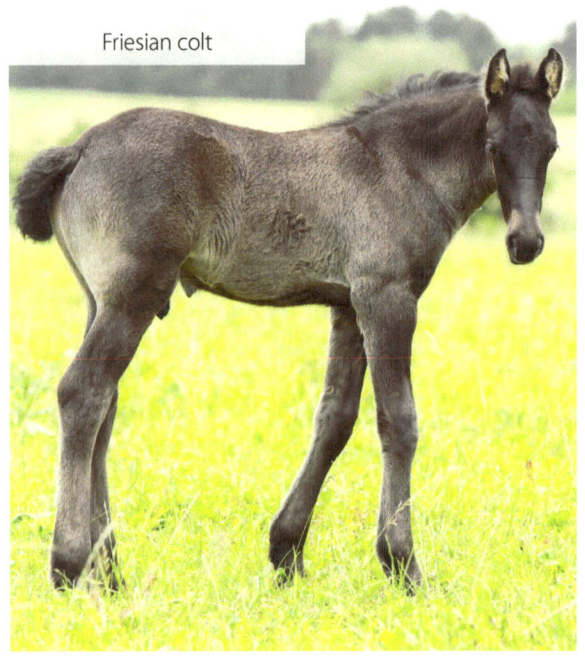

Friesian colt

Playful Friesian foals

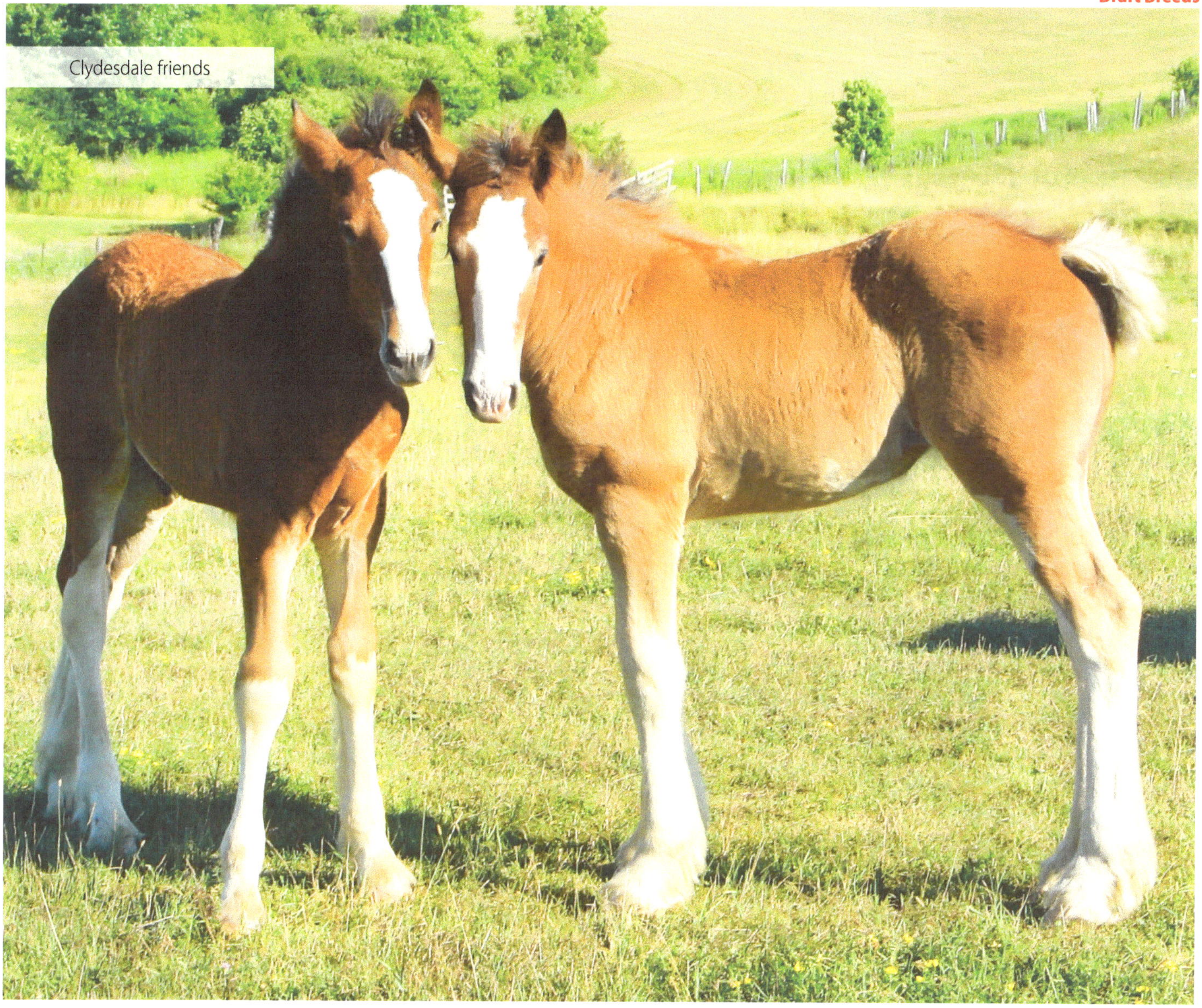

Clydesdale friends

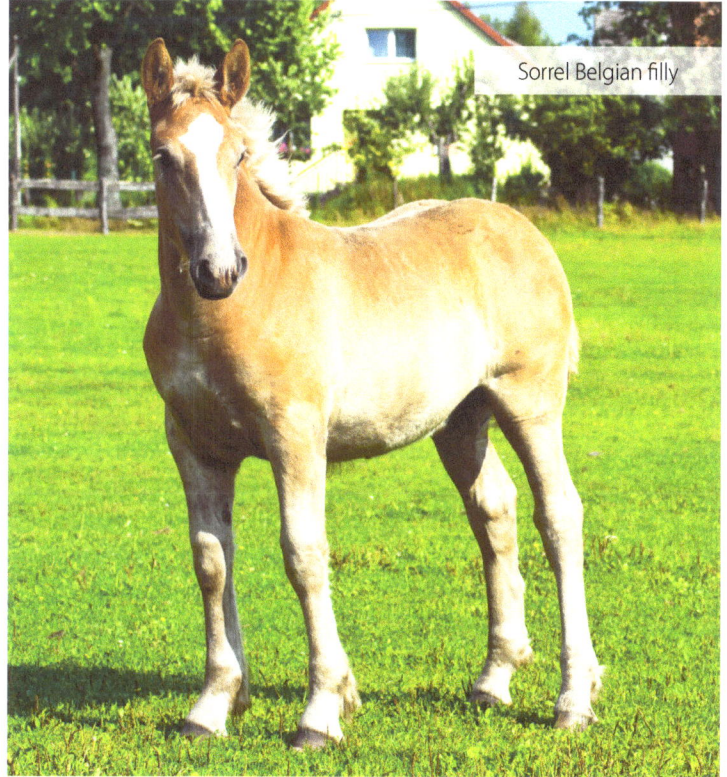

Sorrel Belgian filly

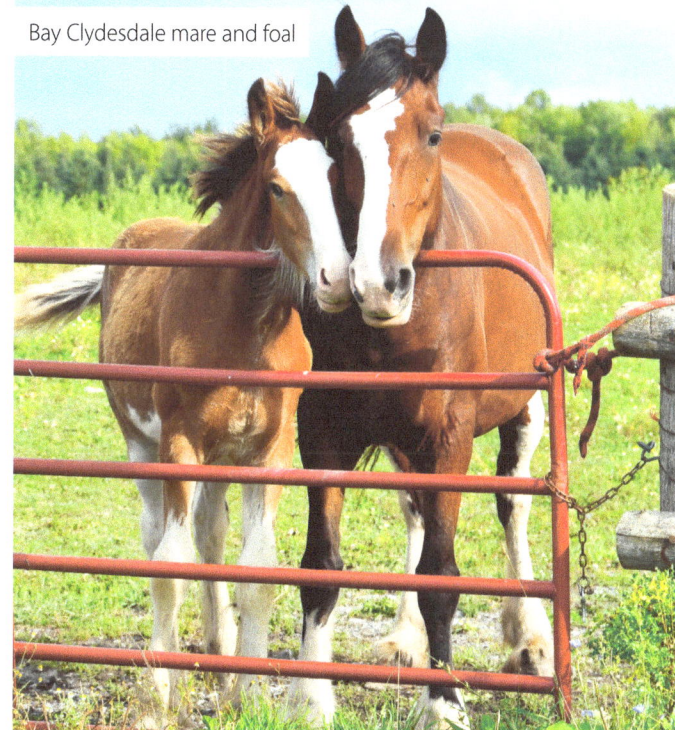

Bay Clydesdale mare and foal

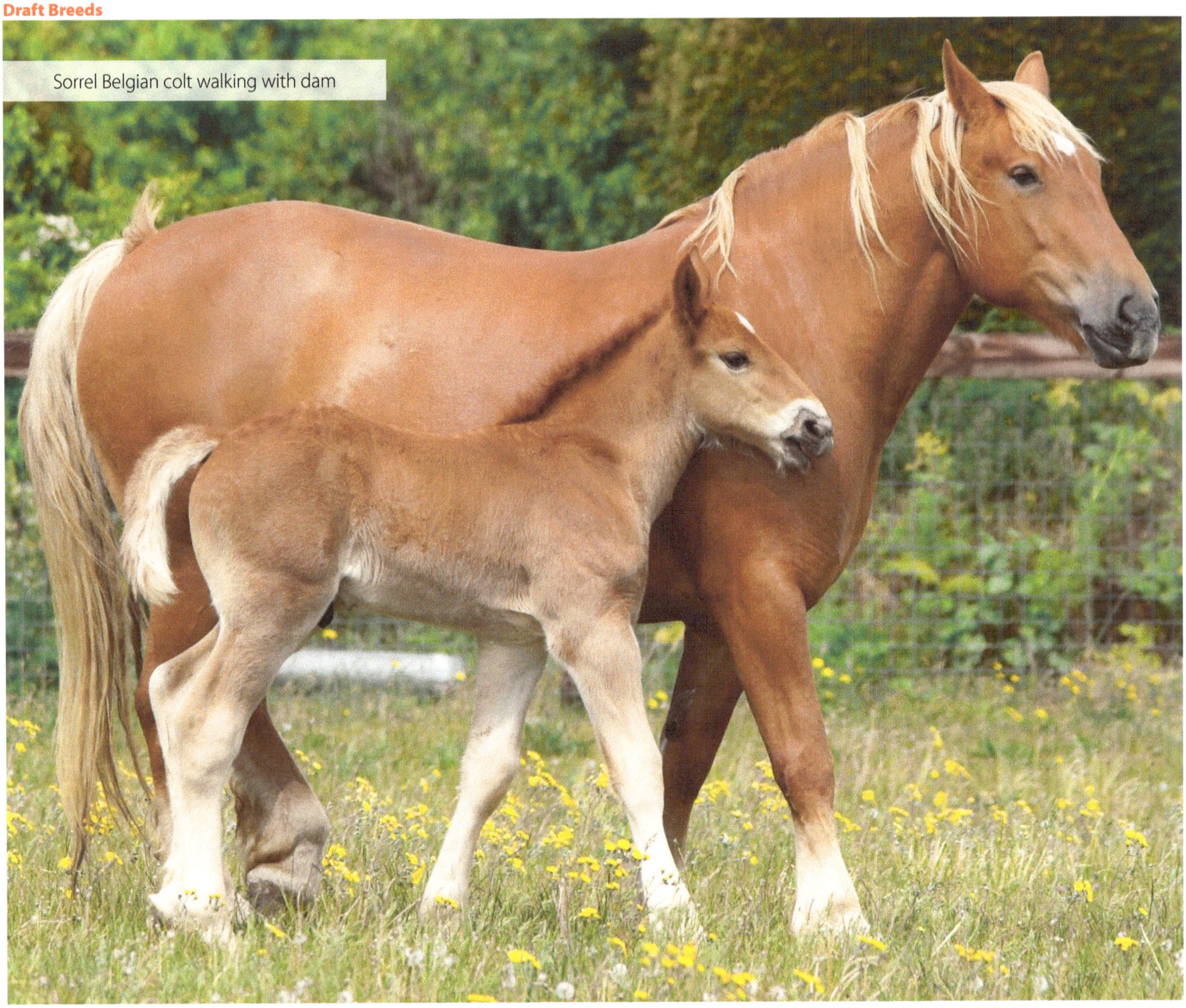

Sorrel Belgian colt walking with dam

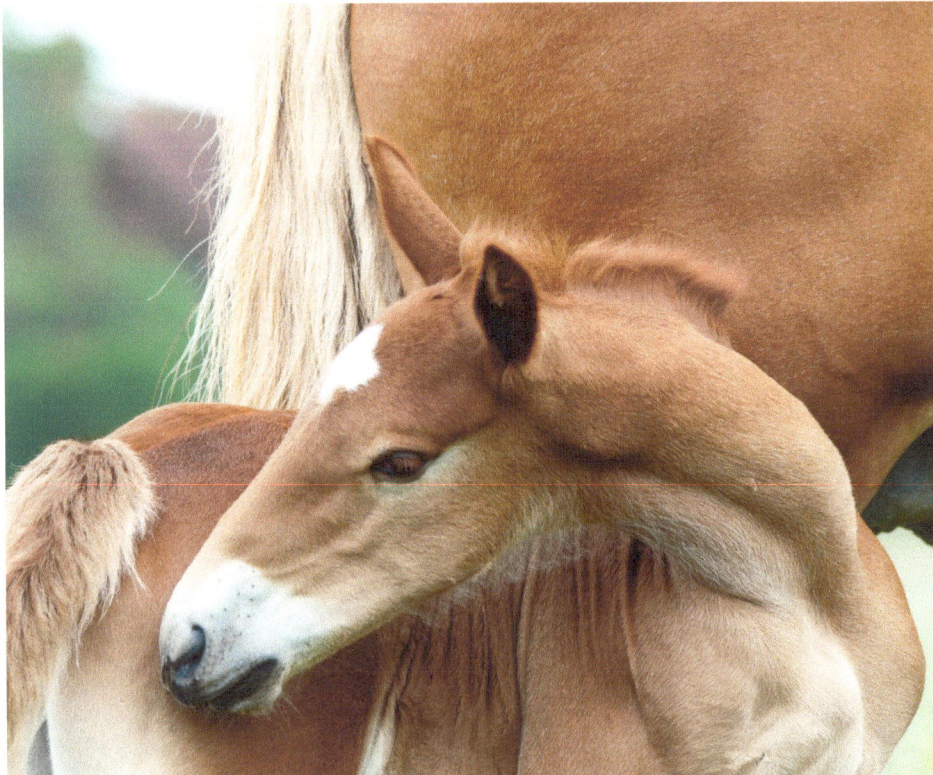

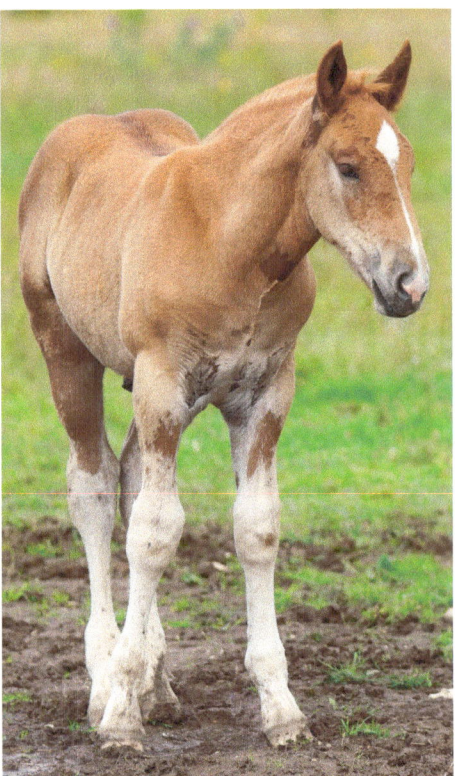

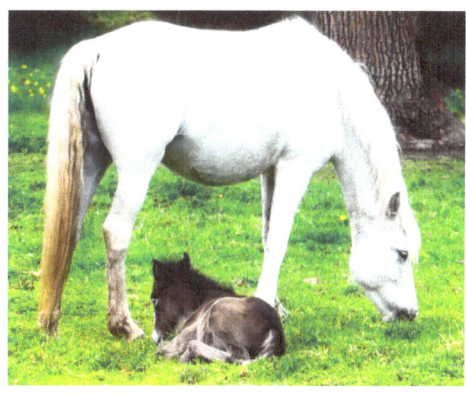

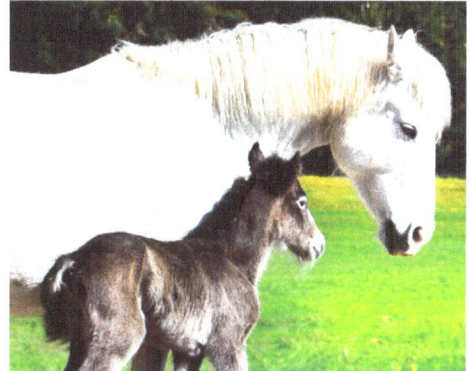

Mare and colt at a walk

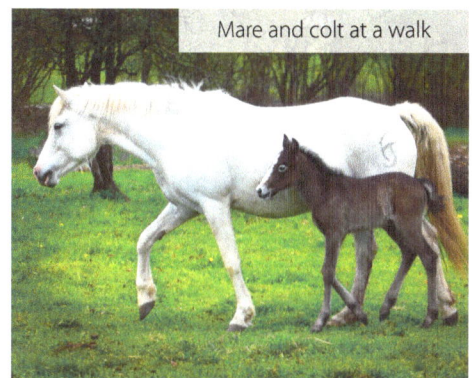

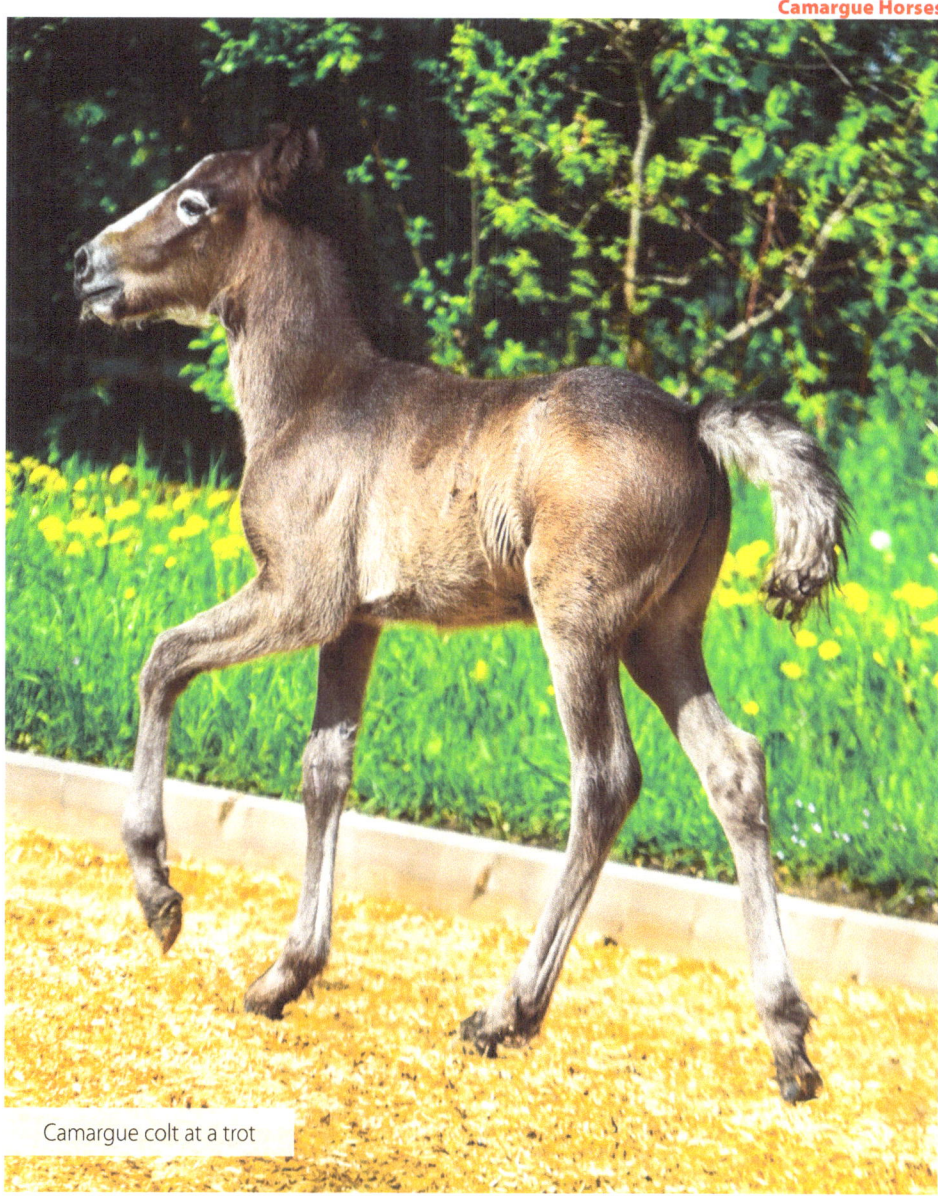

Camargue colt at a trot

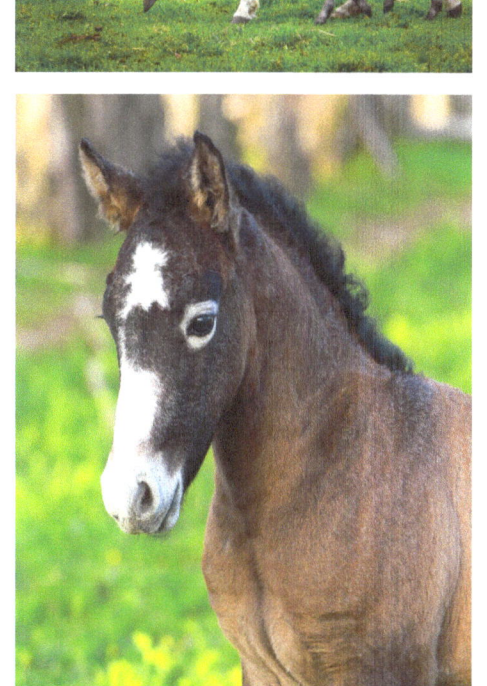

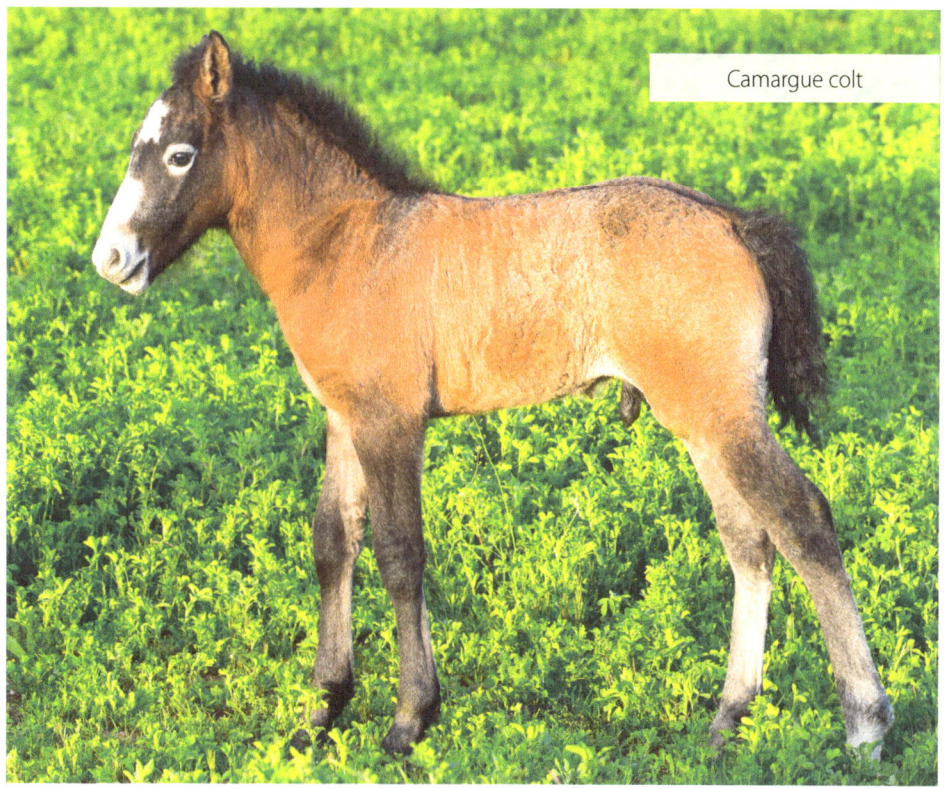

Camargue colt

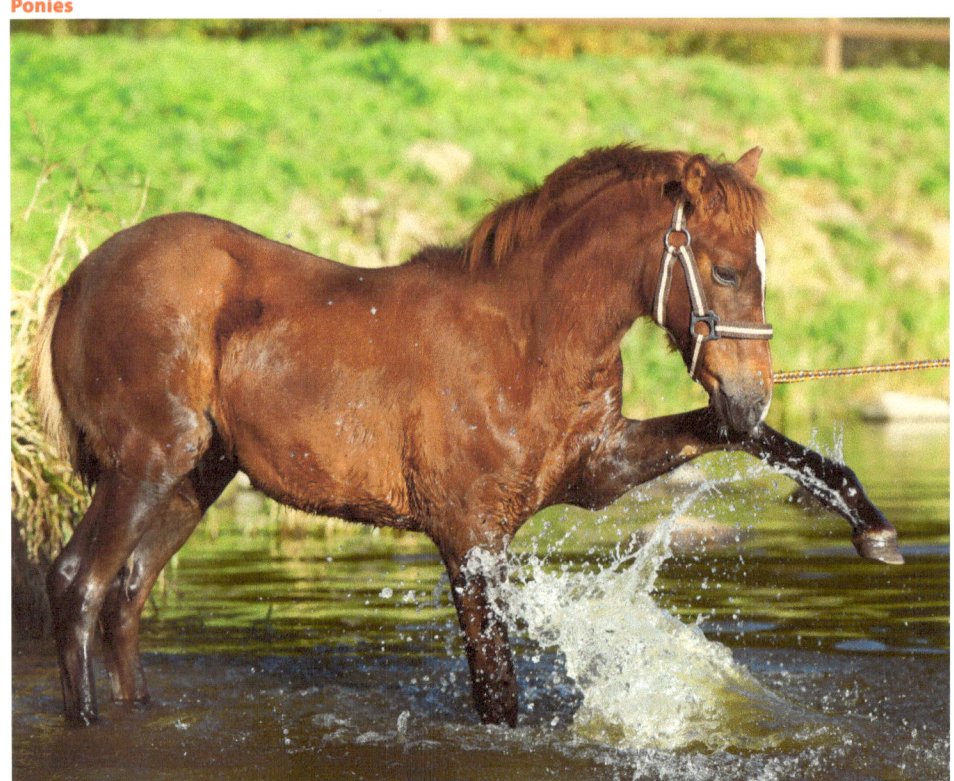

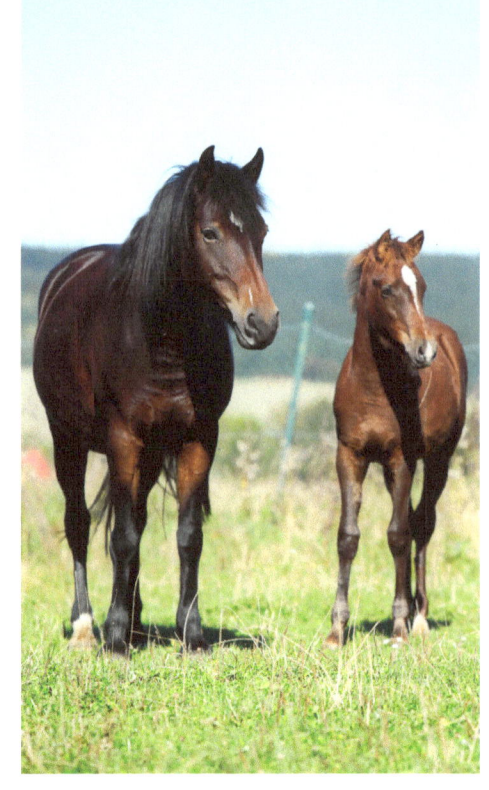

Chestnut Czech sport pony filly and her bay dam

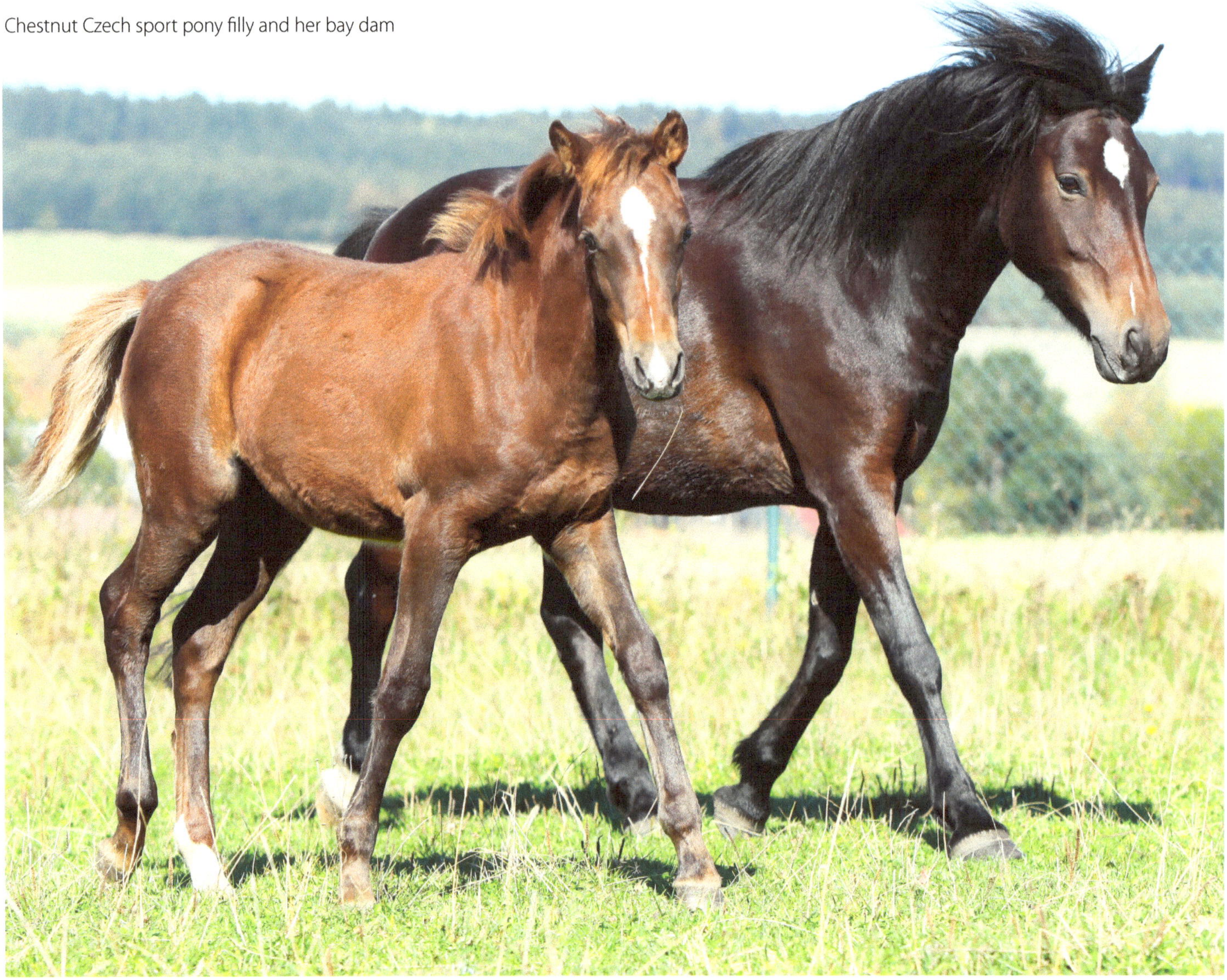

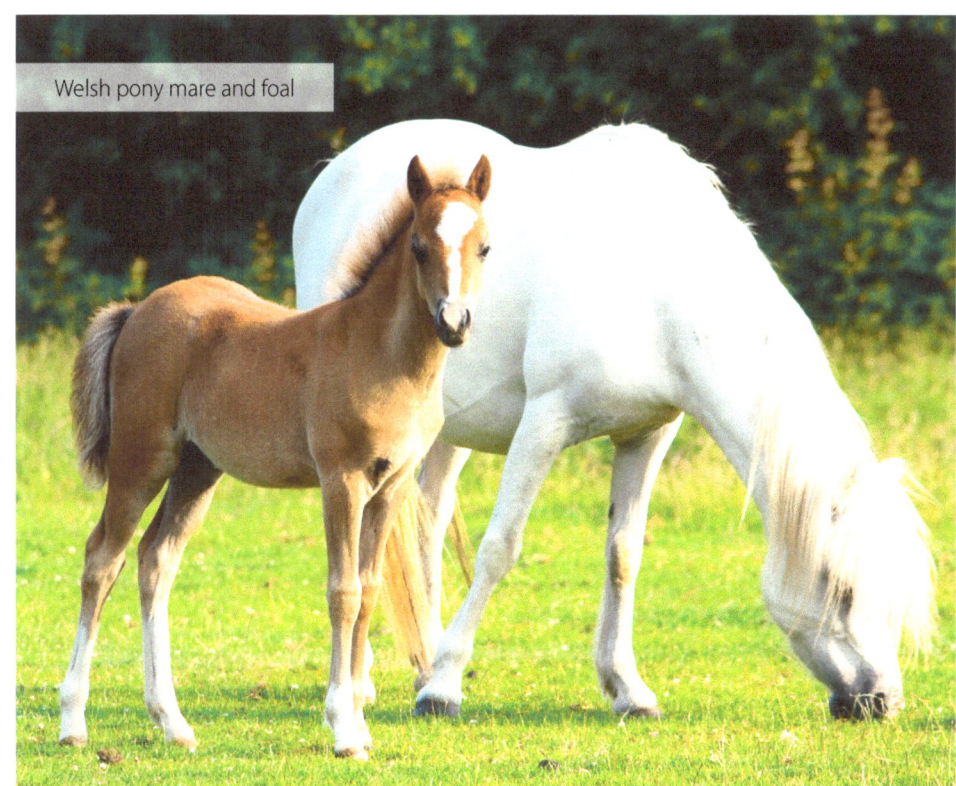

Welsh pony mare and foal

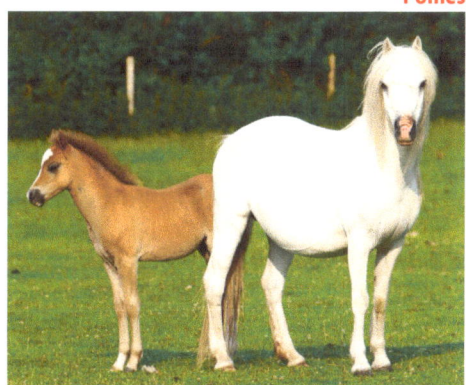

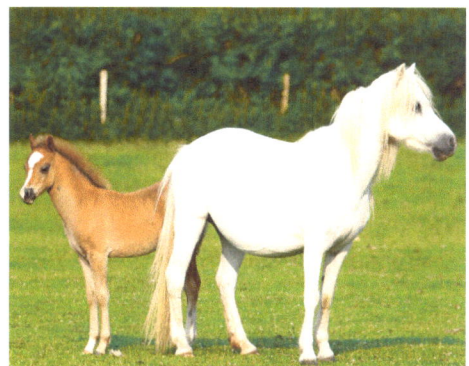

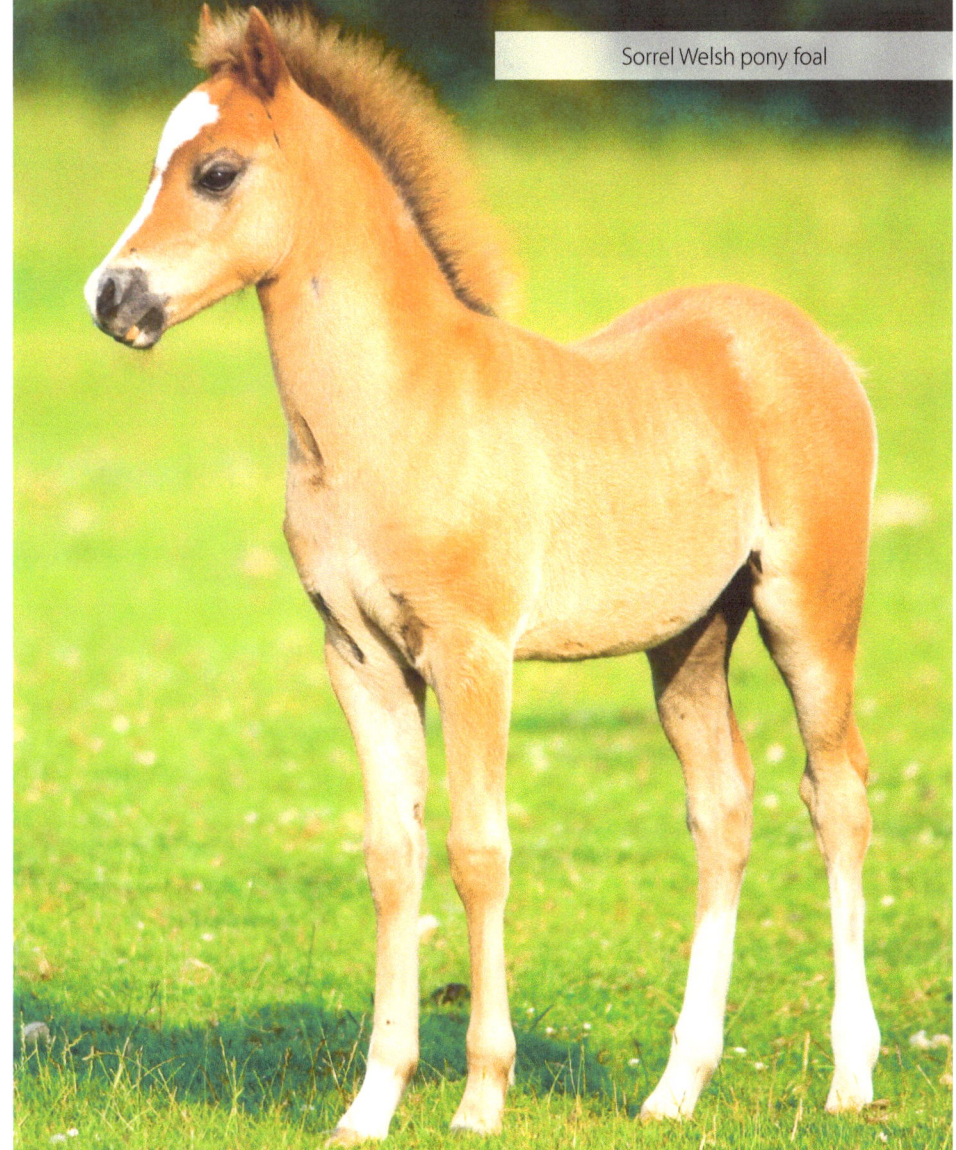

Sorrel Welsh pony foal

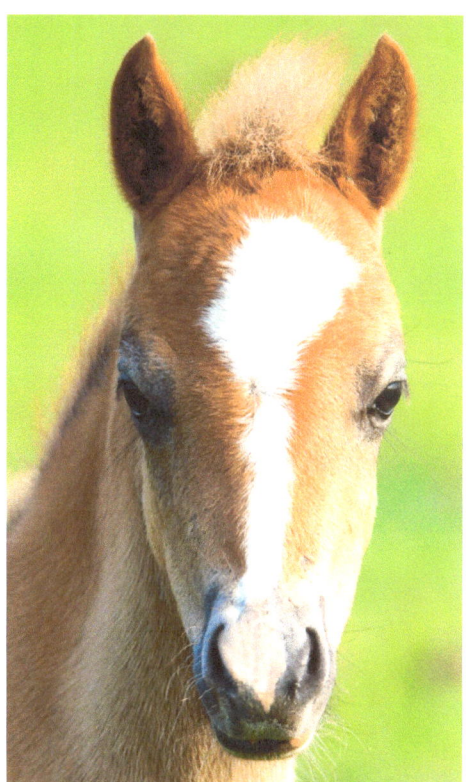

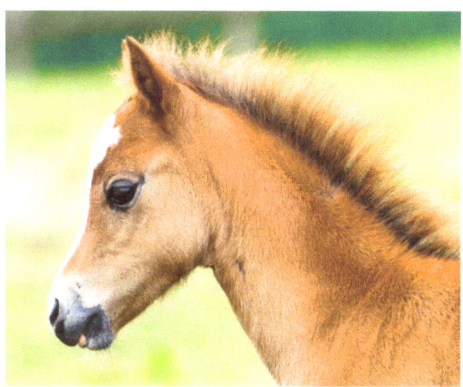

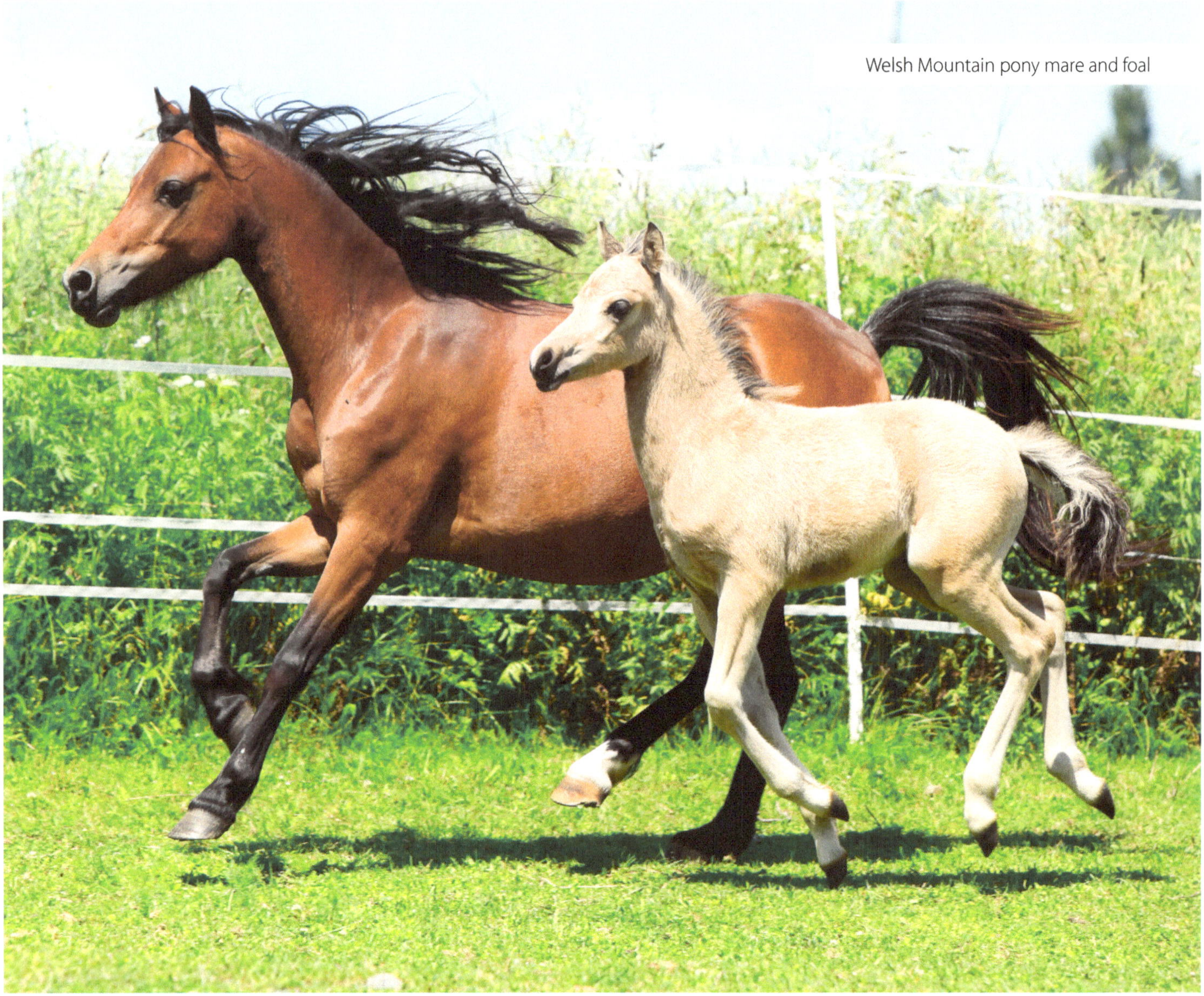

Welsh Mountain pony mare and foal

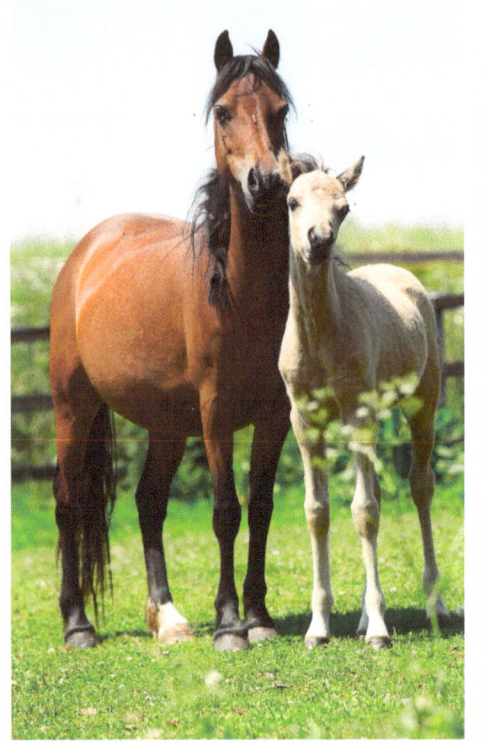

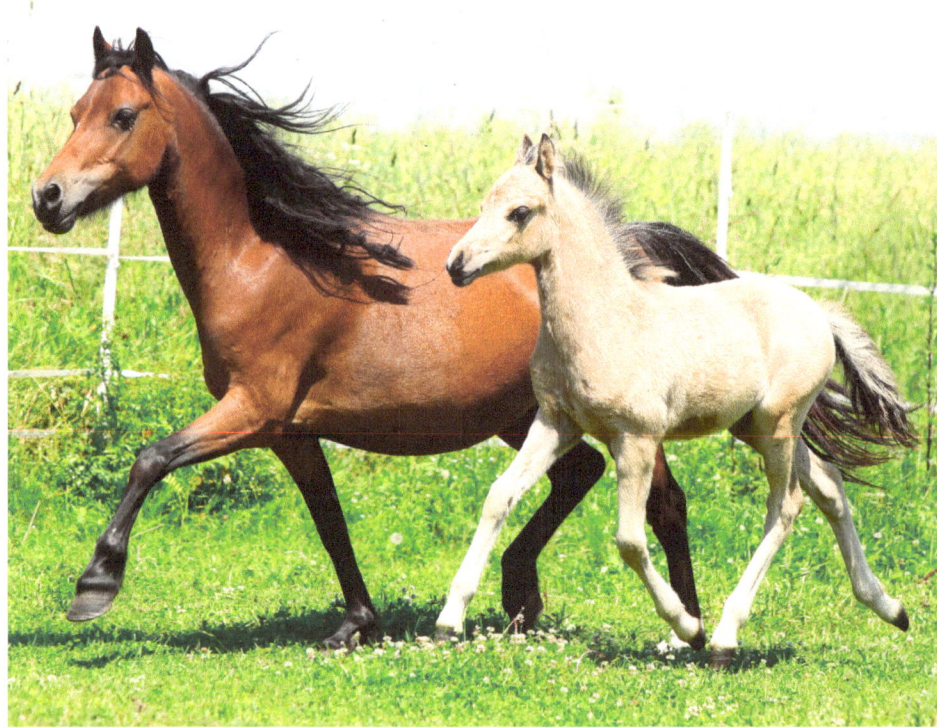

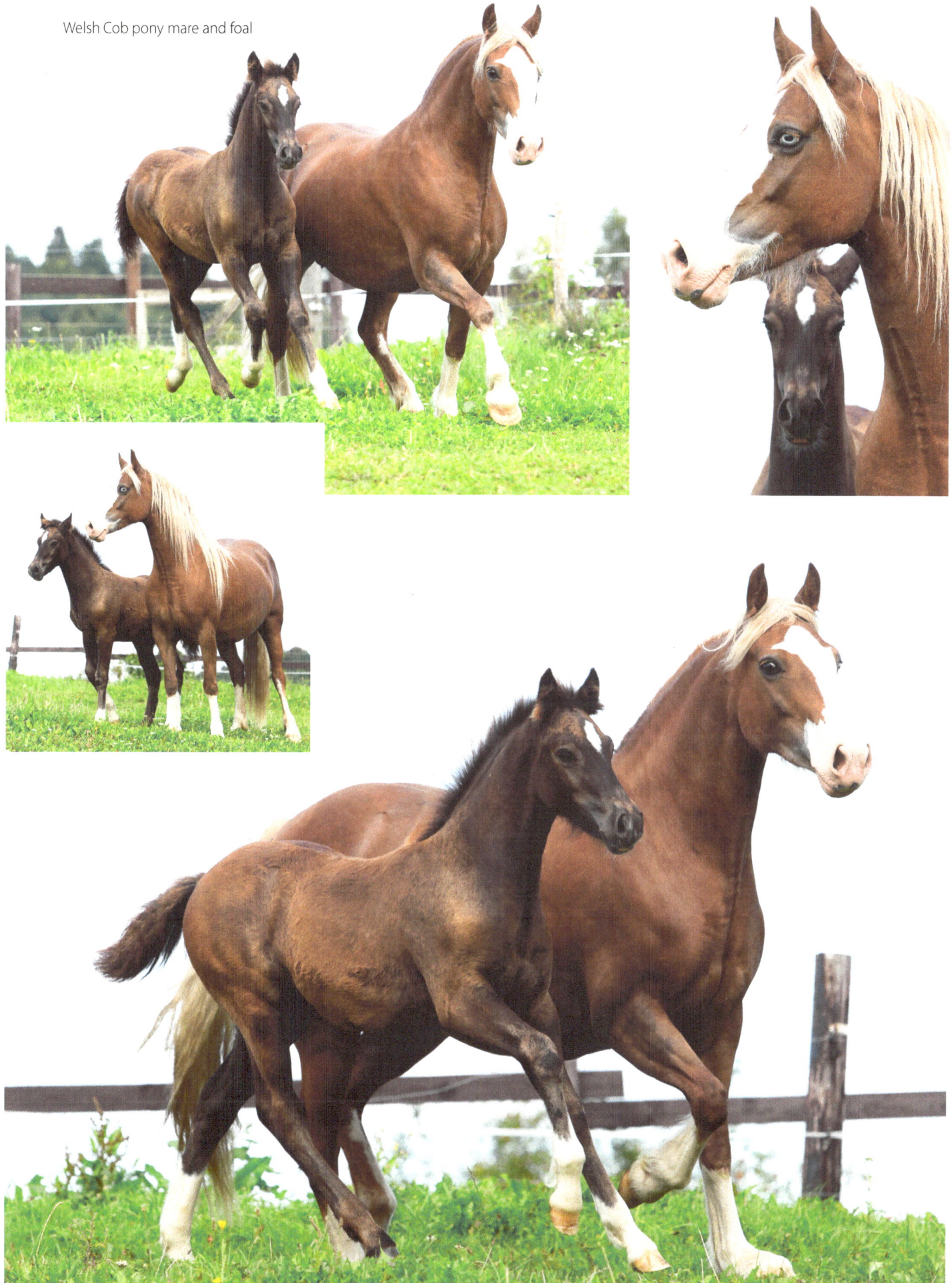

Welsh Cob pony mare and foal

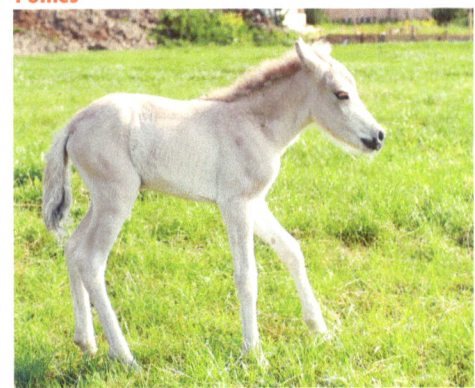

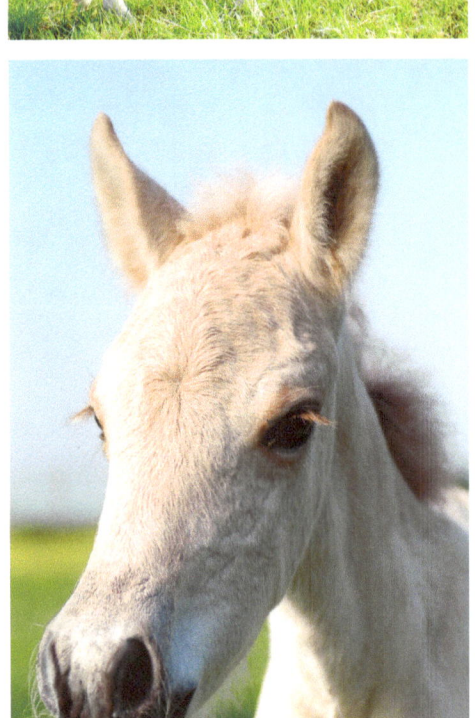

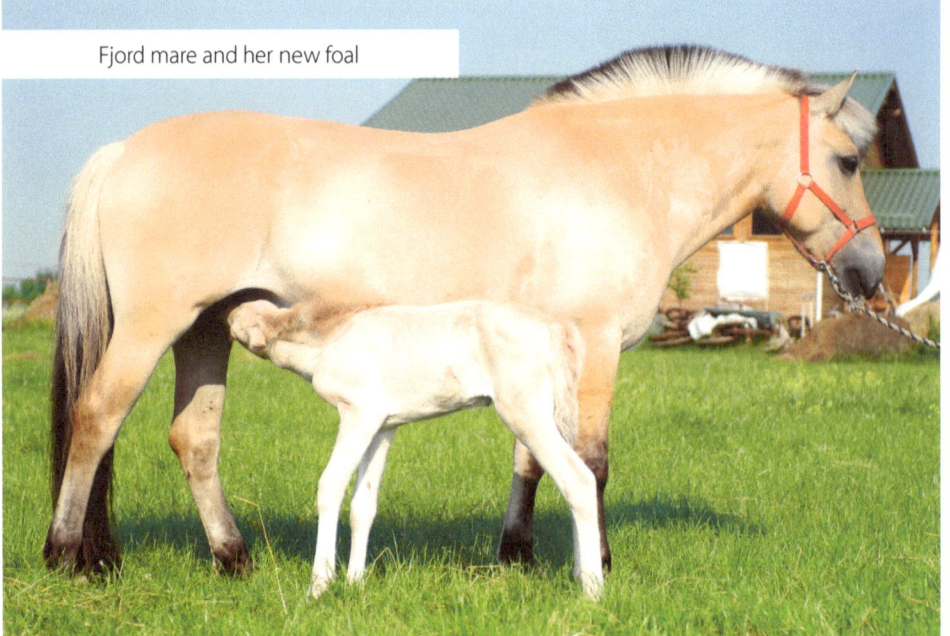

Fjord mare and her new foal

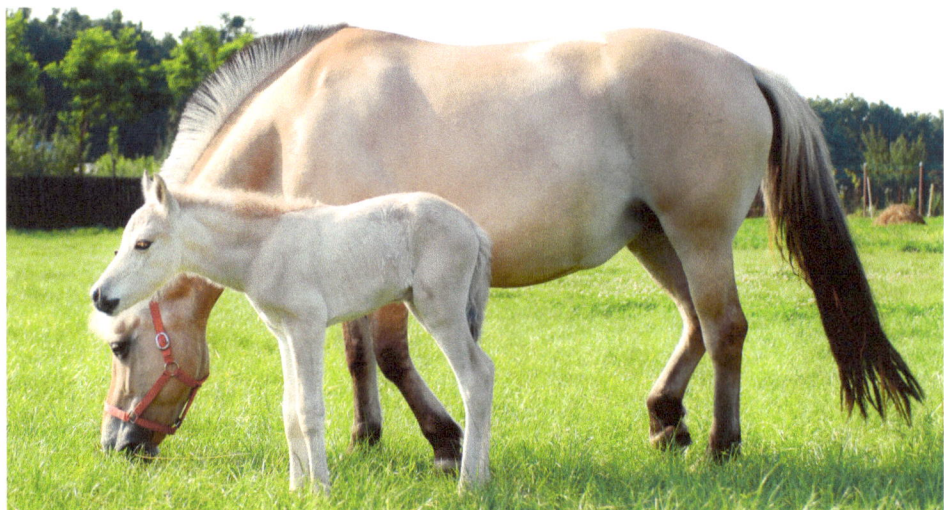

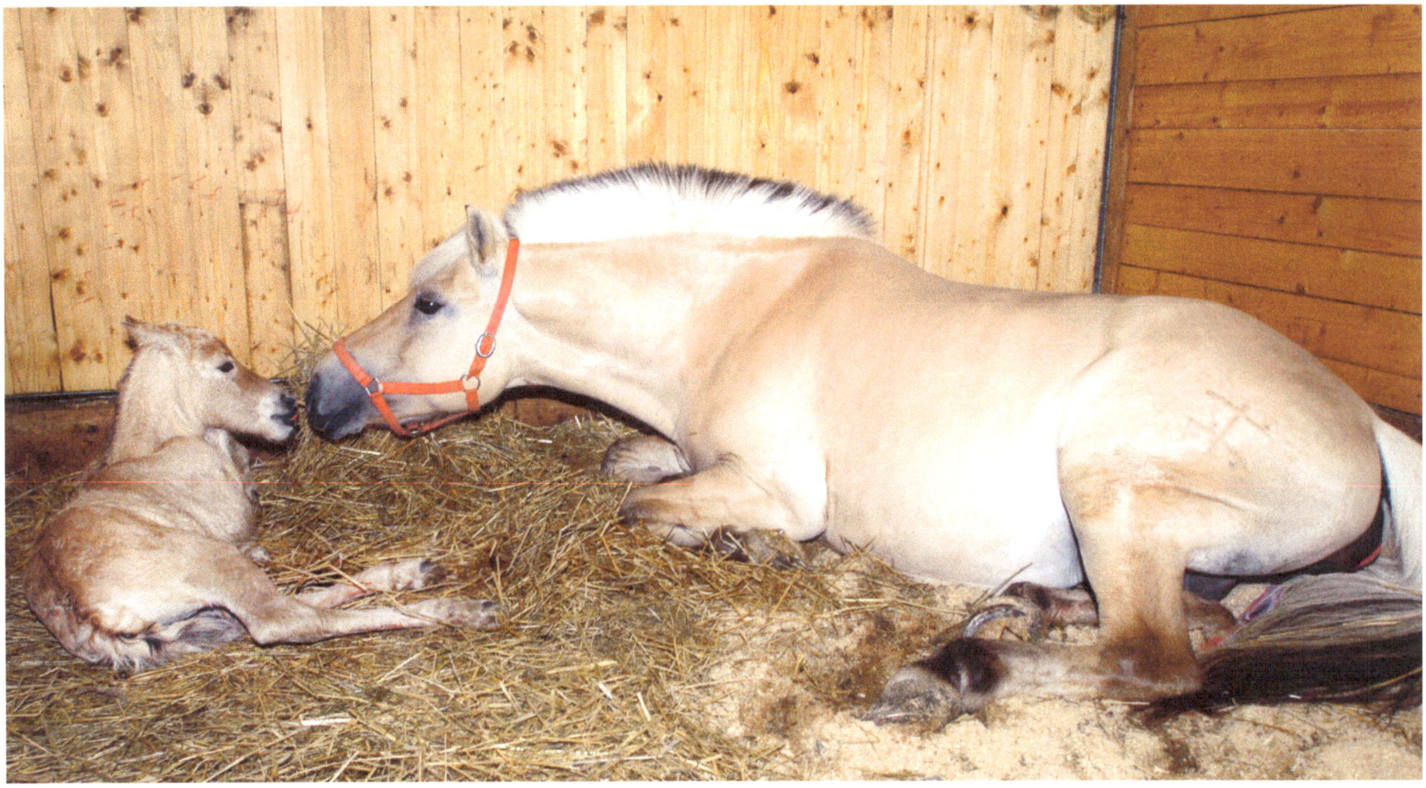

46

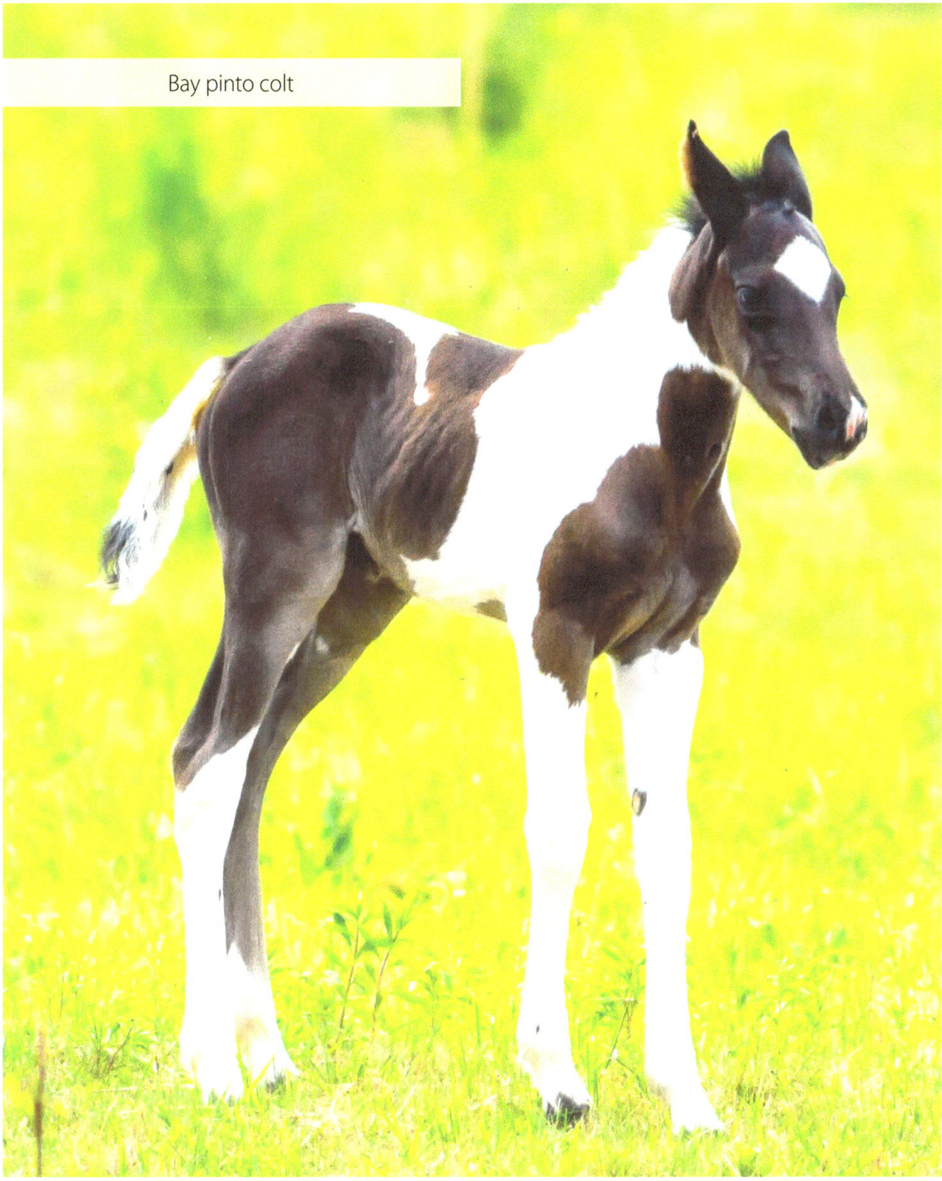

Bay pinto colt

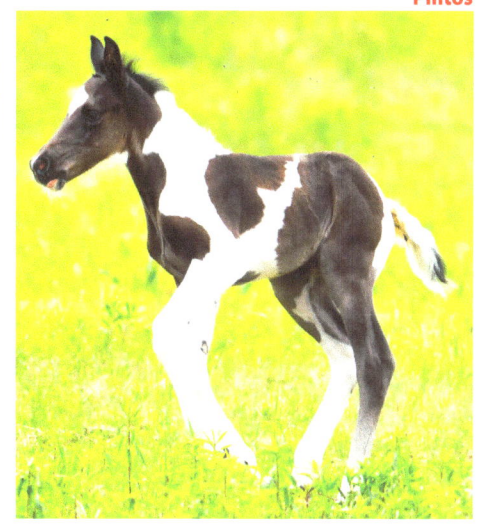

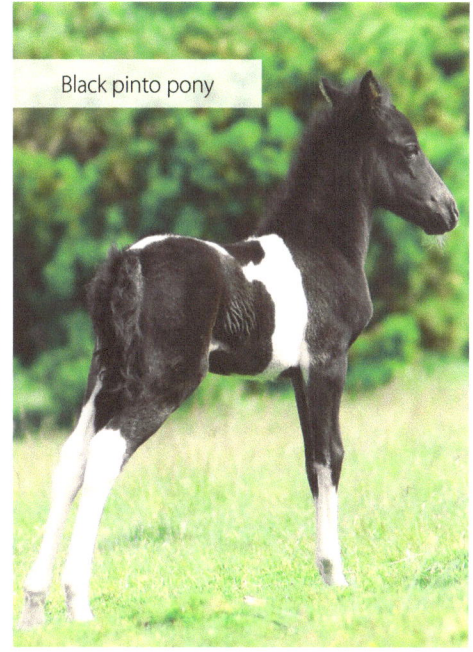

Black pinto pony

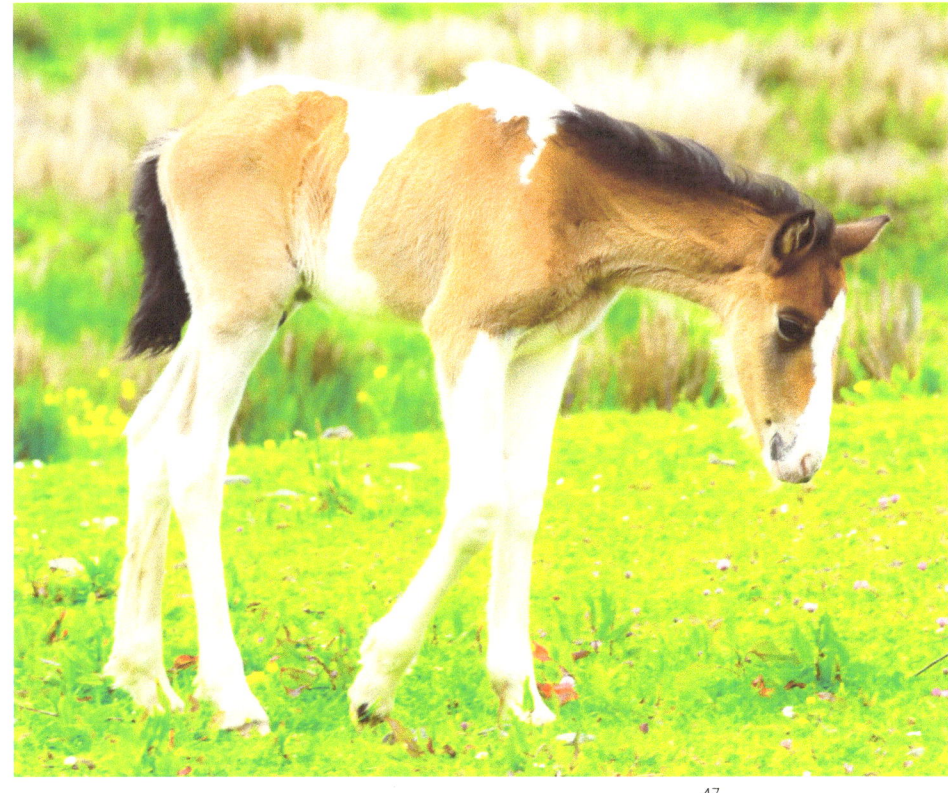

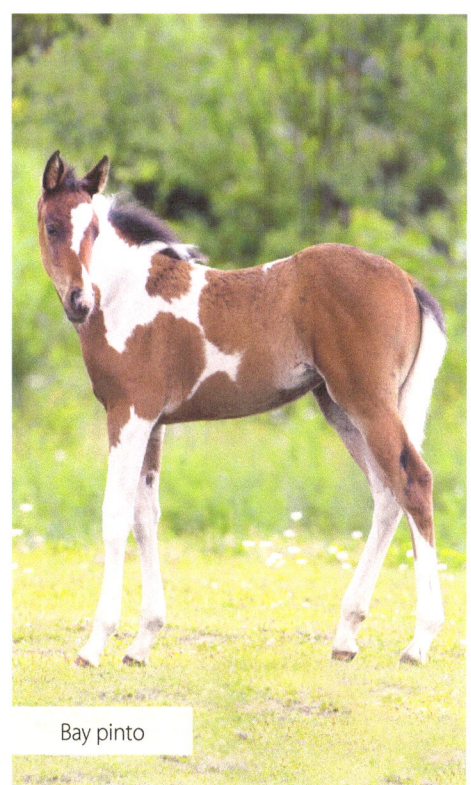

Bay pinto

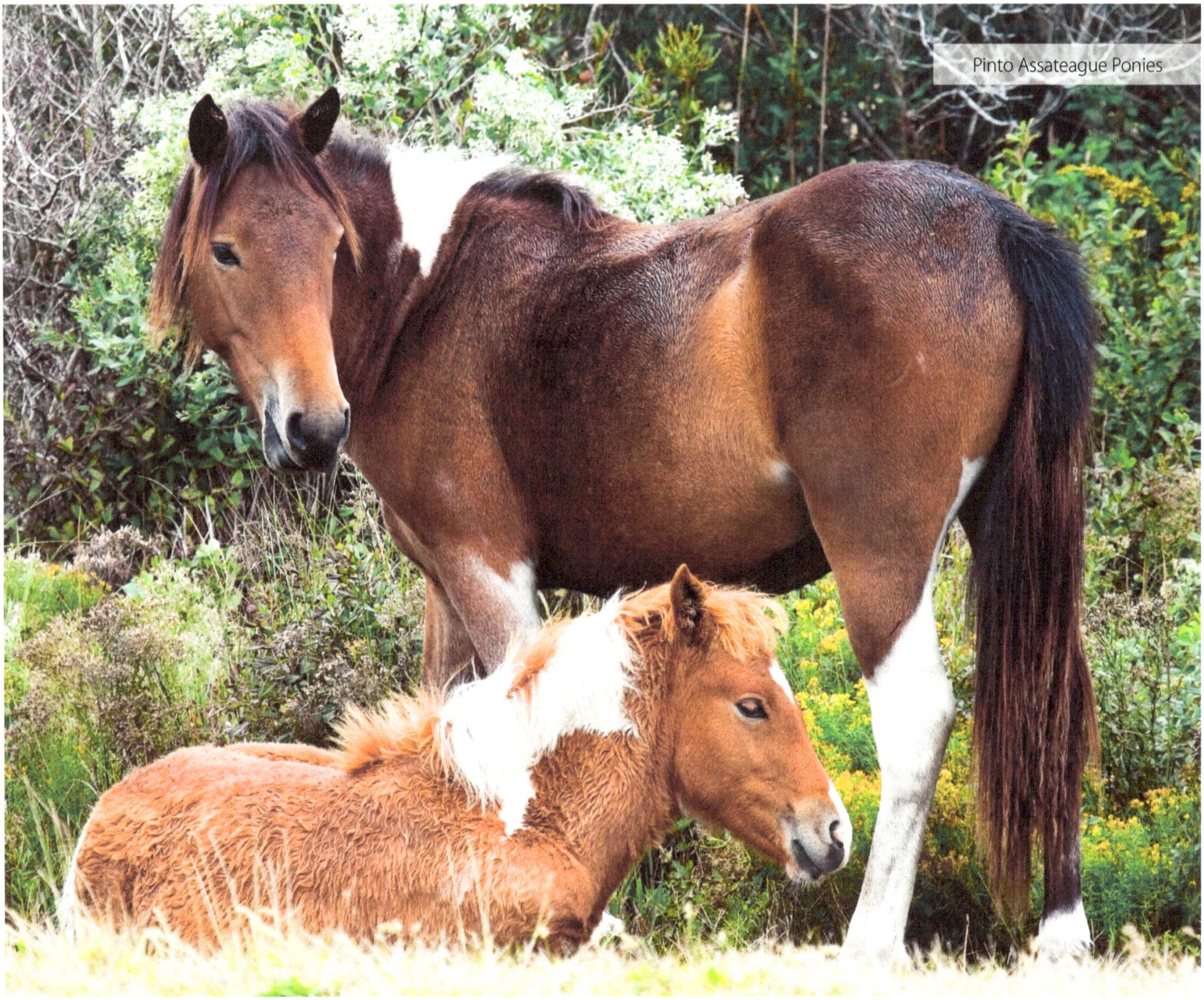

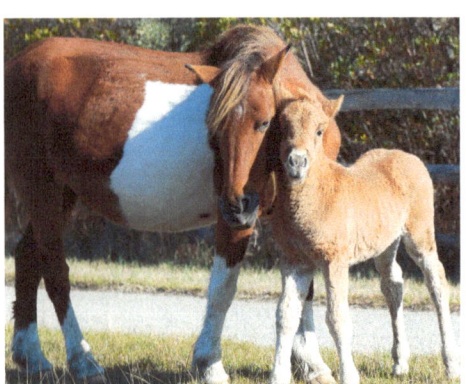

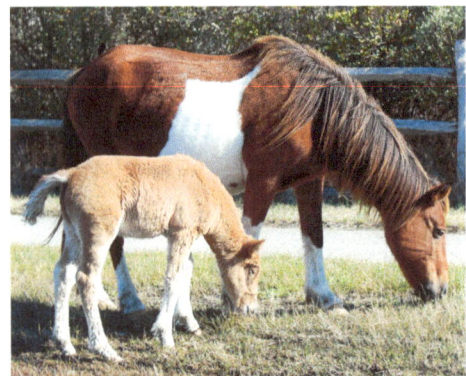

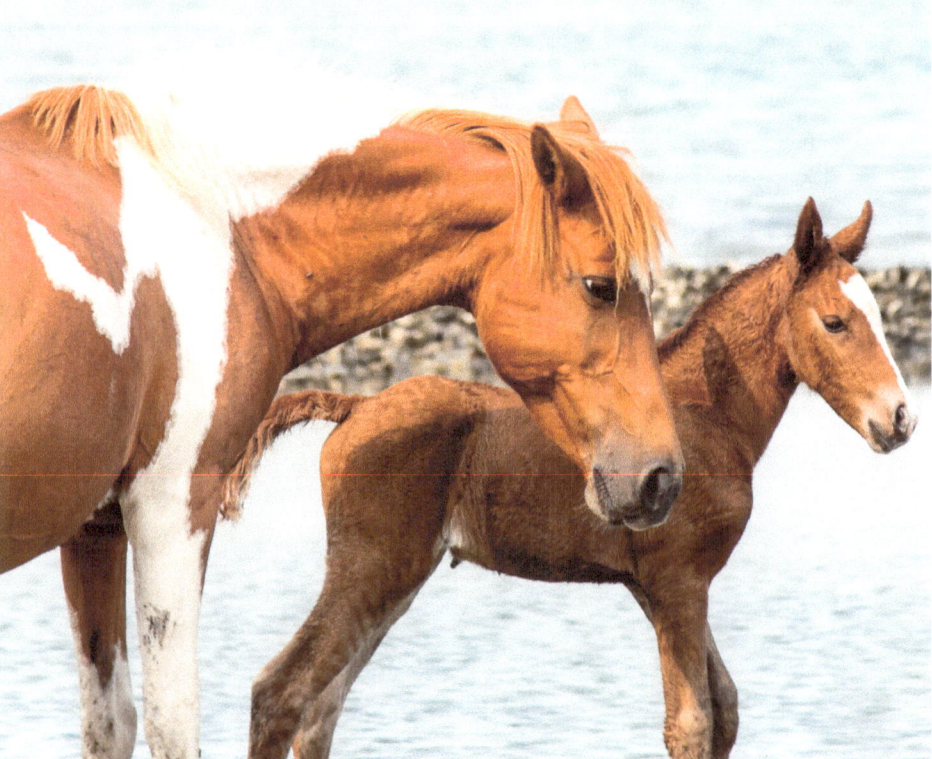

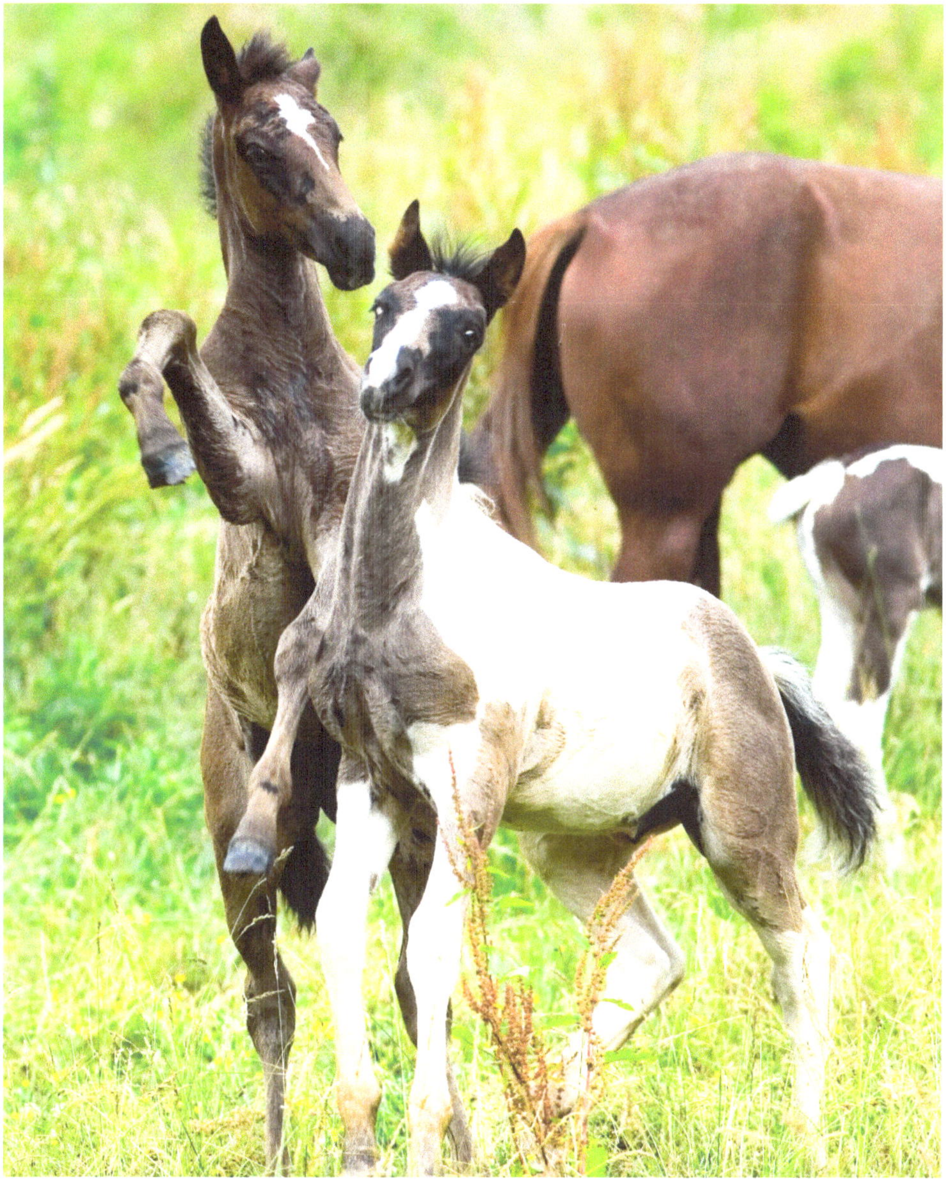

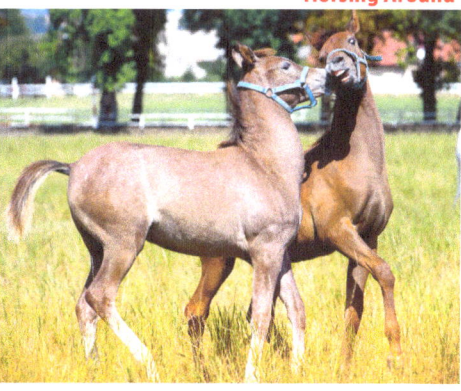

Arabians

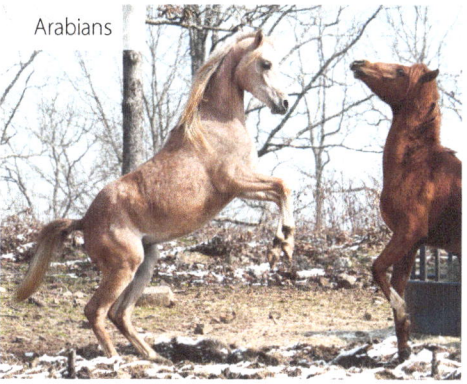

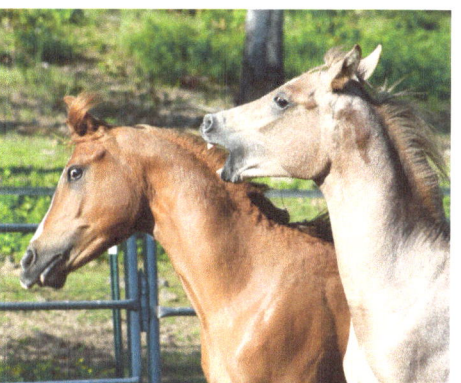

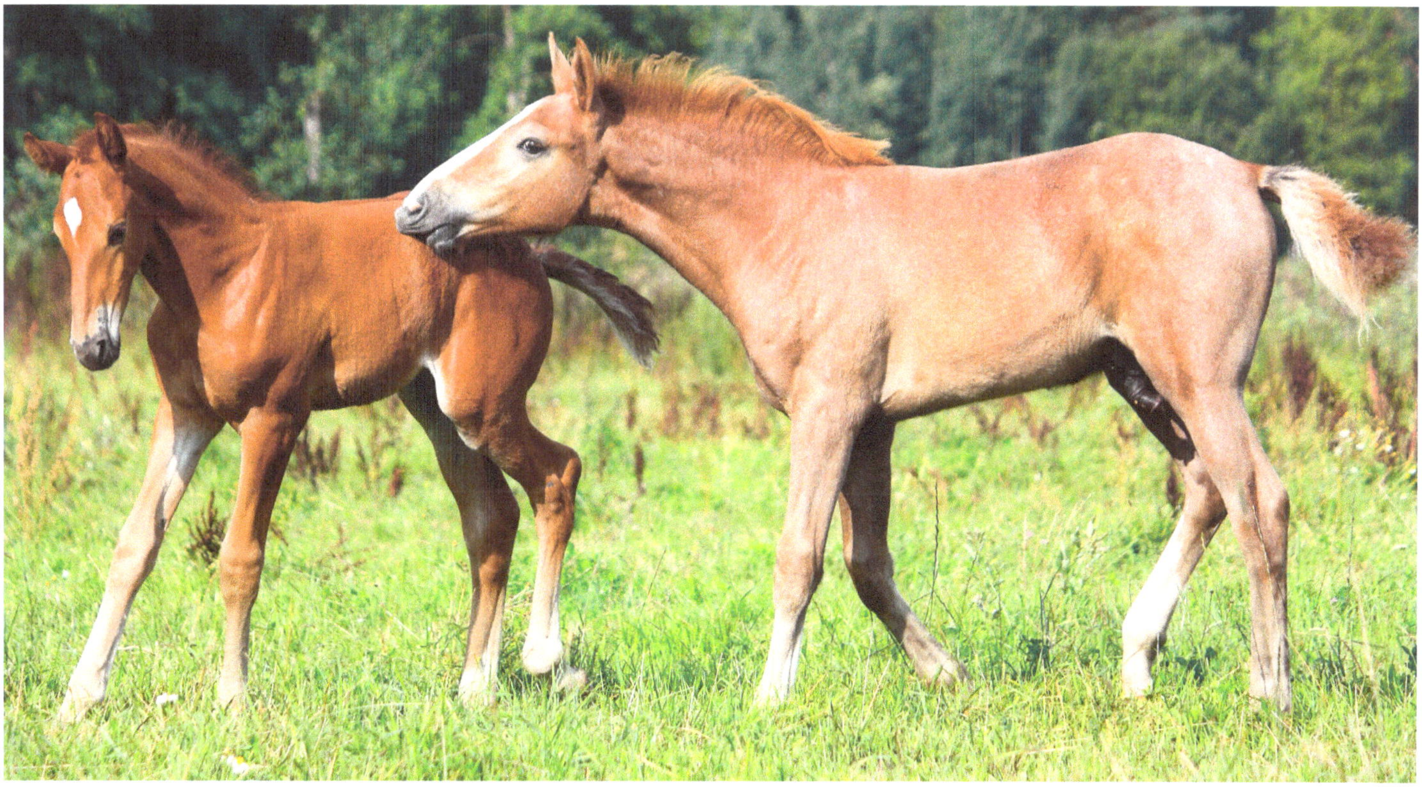

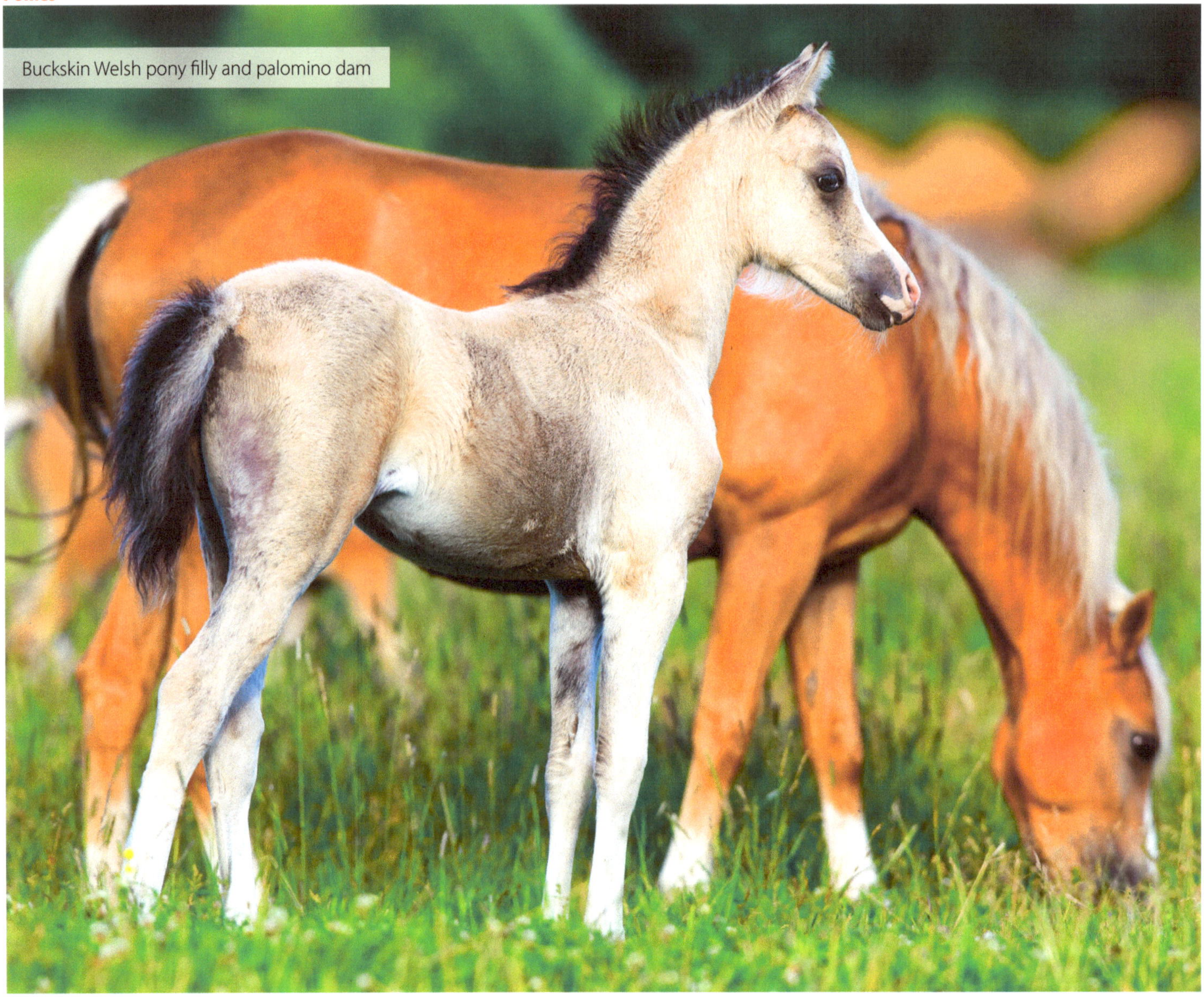

Buckskin Welsh pony filly and palomino dam

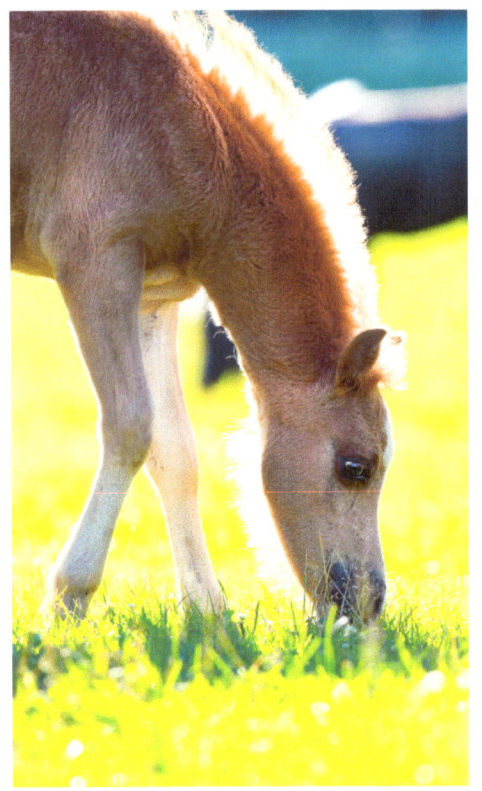

Palomino Welsh ponies

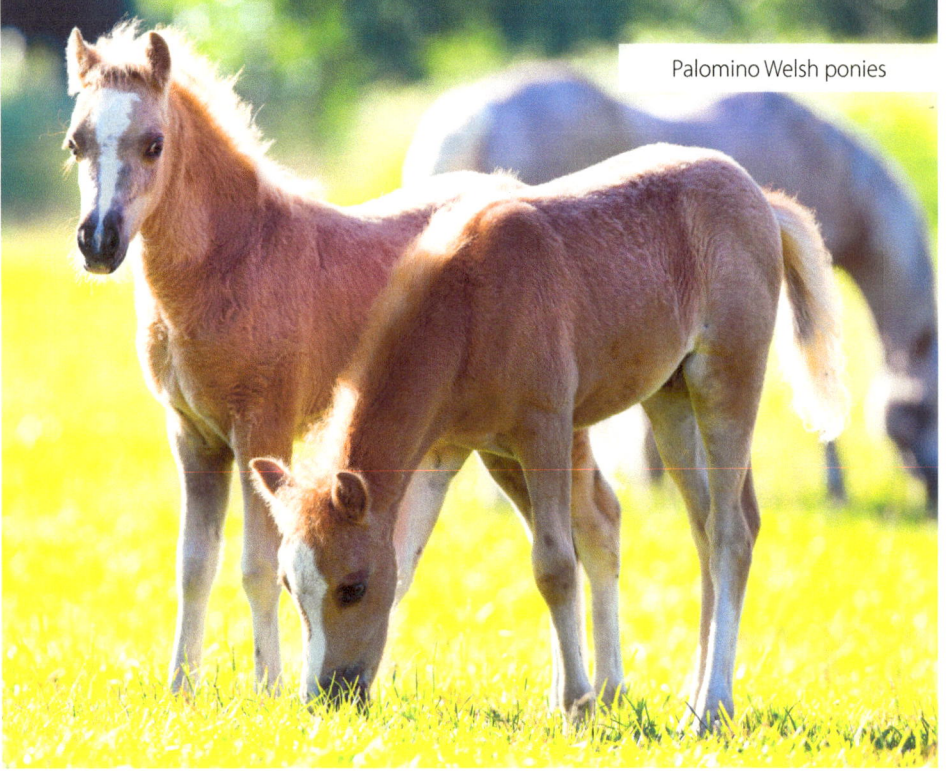

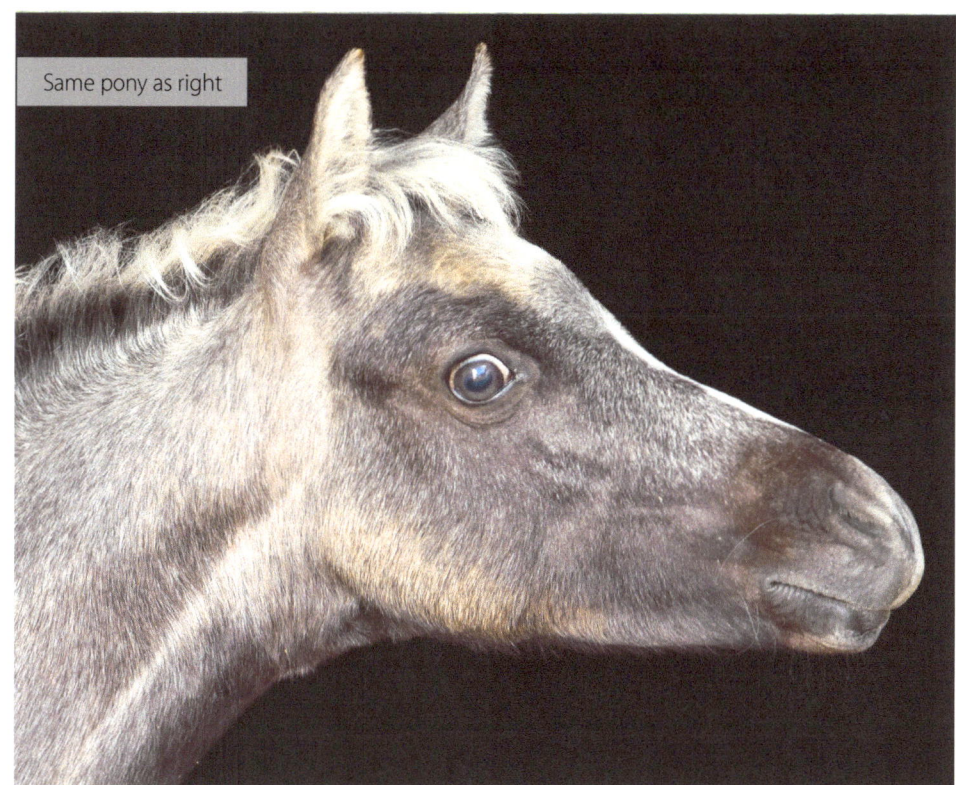

Same pony as right

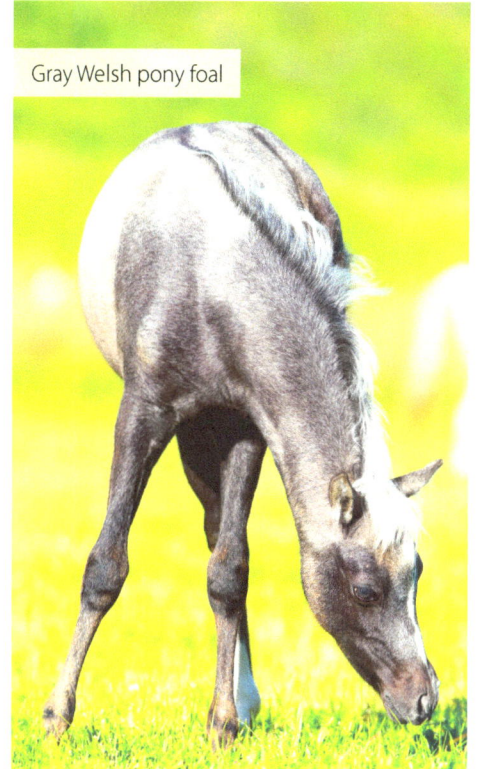

Gray Welsh pony foal

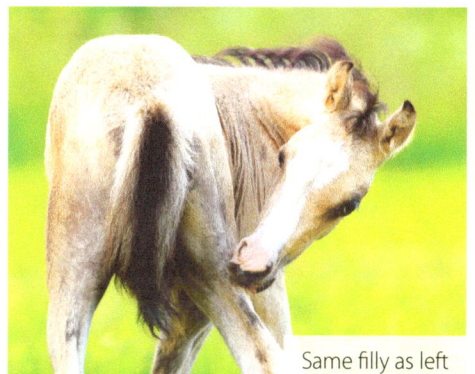

Same filly as left

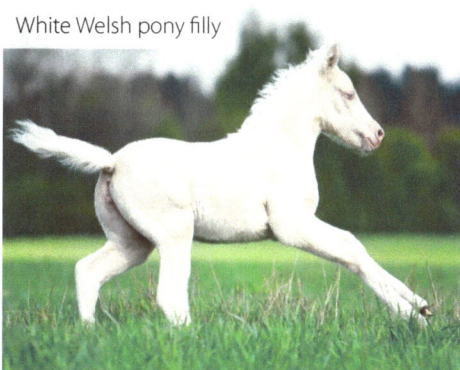

White Welsh pony filly

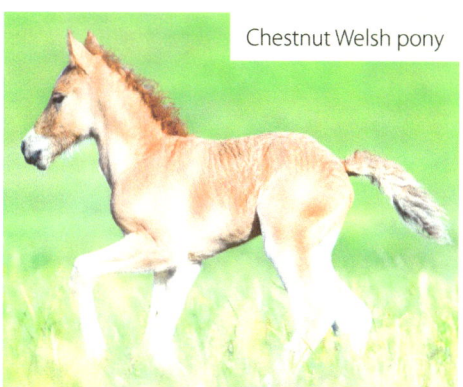

Chestnut Welsh pony

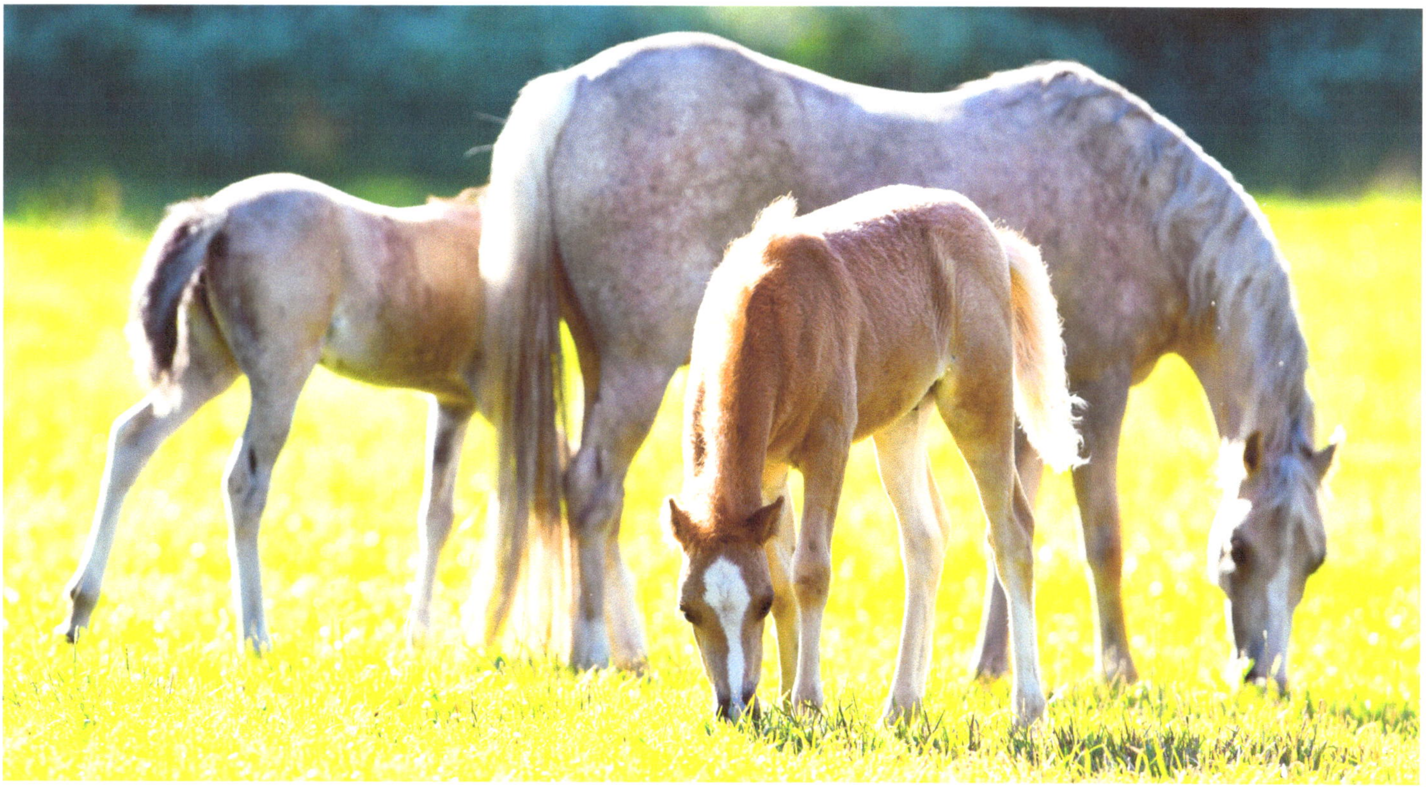

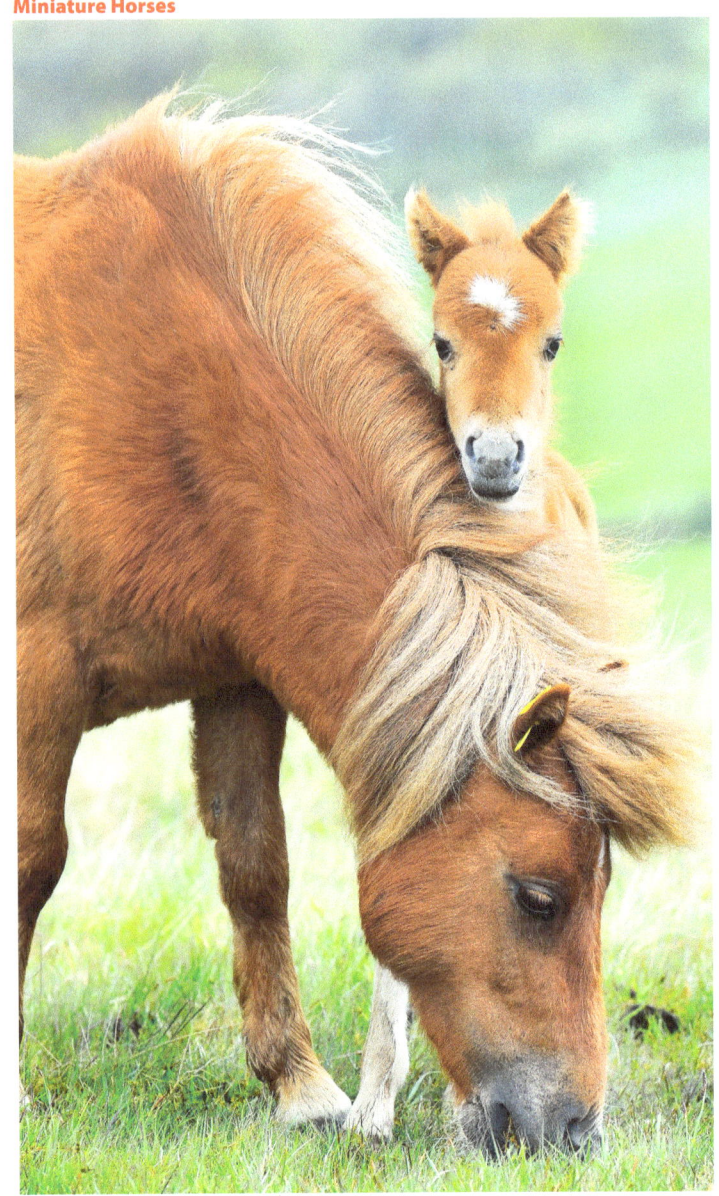

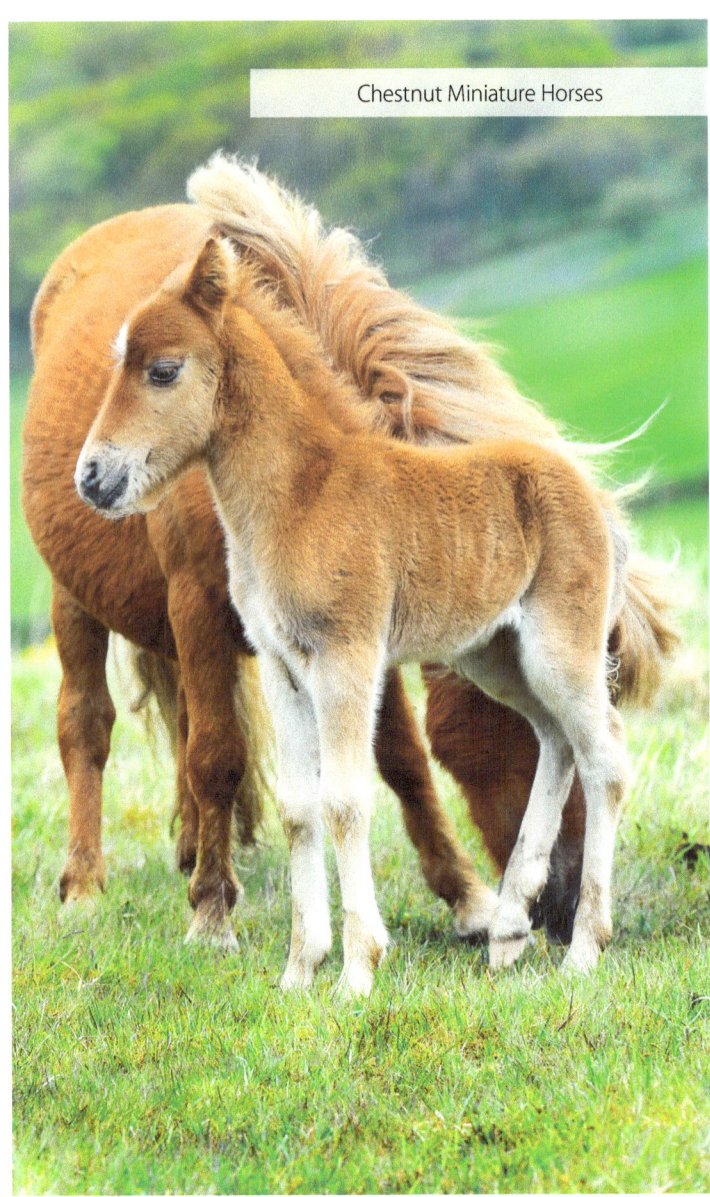

Chestnut Miniature Horses

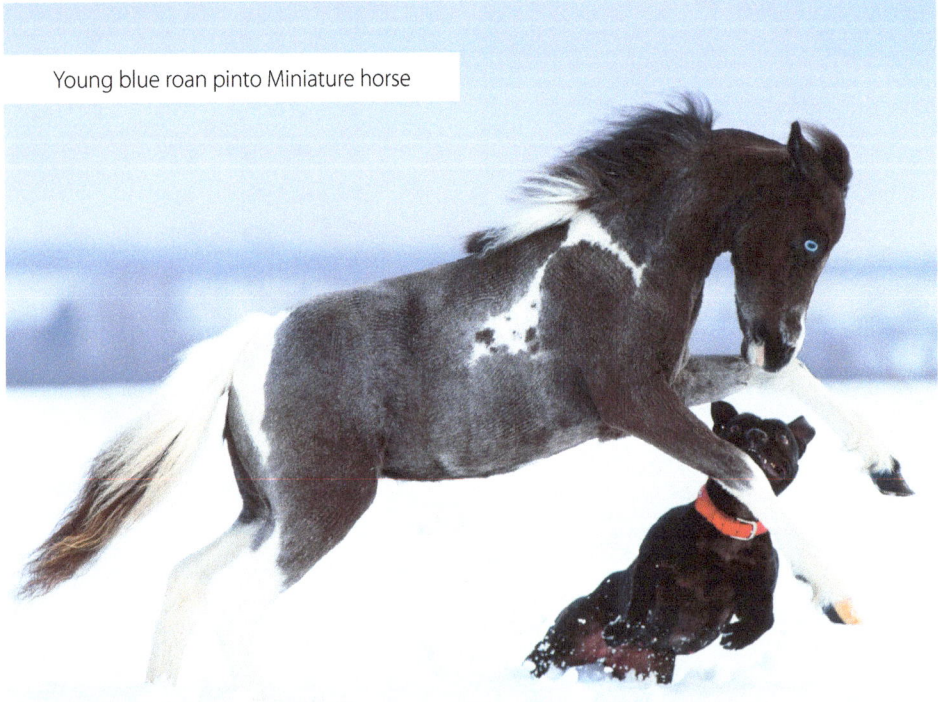

Young blue roan pinto Miniature horse

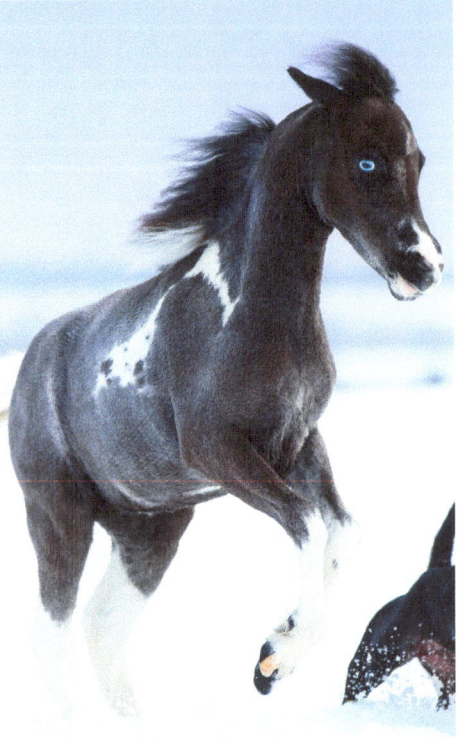

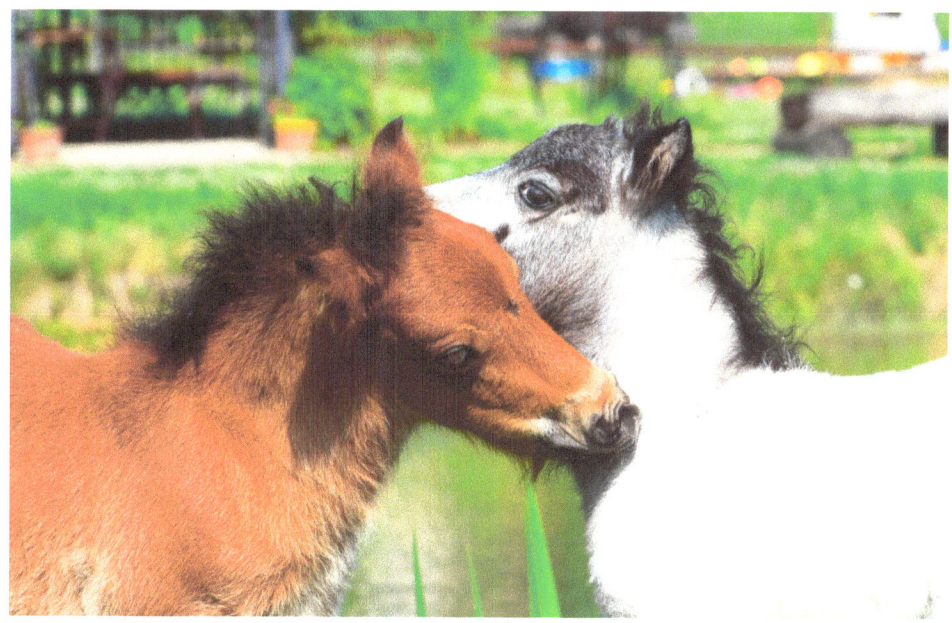

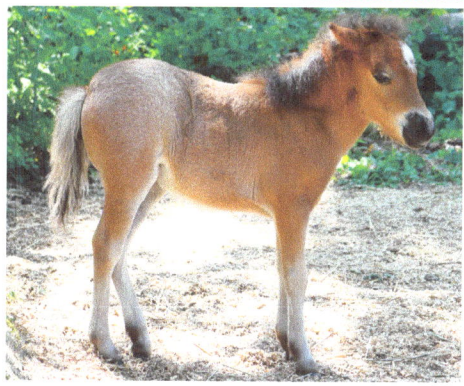

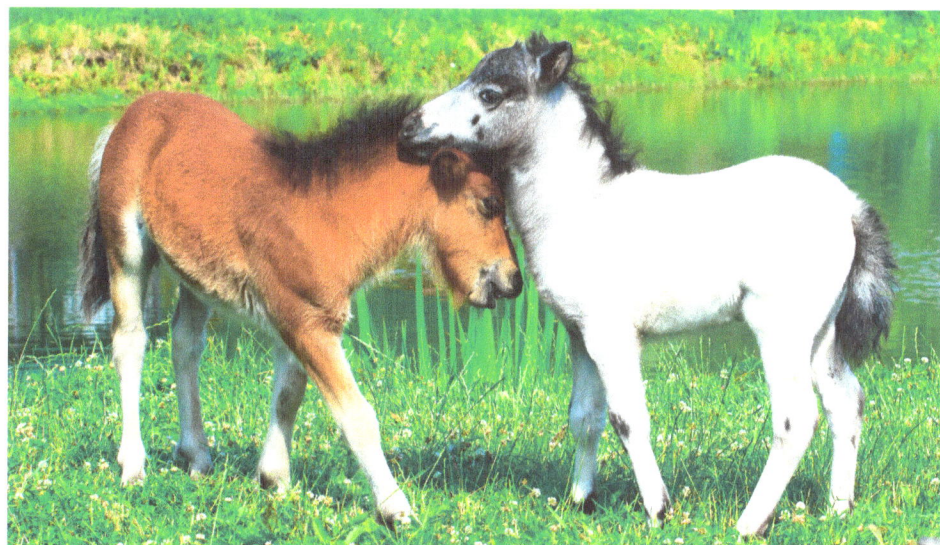

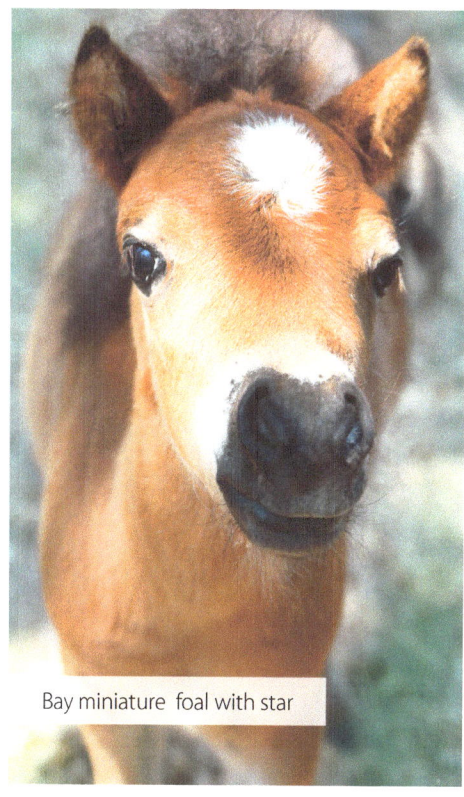

Bay miniature foal with star

Miniature horse foal friends

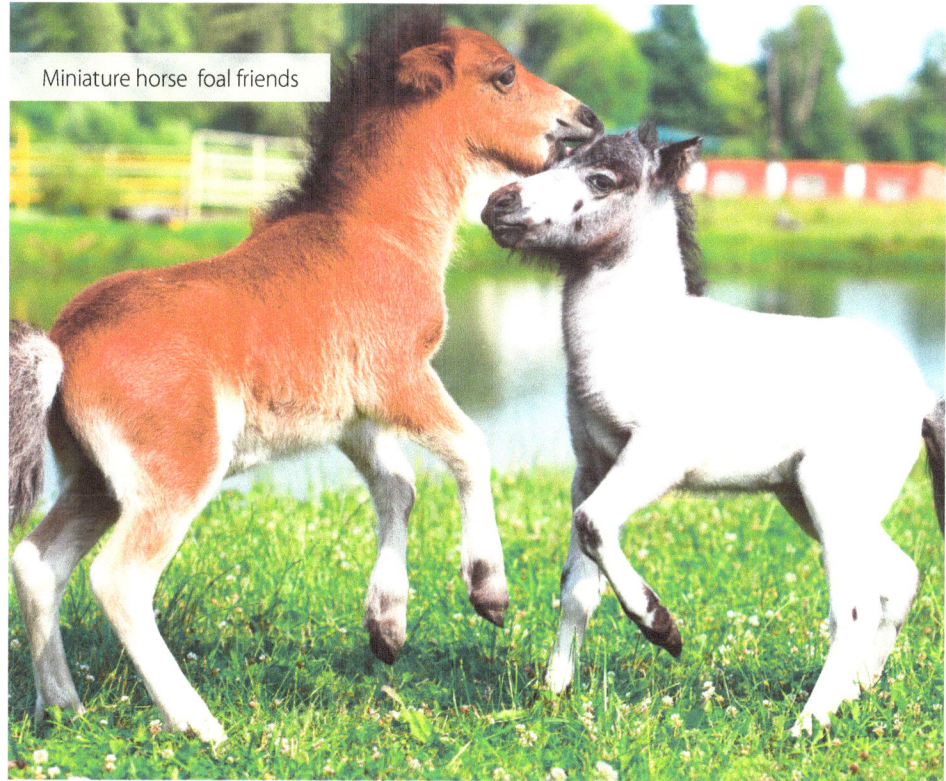

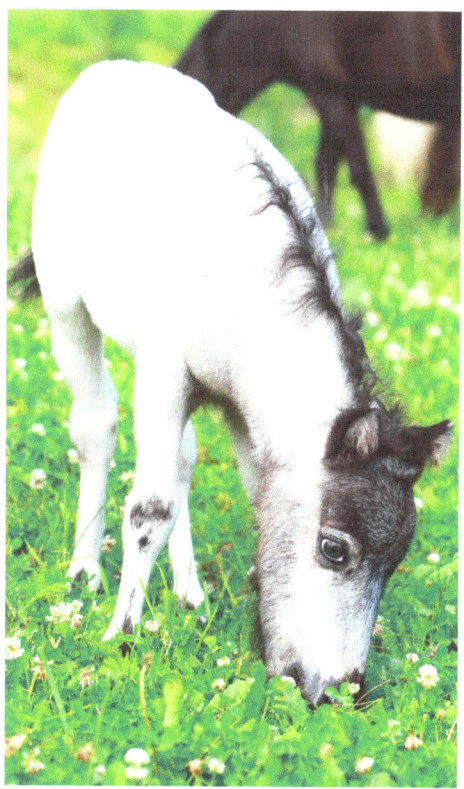

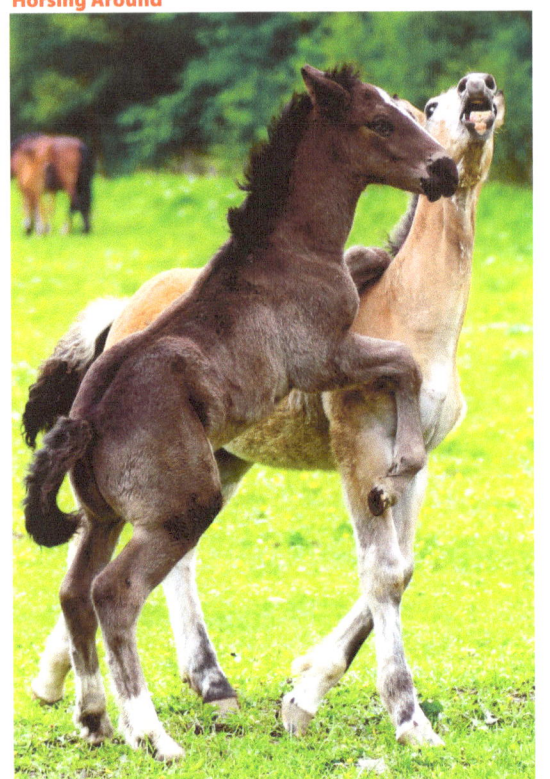

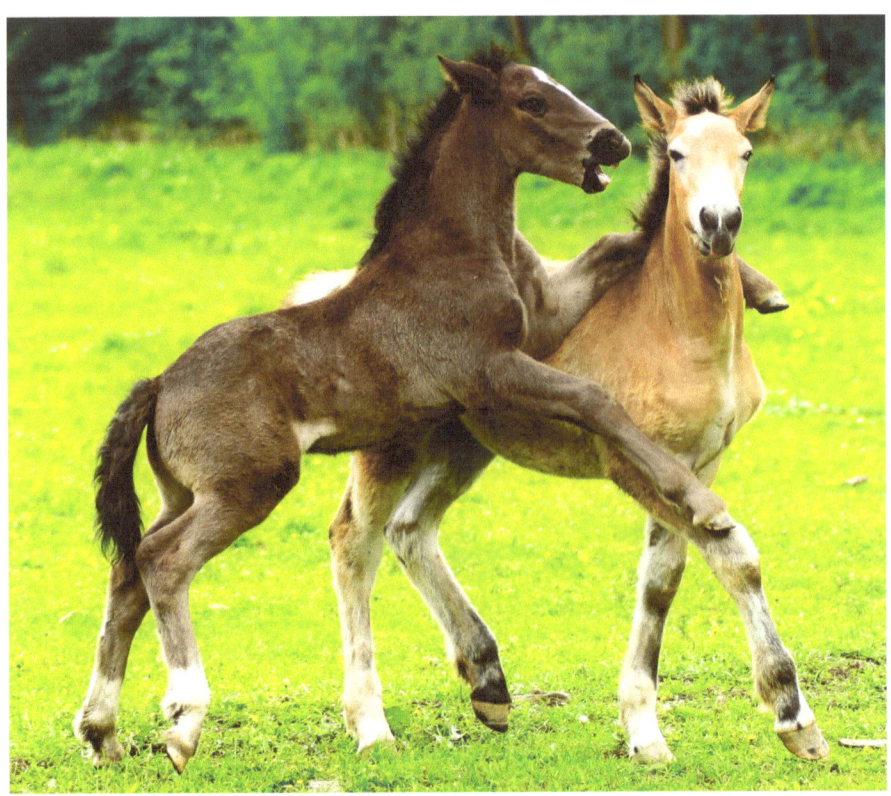

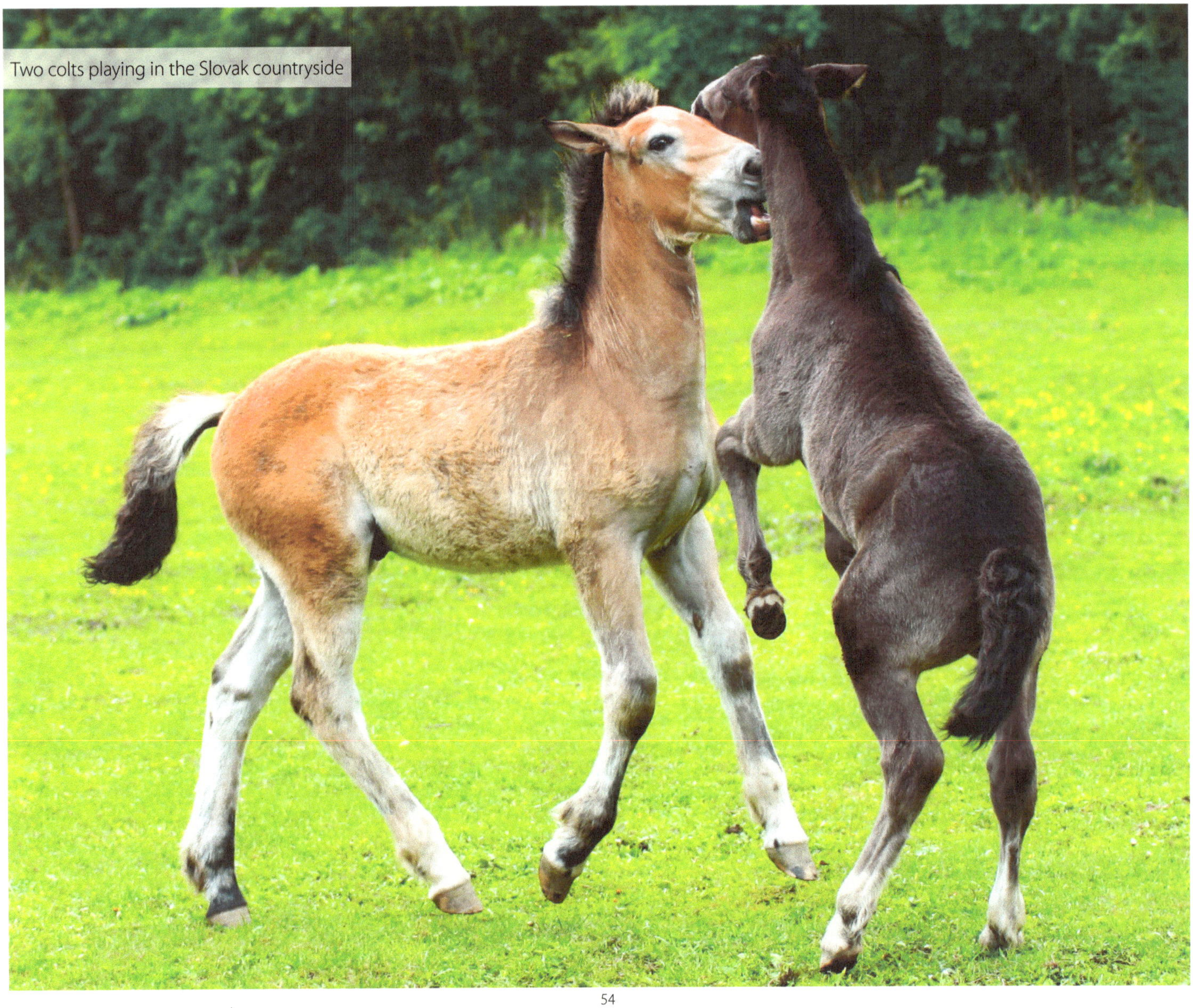

Two colts playing in the Slovak countryside

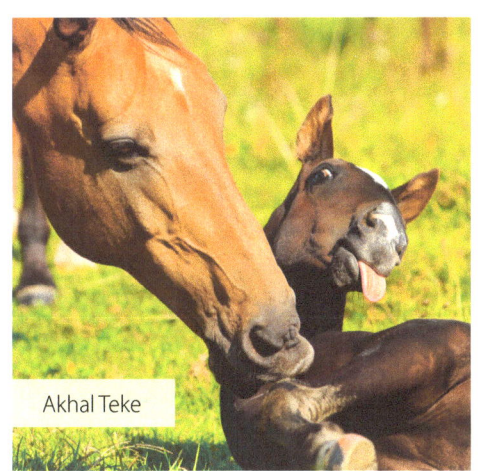

Akhal Teke

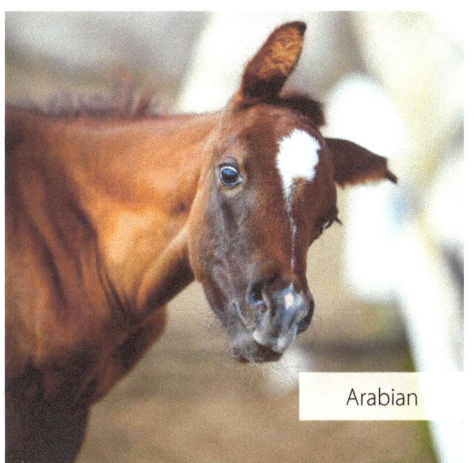

Arabian

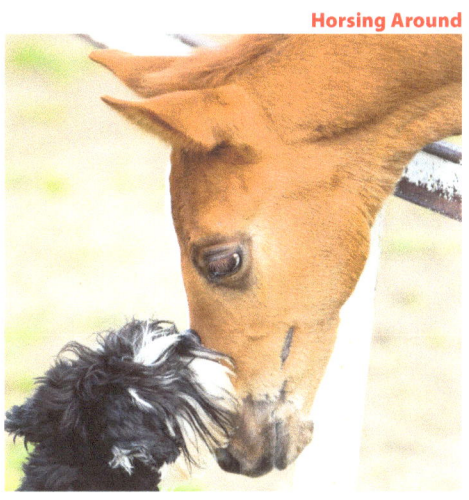

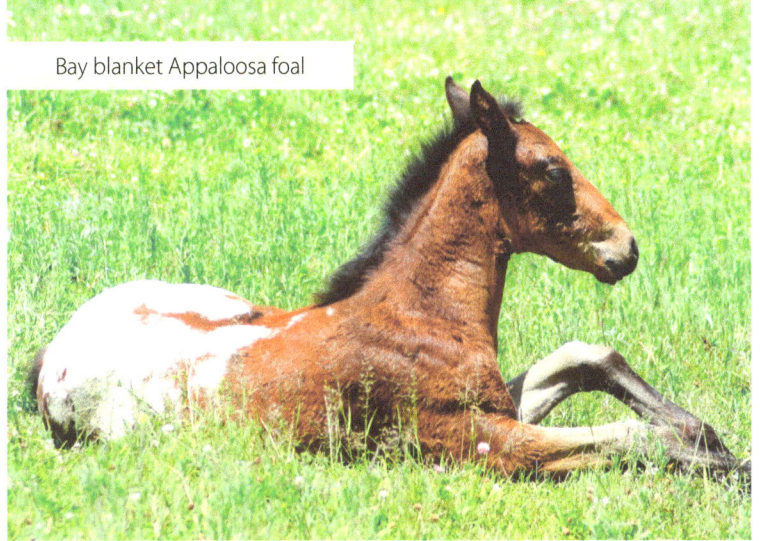

Bay blanket Appaloosa foal

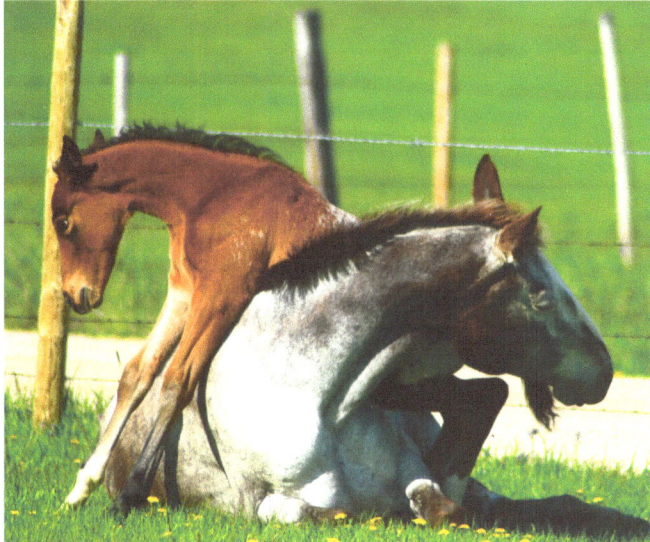

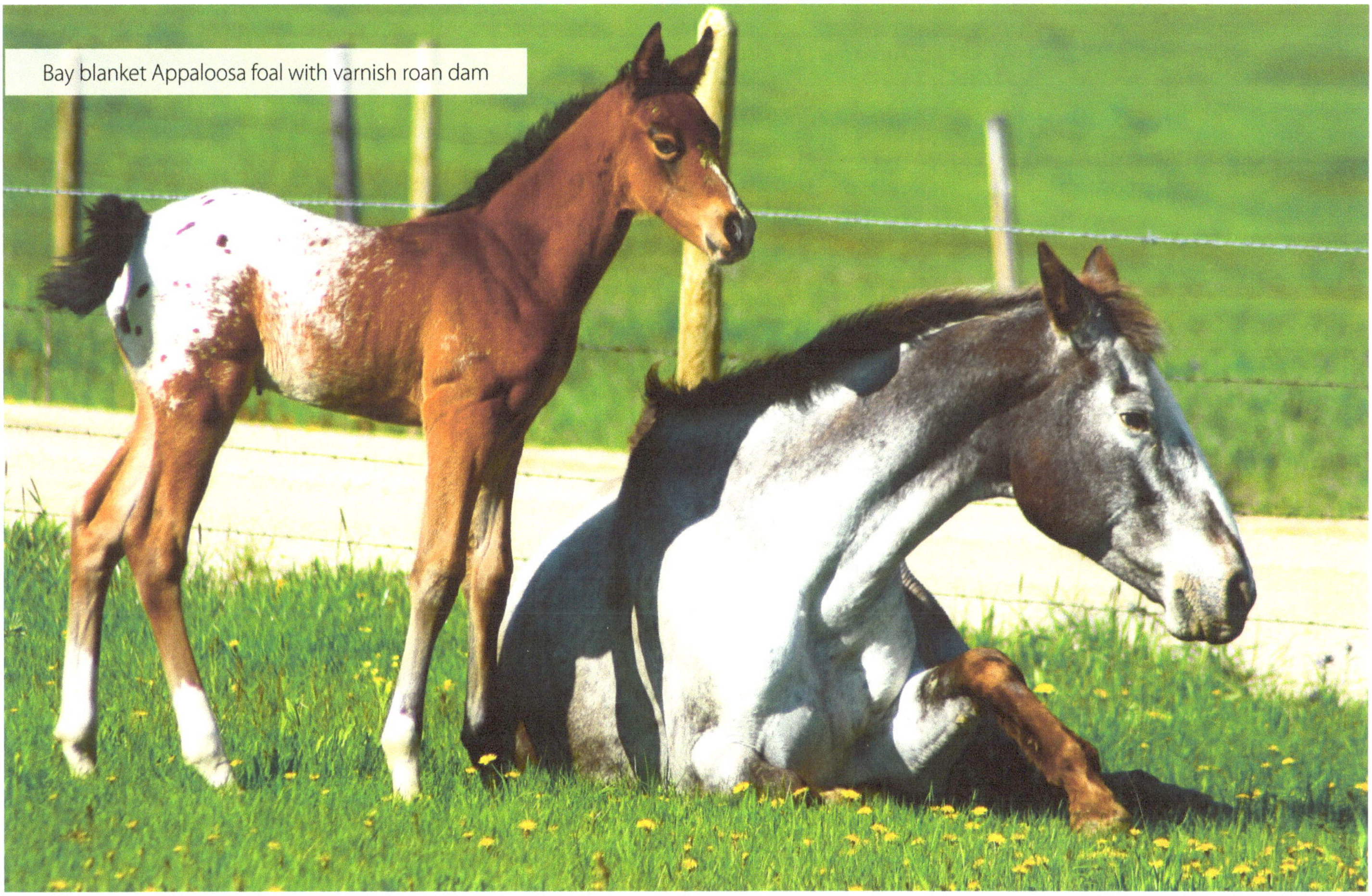

Bay blanket Appaloosa foal with varnish roan dam

Index

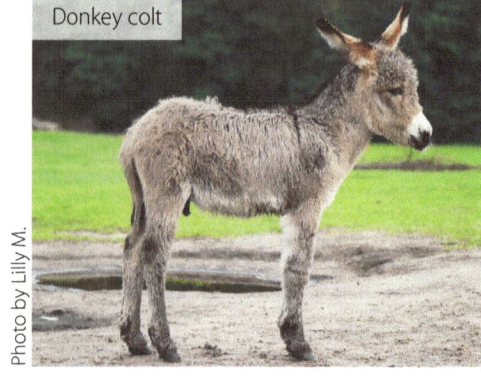
Donkey colt

Photo by Lilly M.

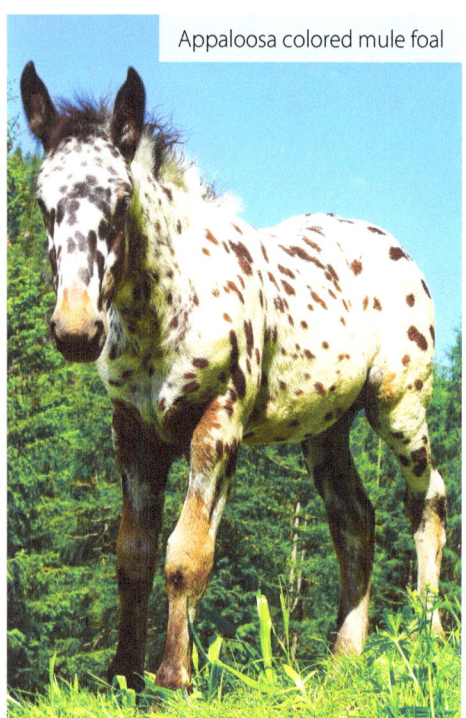
Appaloosa colored mule foal

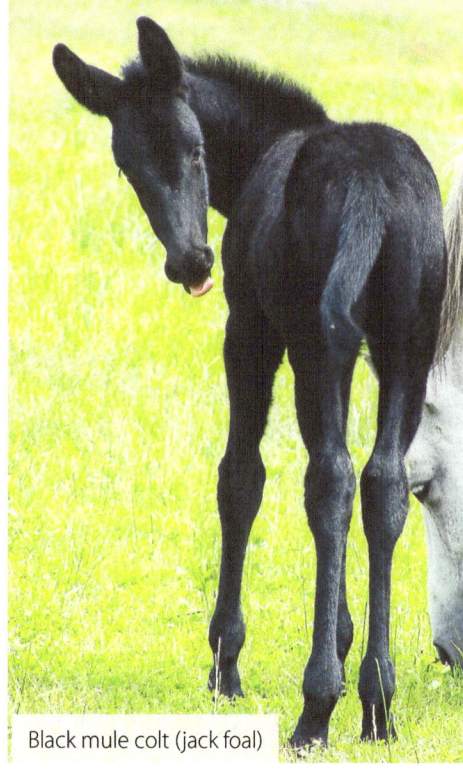
Black mule colt (jack foal)

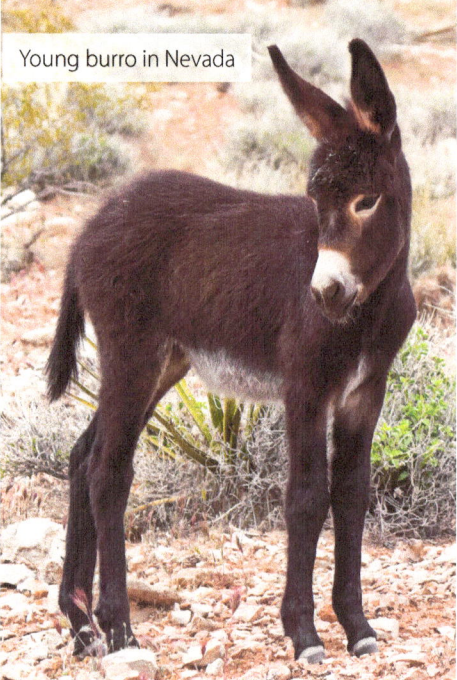
Young burro in Nevada

The same black mule colt as above right. He is older and has a clipped coat—notice that his lower legs are not clipped.

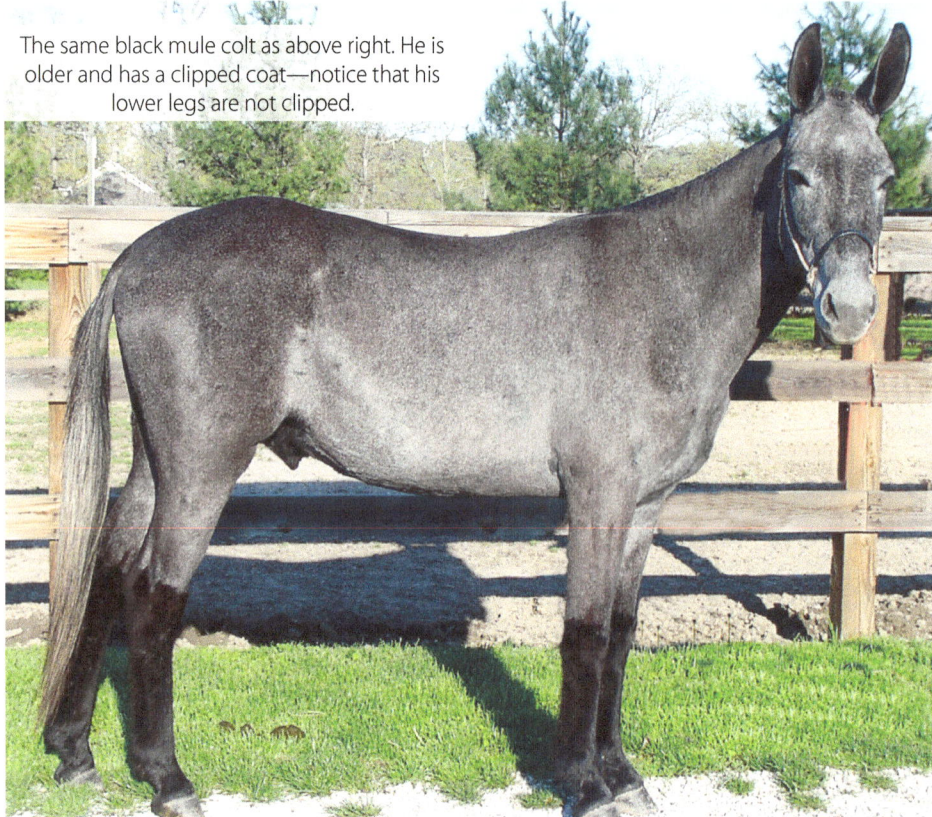

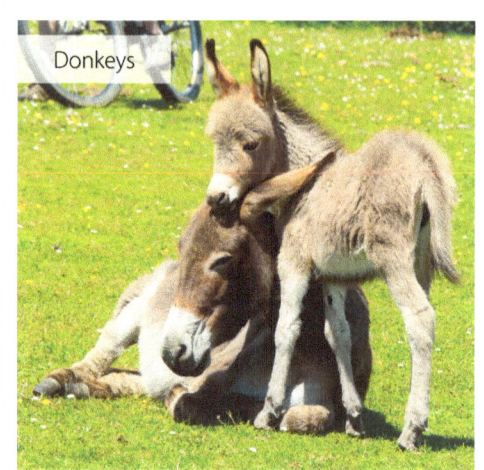
Donkeys